TO BE A CONGRESSMAN:
the PROMISE and the POWER

TO BE A CONGRESSMAN:

the PROMISE and the POWER

Edited by
SVEN GROENNINGS and
JONATHAN P. HAWLEY

Preface by
EVRON M. KIRKPATRICK

Prologue by
Rep. WILLIAM A. STEIGER

Introduction by
Sen. HUBERT H. HUMPHREY

 Published by **ACROPOLIS BOOKS LTD.** • WASHINGTON, D.C. 20009

225619

cıp

Library of Congress Cataloging in Publication Data

Groennings, Sven.
 To be a Congressman.

  1. Legislators—United States. I. Hawley,
Jonathan P., joint author. II. Title.
JK1061.G75   328.73'07'4   73-7946
ISBN 0-87491-352-7
ISBN 0-87491-353-5 (pbk.)

ACROPOLIS BOOKS LTD.

Colortone Building, 2400 17th St., N.W.
Washington, D. C. 20009

Printed in the United States of America by
COLORTONE PRESS Creative Graphics Inc., *Washington, D. C. 20009*

Library of Congress Catalog Number 73-7946
International Standard Book Number
(Cloth) 0-87491-352-7
(Paper) 0-87491-353-5

Contents

PREFACE: Increasing Understanding of Capitol Hill Politics
Evron M. Kirkpatrick **vii**

PROLOGUE: Congressional Fellows in the Congressman's Office
Representative William A. Steiger **xi**

INTRODUCTION: What It Means to Be in Congress
Senator Hubert H. Humphrey **xv**

I.   THE CAMPAIGN
      Joel M. Fisher **1**

II.   THE FRESHMAN FACES CONGRESS
      Gerald D. Sturges **23**

III. SYMBIOSIS: CONGRESS AND THE PRESS
      Delmer D. Dunn **37**

IV.   THE CONSTITUENT NEEDS HELP: CASEWORK IN
      THE HOUSE OF REPRESENTATIVES
      T. Edward Westen **53**

V.   THE CLUBS IN CONGRESS: THE HOUSE
      WEDNESDAY GROUP
      Sven Groennings **73**

VI.   COMMITTEES AND THE POLITICS OF
      ASSIGNMENTS
      Robert Healy **99**

VII. SENIORITY AND COMMITTEE LEADERSHIP: THE
      EMERGENCE OF CHOICE
      Jonathan P. Hawley **121**

VIII. THE POLITICS OF HUNGER: FORMING A SENATE
      SELECT COMMITTEE
      Bertram G. Waters III **151**

IX.   CONGRESS GETS NEW IDEAS FROM OUTSIDE
      EXPERTS
      Ernest A. Chaples, Jr. **169**

X.   LEADERSHIP: THE ROLE AND STYLE OF
      SENATOR EVERETT DIRKSEN
      Jean E. Torcom **185**

XI.   CAN THE INCUMBENT BE DEFEATED?
      Fariborz S. Fatemi **225**

INDEX **255**

In TO BE A CONGRESSMAN: *The Promise and the Power* eleven contributors examine the dominant elements of congressional life. Being a congressman involves constant electioneering, organizing and directing an office and staff, communicating with the public, and responding to its many needs. The legislator works with colleagues on committees and in informal groups, proposes policies, confronts power, accepts leadership, and defends his record against an opponent's challenge.

The contributors discuss these aspects of Congress as they came to know them during service and observation on Capitol Hill. Political scientist Evron M. Kirkpatrick describes their Congressional Fellowship Program. Representative William A. Steiger explains the work of Fellows in his office. Senator Hubert H. Humphrey evaluates this unique experience, offering his personal perspective on what it means to be in Congress.

Increasing Understanding of Capitol Hill Politics

EVRON M. KIRKPATRICK *

TO BE A CONGRESSMAN: *The Promise and the Power* is an outgrowth of the Congressional Fellowship Program, sponsored by The American Political Science Association since 1953. This educational program has provided more than 500 social scientists, journalists and Federal officials opportunities to serve in staff roles in the Senate and House of Representatives. More than 100 national legislators have had Congressional Fellows with their staffs, many of them regularly including the program's participants in their offices.

This program is founded upon the premise that the experience of participant observation will deepen insights into Capitol Hill politics. Whether one enters the program as a scholar, journalist or government official, he or she finds involvement in the processes of Congress to be highly useful and educational. Journalists benefit through increased depth of their future reporting, while Federal Fellows find that their increased understanding of congressional policy-making renders them more valuable to their agencies. For all the Fellows, the education program conveys a unique opportunity to develop contacts and new sources of information.

Political scientists find that their experience with the Congress not only increases their ability to interest and inform their students but also enhances the confidence and credibility of their instruction. Most academics in the program, including most of the political scientists contributing to this volume, have returned to teaching. Almost 70 percent of the 150 former Fellows now on faculties are teaching courses on Congress and legislative behavior, and thus have the opportunity to convey their personal observations as supplement to their theoretical understanding.

* Executive Director, The American Political Science Association.

Social scientists long have regarded participant observation as among the most fruitful of their research methods, particularly for producing seminal perspectives and translating "real world" complexities into scientific refinement. Former Fellows' Hill experience has stimulated some of the most prominent scholarly literature on the Congress, including approximately 20 books as well as numerous articles. Many of the discipline's most productive researchers on Congress received their initial exposure to the legislative process through these fellowships. Their research topics have included civil rights, foreign affairs, agriculture, public education, taxes, and public spending, as well as legislative rules and strategies, committee structures, congressional staffing, congressional ethics, interest group activity, campaigning, elections, and congressional voting. *To Be A Congressman*, intended as an introduction to the practical aspects of congressional life, is the first volume prepared by a group of former Fellows.

During the more than four months that Congressional Fellows work in each body of Congress, they gain personal experience in a variety of congressional responsibilities. Their involvement ranges from the handling of press work and constituent problems to policy research and the preparation of legislation. Prior to undertaking these assignments, the Fellows engage in an intensive orientation seminar with members of Congress, Washington correspondents, lobbyists, political party spokesmen, and political scientists. Reconvening periodically in similar sessions during the year, the Fellows also share and evaluate their experience.

Half of each year's Fellows begin their office work in the House, and the others in the Senate. At the mid-point of the program, each group moves to the other body in order to obtain a comprehensive view of congressional life. As Fellows' service has proven valuable to congressmen and is available to them without cost, many legislators inform The American Political Science Association of their keen interest in having a Fellow. The Fellows are free to pursue and negotiate those assignments which are most in accord with their personal backgrounds and professional interests. This procedure results in assignments which enhance the insights of the Fellows and the capabilities of the offices in which they serve.

About half of the 45 or 50 Congressional Fellows each year are selected in a national competition from among newsmen with an interest in government and politics, political scientists who have completed or are nearing completion of their doctorate, and outstanding law school faculty members. The criteria for selection are superior training, practical experience and professional competence. Political scientists, journalists, government officials and former Fellows interview and evaluate candidates. Designation of Fellowship recipients is by an Advisory Committee consisting of academics, journalists, and Republican and Democratic members of both Houses of Congress. This group also sets overall policy for the program.

The United States Civil Service Commission and the Association share in selecting other Fellows upon recommendation by the Federal agencies in which they are employed. Competition for these Federal careerist awards is similarly intense, and applicants are at middle-management levels. In addition, several foundations, including some which finance study grants for foreigners in the United States, affiliate with the Congressional Fellowship Program and share in selecting persons to gain this experience.

In cooperation with the Democratic and Republican National Committees, The American Political Science Association has additionally sponsored a parallel educational program involving the assignment of one political scientist each year to each national committee. It is appropriate that a former National Committee Fellow, by contributing a campaign chapter, has joined ten former Congressional Fellows in this volume.

Generous support for the program from the Ford Foundation, the Edgar Stern Family Fund, the Poynter Fund, Time, Inc., the New York Times Foundation, the Courier-Journal Louisville Times Foundation, the Shinner Foundation, the

Revlon Foundation, the Helen Dwight Reid Foundation, the Joseph E. Davies Foundation, the Commonwealth Fund (Harkness Fellows), and the Asia Foundation, as well as government training funds from the U.S. Civil Service Commission have provided the means to carry on the program.

In *To Be A Congressman*, the authors have demonstrated the training and educational effectiveness of this distinguished program of the Association.

Congressional Fellows in the Congressman's Office

REPRESENTATIVE WILLIAM A. STEIGER

A congressman's office is small. Unlike the staff of a governor, senator, mayor of a large city, or any major official in the executive branch, a congressional staff has few, if any, specialists. All of the work on literally hundreds of issues and problems is done by a mere handful of people. An assignment as a Congressional Fellow in the House therefore entails a broad range of jobs and experiences rather than a single concentrated research effort.

Over the past four years my office has been the principal workplace for seven Congressional Fellows. One was a lawyer, two were journalists, two were advanced predoctoral political scientists, and the remaining were young professional staff of Federal agencies.

To observe and do as much as possible in an apprenticeship of four and a half months, each Fellow (they are both men and women) has used a desk in my personal office. This is the one location that ensures a part in meetings I have with constituents, colleagues in the House, staff members, newsmen, students, interest groups, and whoever happens to call.

Duties of a Fellow may be determined by the special training and interests the individual brings to an office. More often, however, the work—like so many things—is determined by timing.

The Congressional Fellow sharing my office at present is a Boston newspaperman who has a strong background in manpower planning. Had he come here two or three years ago, his chief role would have been to help in drafting sorely needed manpower legislation. Today, since the arduous writing of the bill is completed, his chief efforts are devoted to garnering support. He is closely involved in all strategy and planning sessions associated with getting the bill passed. He has prepared a few speeches, has met with such organizations as the National

League of Cities and the U.S. Conference of Mayors, and he will cover many more.

Work of earlier Fellows similarly reflects the needs of the time. In early 1968, when pollution of the environment had not yet aroused widespread public consciousness, a Congressional Fellow helped in organizing a public hearing on lake pollution, held in Neenah, Wisconsin. The Fellow drew up a list of witnesses, scheduled their appearances, and handled the many arrangements before and during the hearing. Following the oral and written testimony of state and local conservation officials, biologists from universities, representatives of organizations such as the League of Women Voters, and a number of interested citizens, we compiled and published a record that led to Interior Department support of our legislation, the Clean Lakes Act. The legislation, now part of the Water Pollution Control Act, provides research and demonstration money to fight pollution in small lakes.

In the spring of 1969, when violence erupted on hundreds of college campuses, another Congressional Fellow's efforts aimed to end the alienation between students and Washington. Assisting the Campus Task Force, an ad hoc group of 22 members of Congress, the Fellow assigned to my office paid visits to more than a dozen campuses to arrange quiet meetings between students and members of the Task Force. Altogether we toured 50 campuses and met with students from every part of the political spectrum. We managed to do so without publicity in large part because of the painstaking advance work of a few congressional aides. Reforms we later outlined in a written report to the President were subsequently incorporated into the Reports of the Scranton Commission on Campus Unrest and the Carnegie Commission on Higher Education.

Having illustrated how work changes with the needs of a time, I should note there is one issue, as well as certain kinds of work, that remains a constant for Congressional Fellows. As a group whose underlying interest is, after all, the workings of Congress, it is not surprising that each of the seven Fellows in my office has taken a special hand in efforts for congressional reform. The precise form of the work has depended again on timing. One Fellow helped to write a set of 12 amendments to the 1970 Rules Committee Report on Legislative Reorganization. The most important of these was the proposal which now permits record teller votes in the Committee of the Whole, where most of the business of the House is conducted.

The Fellow currently in my office is rebuilding support for one of the amendments which failed House passage in 1970—a requirement that the *Congressional Record* use different styles of type face to distinguish what is said on the floor during debate and what speeches are merely inserted and not actually made. To revive this proposal, we are seeking cosponsorship from interested members on both sides of the aisle, and most especially the members of the Joint Committee on Printing.

Request handling and letter writing, crucial chores in every congressional office, are other constants in the work of congressman and Fellow alike.

Inherent in the Fellowship program is the notion that we learn by doing. It is obvious that the Fellows return to their teaching and writing with a greater "feel" for the legislative process. As a legislator, I find an APSA Fellow in my office gives me a greater perspective on the operations of a Federal agency, the pressures in a news office, the resources of academic institutions, and the literature of political science. The sharing of different experiences and backgrounds makes these brief Fellowships mutually rewarding and educational.

What It Means to Be in Congress

SENATOR HUBERT H. HUMPHREY

The Congressional Fellowship Program of the American Political Science Association long has had my enthusiastic support. In both my legislative and academic experiences I have been convinced of its substantial contribution to the campus and the Congress. Many Fellows have worked in my office, contributing ideas while learning-by-doing, and several subsequently have joined my staff as legislative assistants. The Program has been invaluable in deepening understanding of congressional operations among Federal officials, journalists and young scholars. It has contributed to realistic appraisal of Congress' work in the agencies, the press and university classrooms. And cumulatively the Fellows have become a distinctive force for realistic reform of the Congress.

This volume reflects the understanding and interests of some of these Fellows who have been involved in the daily life of the Congress. Here the reader encounters the Congress up-close, yet within a conceptual framework which helps to make clear the meaning of each phase of activity for the member of Congress, for the public, and for the political system.

The authors' involvement in congressional work has enabled them to discuss practical congressional politics. My own teaching and lecturing have repeatedly revealed the curiosity of students and general audiences about the how and why of congressional procedures. Their curiosity indeed is one of the vital strengths of our democracy.

Despite the growing interest among people in national politics, opportunities to see Congress at work through the eyes of a participant are rare. Not many people see a campaign from a candidate's point of view, face the problems of establishing and maintaining a representative's office, or attempt to become influential within the world of policy-makers.

It is therefore important not only that our government professors, political journalists and career government administrators have an opportunity to participate in congressional activities and share in "congressional thinking," but also that they contribute to the literature to which our students and interested citizens are exposed.

Based in large part on the pioneering program of the American Political Science Association, I have introduced legislation that would set up an ongoing internship program called Interns for Political Leadership. This legislation would establish intern programs at all levels of our government—local, state and Federal.

I believe that we need more programs like the American Political Science Association's Congressional Fellowship program. And, I certainly hope that more Fellows will use their professional talents to explore in one collected volume such as this, their congressional experiences and analyses.

The Fellows' book includes several topics seldom discussed in studies of the Congress. In opening and concluding chapters illuminating the campaign context of congressional life, the book appropriately links congressional processes to our representative function. Included are chapters on subjects basic to our work in both Houses, such as the fundamental service of handling constituents' problems and the techniques of press relations. The chapters on the House treat the little studied, but important, informal groups as well as the seniority reforms of the 91st, 92nd, and 93rd Congresses. Senate chapters discuss the establishment of Senator George McGovern's Select Committee on Nutrition and Human Needs, and the memorably skillful leadership of my late colleague, Senator Everett Dirksen. It is noteworthy that most of the illustrations and references in this volume stem from the 1970's.

These chapters afford the reader sound insights into a demanding, often controversial, and important career. They tell what it means to be a congressman. Few careers open such remarkable opportunities for translating dreams into reality. A new bill, a creative amendment, a wise appropriation, may mean the difference between health and sickness, jobs and idleness, peace and war for large numbers of people. Stemming from ancient parliamentary origins, the main job of Congress is to redress grievances, to right wrongs, to make freedom and justice living realities for all. This is the essence of politics: to translate the concerns and the creative responses of a vast citizenry into effective and humane laws.

I welcome this book; it will contribute significantly to public awareness of our job.

I | The Campaign

JOEL M. FISHER

Through his campaign, the congressional candidate develops his concepts of representation. He seeks to extend his public recognition and demonstrate his suitability as the constituency spokesman and decision-maker. To compete he must attract and organize supporters, raise money, define policy positions, and employ the increasingly sophisticated methods of modern campaign management. The chapter concludes by discussing the campaign's impact upon a congressman's behavior in office.

The author is Associate Professor of Political Science at California State University, Fullerton. He holds both a Ph.D. from Claremont Graduate School and a J.D. from the University of California Law School in Berkeley. President of the California Young Republicans in 1961, he was Chairman of "Win with Nixon" in 1962 and worked extensively in the 1968 and 1972 Republican Presidential campaigns. He also has worked on several congressional campaigns and in 1964 was regional campaign director in New York for the Keating for Senate Committee. He was the American Political Science Association's Republican National Committee Fellow in 1968-1969. For the following two years he served with the Department of State and on the White House staff.

1

A CITIZEN'S CANDIDACY for a seat in the House of Representatives or Senate is at once an exciting and promising event in his life and an important element in the nation's democratic process. The patterns of partisanship and the advantages of incumbency are such as to enable most victorious congressional candidates to serve in their posts for extensive periods of time. A successful campaign is commonly the opening event in a lengthy congressional career.

But the first campaign is of more than personal importance. As the candidate appeals for votes throughout a district whose population approaches a half million people, he gains understanding of the constituents' needs and aspirations. He develops sources of information, makes acquaintances, and achieves the support of various interest groups whose loyalties often become very durable. It is probable that citizens who gave a candidate his first significant assistance will maintain a feeling of closeness to him, and certainly the office-holder will strive to be continuously responsive to them.

In a discussion of congressmen's first successful campaigns, it is important to mention some contextual considerations. Many districts are not closely competitive; customarily, the overwhelming majority of incumbents are re-elected with more than 55 percent of the total vote. Candidates who oppose an incumbent face a very formidable challenge. To be successful they must overcome a heavy tide of traditional support for the incumbent and his party. Moreover, a candidate making his first race, particularly if he is opposing an incumbent, can expect difficulty securing sufficient funding for adequate media exposure. Similarly, he may lack the assistance of a helpful multitude of well-organized and experienced campaign workers. Nonetheless, even powerful incumbents occasionally are upset by resourceful challengers. When Margaret Heckler (Mass.) defeated 81-year old former Speaker Joe Martin in the 1966 GOP primary, she recited Martin's 1924 speeches against an incumbent who also was in his eighties. She asserted that the increasing complexity of government had made Martin's prescription for vigor far more compelling in 1966 than it had been during the Coolidge administration.

Because congressional elections are not necessarily held when there are great issues at stake but rather at fixed intervals, candidates may have difficulty defining issues suitable for their appeals. An absence of lively issues may significantly affect the election outcome.

A candidate's fate may be determined by voters' responses to developments beyond his control or influence. With the exception of special elections, congressional campaigns are conducted simultaneously with other races. Every four years they occur in the context of presidential elections which not only dominate the public's attention but swell turnout by a third or more. In other years a congressional candidate may find that constituents are particularly interested in local issues or candidacies.

All external influences aside, the congressional candidacy plays a particularly vital role in the American system of representative government. The voters' biennial choices for all House and one-third of the Senate seats constitute their principal means of shaping national policy.

The victorious congressional candidate is embarking not only upon a fascinating experience of representation, but also a new way of life. He will find the doors of Washington open to him, yet encounter heavy demands upon his time and family living habits. His office becomes central to his life style, determining most of his relationships with other people.

WHO RUNS AND WHY?

The open primaries and frequently weak party organizations which are characteristic of the American system permit candidates of greatly varied backgrounds and motivations to seek election to Congress. Representatives have been of all ages between 25 and 95 and from nearly as wide a range of ethnic, religious, educational, and occupational backgrounds as the population in general.

Some generalizations are nevertheless possible. As usual, a majority of the 93rd Congress, 1973-1975, are lawyers. For example, both senators and 27 of the 39 representatives from New York were trained in law. In rank order, other backgrounds are in business and banking, teaching, farming, and journalism. While the legal profession is over-represented, clergymen, workingmen, and most scientific fields are under-represented. Only 15 blacks were elected to the House in 1972. Of the only 85 women who ever have served, 35 were preceded in office by their husbands.

Very few are newcomers to political life. Campaign work or management for others is common seasoning for congressional candidates. Many aspirants to Congress have previously occupied the position of state legislator, mayor, or prosecuting attorney. For example, of the 19 current Michigan congressmen, 8 have been state legislators. Young candidates sometimes have found leadership in their party's youth organizations to be a helpful springboard. Among them have been John Ashbrook and former Congressman Donald E. "Buzz" Lukens, both of Ohio and both former Young Republican National Federation chairmen. In sharp contrast are the few, among them former member Allard Lowenstein (D., N.Y.), whose candidacies have been expressions of opposition to established party leaders. Some candidates have the advantage of local name recognition as they attempt to succeed to their fathers' seats, while a few belong to families which are politically famous across the country. The present Congress contains a new generation of Tafts and Stevensons, Symingtons, and Goldwaters.

A considerable number of House and, more commonly, Senate candidates have held state offices, among them governor, lieutenant governor, and attorney general. Of those presently serving in the Senate, 14 have been governors. Two-thirds of the senators have had previous experience as legislators at either the state or the national level. Perhaps surprisingly, however, only 39 have served as congressmen. Many candidates for both Houses have had prior experience at the national level, some

4

having served in congressional staff positions, others in positions with the executive branch. In contrast, Senators Frank Church (D., Idaho) and Charles Percy (R., Ill.) are examples of men whose first public employment beyond youthful military service followed their election to the Senate. Neither, however, was new to political life. In recent years, several prominent athletes have entered politics with successful congressional bids: Olympics champion Robert B. Mathias in California, baseball pitcher Wilmer "Vinegar Bend" Mizell in North Carolina, and Buffalo Bills' quarterback Jack F. Kemp in New York. Tennis star Joseph H. Blatchford, an unsuccessful candidate in California, later became director of the Peace Corps and Action. There are very few members of Congress who have not served an apprenticeship in some segment of political activity. Successful candidates commonly are veterans of military service and have engaged in prominent civic activity.

In discussing candidate motivations, one must first acknowledge that most seats are practically invulnerable to conquest. But the fact that incumbents are overwhelmingly re-elected does not preclude them from challenge, and few races are uncontested. Candidates running against secure incumbents are often motivated more by desire to achieve prominence useful in their legal or business careers than by chance of victory. Others may be running because of a sense of civic duty or to strengthen the overall appeal of their party's ticket. Even in such unpromising races, however, the possibility of a startling triumph can sustain a candidate's efforts and inflate his hopes.

The possibility for victory over an incumbent may be considerably enhanced by the presence on the challenger's ticket of extraordinarily popular candidates for other offices. Presidential "coattails" help a congressional challenger not only by attracting voters to his party's ticket but also by increasing turnout at the polls.

Other circumstances which may increase an incumbent's vulnerability include re-districting, the alienation of a key element of his traditional following, his age, and even scandal. A candidate's prospects are brightest, of course, when he is either seeking a vacant seat or challenging one of the fewer than 100 incumbents who occupy "swing seats." For each of these prized opportunities there frequently are several major aspirants.

Anyone considering candidacy must appraise its implications for his personal and professional life. The campaign will impose physical and emotional strain which he must have the health and stamina to endure. His family must be prepared to face continuing public scrutiny, and he may face the hardship of financial disruption while waging his campaign. He must also evaluate his potential for attracting the support and skills which an aggressive campaign will require.

STRATEGY

Information-gathering

The first task of any candidate for Congress is to obtain information basic to developing an effective strategy for winning the primary election and thereby his party's nomination. All candidates must inquire into the availability of workers and finances, approaches to the media, issues to be emphasized, and characteristics of the electorate. Those consulted may include party leaders; past and present candidates for office; spokesmen for the local press; and leaders of business, agricultural, labor, and professional groups and civic organizations.

Candidates without political experience or extensive personal familiarity with their district may find these explorations difficult. Others, particularly incumbent state legislators or local officials, are likely already to have such social contacts and to have little difficulty in gathering an initial response to their potential candidacy. A candidate challenging an incumbent congressman for nomination may find almost immediately that the bulk of the party and community leaders are predisposed to support the incumbent and not inclined to cooperate with his efforts. But where an incumbent somehow has antagonized these leaders, or where there is no incumbent, these discussions may be particularly fruitful.

In addition to the information provided by local notables, the candidate may review statistical data affording him insight into the political, social and economic composition of the district. Past election statistics are readily available from state and local governments. These data will reveal areas of party strength and weakness, as well as voting trends. Census statistics are helpful indicators of the composition of new communities, population growth and ethnic diversity. Government as well as chamber of commerce surveys provide information about local employment and income trends, the movement of businesses into or away from the area and the impact of Federal spending.

The public opinion poll is an increasingly utilized form of information-gathering. In general, polls have three kinds of utility: they can extend voters' recognition of the candidate's name; they can indicate the issues which most concern the public and how intensely people feel about them; and they can be of value in the development of campaign themes and in focusing the campaign upon the geographic areas where it is likely to have greatest effect.

Some candidates do not have sufficient need or resources to employ this technique. However, those who are running in new districts or areas of rapid social change or intense party competition will find it tremendously helpful in formulating campaign strategy. By the mid-1960's, 85 percent of the winning Senate and half of the winning House candidates used polls.[1] Depending upon the size of the sample and whether the polling is by interview or by mail, a single survey is likely to cost between $1,000 and $5,000. A candidate who has a money problem may feel that he can spend his funds in more effective ways. Furthermore, unless polls are carefully prepared and conducted, they can be misleading. Even if the results are accurate, indication that a candidate is either well ahead or trailing badly may be dysfunctional to his efforts, inflating the confidence or undermining the dedication of his organization. In some cases, polling data indicating that one candidate commands a handsome lead can discourage his opponent and incline voters toward the likely winner.

Because the characteristics of candidates and districts vary greatly, every campaign must be individually planned if it is to be effective. It is for this reason that the information-gathering process is so vital. The information is basic to the assessment of how the candidate can best spend his time and resources, what he must emphasize, and where he can obtain help. The general purposes of campaigning are the same for all candidates: to gain recognition among the voters and to make sure that those who are most likely to be supportive actually vote. The campaign plan is a schedule for the optimal utilization of the candidate's time, his team of co-workers, and the available finances as allocated to the media and other instruments for reaching and persuading the people. All plans must be flexible, as early assumptions about resources usually are not accurate and what one does depends on what other candidates do.

Campaign Organization

The candidate normally must rely totally upon his personal organization of friends and supporters as he battles for nomination. Thereafter, he gains the additional organizational support of his party.

In a very real sense, politics implies organization. Fundamentally, it is an arranging of individuals and groups into a team or coalition having the power to achieve an objective. The old-style "boss" typically was a master at campaign organization. Modern campaign strategists continue to regard organization-building as the "nuts and bolts" of politics.

While district variations make it impossible to outline precisely an organization suitable for every congressional campaign, it is instructive to examine the basic features of effective campaign structures. These include the campaign manager, the executive committee and other key personnel, and the headquarters from which campaign activities and materials emanate.

8

A personal organization offers an opportunity for the candidate to appeal broadly for assistance and votes without regard to parties or local political biases.

The executive committee meets regularly throughout the campaign. Breakfast sessions are frequently particularly productive, bringing people together when they are alert and aggressive, rather than late in the day when they are tired. These sessions review the activities of the previous week, assess their impact, and project ahead to assure that proper planning accompanies all campaign activities.

While the sessions of the executive committee typically are private, the campaign headquarters is the visible nerve center of the campaign. Its location must be convenient to workers and persons who may wish to visit during the course of the working day or while shopping. It should have adequate parking space and be large enough to accommodate meetings of campaign workers. The headquarters should be attractive and reflect *esprit de corps*. To maintain personal association and a spirited group of volunteers, the candidate should regularly appear at the headquarters and spend some time with the volunteers, perhaps having coffee with them and with visitors.

One of the more important tasks at the headquarters is that of answering the telephone. Most of the people who call will not have an opportunity to talk to or hear the candidate anywhere, but will form an impression of him through a phone conversation with someone at the office. A pleasant and cheerful voice symbolizes a friendly, interested, and optimistic candidate.

The good headquarters is one which the public steadily visits. If voters aren't coming in for literature, to meet the candidate and his followers and show interest in his program, the campaign is likely to be in serious trouble. In this sense, the headquarters is not only a place from which campaign efforts initiate, but a source of feedback as well.

11

Finances

Money, tellingly dubbed "the mother's milk of politics," determines a candidate's ability to pursue each stage of his strategy and each major decision on personnel utilization and media exposure. Some closely competitive House races cost between $100,000 and $150,000. Senate campaigns in the most populated states now often exceed $1 million.

Professional campaign managers commonly advise candidates to spend half of their resources on the media and the remainder on other needs. Thus, one expert budgeted a $50,000 House campaign in the following manner: advertising and promotion, including mailings, billboards, newspapers, radio and television as well as brochures and associated photographic needs, $25,000; headquarters, $4,000; personnel, including a paid manager, $11,000; candidate's travel and other campaign expenses, $2,500; and special events and party organizational activities, $7,500.

Raising funds to challenge a long-time incumbent can be a frustrating task. Obviously, non-incumbents have a greater need for money than do incumbents, who are better known, enjoy the franking privilege, which accords them free postage, and have the advantages of congressional staff. It is particularly difficult to raise funds for the primary election, as party support is normally unavailable prior to nomination. Occasionally, an extra-legal partisan group such as the California Democratic Clubs or the United Republicans of California will endorse and support primary candidates, but normally such candidates must obtain funds from those who are known in the community for past political activities or for community service.

Party contributions for congressional nominees range from very little to more than $10,000. Each party's congressional and senatorial campaign committees generally allocate funds to those non-incumbents whom they believe to have a reasonable chance of victory. Some funds may be provided by the state party, although its major interest is in campaigns for state offices. Despite these contributions and support from national groups such as the AFL-CIO's Committee on Political Education and the National Committee for an Effective Congress, most congressional campaign funds must be raised locally.

The candidate's finance chairman assumes responsibility for raising funds to sustain the campaign. Personal solicitation of potential donors by a member of the finance committee or someone acting in its behalf is essential. The proverbial barbecues, chicken dinners, and similar local events are not only effective financially, but also permit the candidate to mingle with his friends and supporters and to meet others in attendance. While expensive and somewhat risky, direct mail solicitations enable a candidate to express his objectives as well as his need for broad public support.

During the course of the campaign, the finance chairman must work closely with the other members of the executive committee to assure that campaign activities are scheduled so as to maximize cost effectiveness. While there is compulsion to spend heavily at the outset of a campaign, this pressure must be restrained. The greatest needs for media advertising, mailings, and telephone services occur in the final days of the campaign. Victory may depend upon the availability of adequate resources for this crucial period.

To maintain financial controls, the finance chairman or treasurer is often solely responsible for bookkeeping and for approving all payments. As the nominal campaign accountant, he must comply with the increasingly complex and detailed requirements for reporting contributions and expenditures to the appropriate legal authorities.

Many are the candidates who find themselves $5,000 or $10,000 out-of-pocket at the conclusion of their losing campaigns. In 1972 one well known first-time candidate in Connecticut suffered the misfortune of having his house attached by a New Haven public relations firm and nine unpaid members of his staff.

The Role of the Candidate

A candidate's foremost concern is the manner and extent of his communications with the public. Indeed, a campaign is a planned series of communications between candidate and voters. He is the focus. As leader of people, he must coordinate and inspire his co-workers on a schedule of personal strategic design. As "salesman" of ideas, he must determine the few simple themes to dominate his campaign. As one who must win the confidence of the public, he must decide how to maximize his appeal as a person, perhaps in contrast to his opponent. Normally, the more personal the communication, the more effective it is. He must maximize his personal contacts in the constituency, concentrating upon the groups whose combined support are essential to victory. The demand for stamina can be almost merciless, yet he must also maintain poise and good cheer.

Voters desire candidates who are dynamic, demonstrate integrity and capacity for leadership, are personable and willing to listen, understand and articulate their sentiments, and have relevant experience. It is common to present strength by implicit contrast. For example, if an opponent is inconsistent or weak in credibility, it may be advantageous to stress one's own reliability or that "Joe is a man you can trust."

It is common also to counter impressions of one's own weakness. The winning 1966 campaign of former Representative George Bush (R., Tex.) is illustrative. He had learned from pre-campaign polls not only that he was not well-known but also that he was perceived as lacking warmth and sincerity. Following the pollster's advice, he sought to project warmth and dynamism in his billboard and television advertising. "Vote for Bush and Watch the Action" became the theme of illustrations depicting him as a man of action, with jacket slung across his shoulder as he mingled with children.[2]

In planning a campaign, a candidate may wish to follow the advice of many professionals who believe it is wise to avoid

14

publicizing his opponent. As the purpose of the campaign is exposure, it is counterproductive to call voters' attention to a rival. For this reason, experts commonly advise avoidance of debates, which not only grant visibility to the opposition, but also may confuse the basic themes which the candidate is striving to project.

The candidate's development of policy positions is an integral part of his strategy. An issues committee consisting of task forces concentrates on the concerns closest to home, on national issues, and on the record of the opponent. An incumbent's record may reveal considerable vulnerability in his voting as well as in his service in securing Federal assistance for the district's media. An advantage of having a task force is that the candidate can defer taking a position on a particularly sensitive issue pending its report, while still being able to supplement the work of one's own volunteers in developing positions. Local academicians, who generally lack sufficient understanding of the practical aspects of campaigning to be good managers, can provide valuable research assistance. The superb task force is one which can reduce findings to a few "talking points" of tactical utility.

The candidate must give his campaign a sense of motion and vitality through personal appearances, yet not "peak" too soon. The effective campaign schedule includes its entire span, beginning with the initial covert activities prior to public announcement of candidacy and outlining where the candidate is to concentrate his personal efforts until election day. The purpose of scheduling is to maximize the candidate's exposure where it is likely to have broadest impact. A county characterized by "ticket-splitting" offers a special opportunity for winning new support to augment the party faithful and the candidate's personal supporters. The candidate's presence at country fairs, other civic events, service clubs, railway stations, and factory gates must be carefully planned. Shopping centers provide opportunities to shake hands with great numbers of people, and it is similarly useful to become known in the barber shops. An "advance man" can help to gather crowds to hear the candidate and bring passers-by to him. Similarly, a banjo player or band can help attract an audience.

Media and Public Relations

Media use is governed by the budget. The opportunity to reach massive numbers of people through television advertising must be weighed against the realities of the treasury and the fact that the most costly campaign is not necessarily the most effective. Weekly papers and throwaways may offer an effective advertising opportunity at far less cost than some major daily newspapers. Advertising in a newspaper whose circulation covers several congressional districts means that little of the expense is on target. Metropolitan television coverage has similar drawbacks. Moreover, it is very expensive: 30 seconds of prime time in Los Angeles or New York may cost $1,500 to $3,000. Radio advertisements broadcast during commuting hours, and popular musical programs or "talk shows" enable a candidate to reach many people at far less cost. Because television and radio advertising is the most expensive element of the campaign, scheduling for concentrated impact at its climax is imperative. A candidate's press aide can make a crucial contribution by making sure that the candidate does things that are newsworthy, that the press knows his schedule, and that the papers receive bulletins in a useable format at the appropriate times.

Increasingly, well-financed congressional candidates are turning to professional public relations firms for either total management of their campaign, for direction of media services, or for polling or strategic counseling. In some states, notably California, their role as campaign specialists has virtually supplanted that of the party organization. Major firms undertake accounts for candidates for various offices in several states. A pioneer among campaign management firms was Whitaker and Baxter, which began in 1933 and specializes in Republican campaigns. Well-known campaign managers include Joseph

16

Napolitan of Pennsylvania, who handles Democratic candidates, and F. Clifton White, who has been associated with many prominent Republicans. An example of a specialist performing campaign services is Harry Treleaven, who prepared television commercials for George Bush's successful 1966 House campaign and for Richard Nixon's presidential campaigns of 1968 and 1972.

Sources of Organizational Support

The weaker the candidate's financial resources and media capability, the more he must rely on his organization of volunteer workers. Indeed, volunteers are essential for the personal contact and enthusiasm needed to win. One needs the efforts of a multitude. The sources of such help are personal supporters, the local party organization, and interest groups. Campuses and service clubs are common bases for recruitment.

The functions performed by such workers include door-to-door canvassing, telephoning, stuffing envelopes for mailing, hosting of teas, manning the headquarters, serving as baby-sitters to free others for constructive effort, driving voters to the polls, and watching the polls to guard against irregularity in the balloting. The volunteers and their effective coordination become crucial in the closing days and hours of the campaign, especially as the "victory squads" canvass the key districts. The importance of their services, however, transcends the functions named. The volunteers' activity conveys the impression that the candidate organizes well and has the confidence of great numbers of local residents. Moreover, every volunteer recruited is not only a commitment gained but also a key to obtaining the support of that person's friends and associates. Volunteers render invaluable service in introducing the candidate in their own communities and extending his reputation.

Recruitment incentives for prospective workers include desire to support the party, exposure to the candidate, perhaps an opportunity to influence him, as well as occasions to observe or associate frequently with other politically important people.

17

For many, a campaign provides opportunities to make friends and feel useful. Volunteers may be trying to learn about politics, work their way into positions of party responsibility, acquire titles, gain exciting assignments, or even prepare for their own future candidacy. A few are enticed by the prospect of going to Washington as a member of a congressional staff.

Congressional candidates always attract some workers who are motivated by ideological or issue preferences. In some instances, as in the anti-Vietnam War and pro-domestic reform campaigns of Allard Lowenstein, these persons are the prime source of volunteers. They exist on the right as well as on the left side of the political spectrum, and among collegians, middle-aged persons, and senior citizens.

Once a candidate has won the party nomination, he will seek the support of his party leaders for the general campaign. In a year of a presidential election or when there are important state-wide contests, the party will work on his campaign as part of its total effort. In many instances, because of the size of the district, the candidate will be coordinating his efforts with those of several party units, often several county chairmen. If there are no state-wide elections, the congressional candidate gains the advantage of becoming the leading figure, but lacks the potential benefit of association with state-wide candidates.

Party support results in acquiring experienced people who have an established communications system and can provide research, money, a usually hard-working women's auxiliary, and an occasionally effective youth organization. The national party organizes training schools for non-incumbent candidates as well as fieldmen to advise on campaign techniques and procedures. Local party auxiliary organizations, such as Republican Associates of Los Angeles County, have also conducted campaign schools for candidates and managers. The California Republican State Central Committee conducts a periodic "Winners Round-up" to advise the various candidates on the newest techniques. The local party can also attract letters of endorsement and appearances by prominent office-holders.

With increasing frequency, national leaders are becoming involved in congressional campaigning. Candidates are invited to the Hill or to the White House for photograph sessions, and the presidential plane may touch down in the district to demonstrate the Chief Executive's interest. Vice Presidents regularly assume extensive congressional campaign responsibilities. Former Presidents and presidential candidates, as illustrated so vividly by the nationwide activity of Richard Nixon between 1960 and 1968, frequently travel widely in support of their party's congressional candidates. They also participate in 30-second radio endorsements and similar supportive techniques. Sure winners, competitive candidates, or those opposing incumbents who have been selected for all-out attack are more likely than almost certain losers to have their pleas for assistance approved.

The candidate must look beyond the party organization and his personal campaign team to secure the broad following required for victory. The support of interest groups is essential and requires aggressive cultivation. Social, professional, and ethnic group leaders are often pivotal in election outcomes. They provide endorsements, audiences, volunteers, finances, and special media publicity.

Prominent members of community interest groups can provide a nucleus for special campaign structures and appeals, such as "Senior Citizens for X." Endorsements of groups of doctors, educators, leaders of commerce and industry, and others trusted throughout the community will be useful in imparting widespread confidence in the candidate. A Republican in a Democratic district will often seek to form a "Democrats for X Committee." For Democrats, organized labor is a significant source of support, although unions do help some Republicans. Business groups are more likely to assist Republicans. In the biggest cities, the minority groups' vote may be fundamental to forming a winning coalition, and in such constituencies the ethnic press can be highly influential.

In addition to the opportunity for increased candidate contact with the public, interest groups perform a more subtle function. By providing information through dialogue, they not only help him frame his program but also enable him to avoid unwittingly offending a segment of the public. Among other specifics, he is likely to learn how current or potential government actions will affect interested groups. Before approaching a group, he may prepare himself by studying his opponent's voting record and public statements so as to point out weaknesses and, by comparison, his own strengths in advancing the group's interests. Having a good working relationship with a group will help him to prepare answers to questions as thorny as that of the farmer who asks: "Will you help us retain the right to use pesticides on our crops?" Contact with groups should help the candidate to recognize how his answer will be evaluated by the environmentalists as well as by the farmers whose incomes may be affected.

Such dilemmas are the recurring peril of the aspiring candidate. They test his adroitness in responding to the multi-faceted interests and pressures of congressional politics.

CONCLUSION

To be a congressman is to be a campaigner. The campaign is not an isolated event in his career. It is his building block. It educates him in the substance of representation, illuminating the nuances pertinent to his district while teaching him what to emphasize, what his constituents expect, and what would be imprudent. Procedurally, the campaign establishes a system of contacts, a network of helpful advisers. Thus campaigning defines the congressman's representative function. It accordingly should not be surprising that any congressman seems to be campaigning continuously while in office. As campaigning is basic to representing, it is an integral part of the congressman's job.

1. Robert King and Martin Schnitzer, "Contemporary Use of Private Political Polling," *Public Opinion Quarterly*, XXXII (Fall, 1968), p. 21.
2. Dan Nimmo, *The Political Persuaders: The Techniques of Modern Election Campaigns* (Englewood Cliffs, N.J.: Prentice-Hall, 1970), pp. 90-91.

II | The Freshman Faces Congress

GERALD D. STURGES

The newly elected congressman immediately confronts a variety of problems. For the representative who wins a seat in a special election and thus arrives in Congress during a session, the needs are particularly pressing. This chapter discusses the first-term aspirations, challenges, adjustments, and satisfactions of such a member, and the conditions of his effectiveness.

The author is Legislative Assistant to Congressman David R. Obey (D., Wis.). A graduate of the University of California in philosophy, he was for nine years a reporter for the Oakland Tribune, covering the city of Berkeley and the University. He also has contributed articles to numerous periodicals. In 1968-1969, he was a Congressional Fellow of the American Political Science Association, serving in the offices of Senator William W. Proxmire (D., Wis.) and the Subcommittee on Foreign Operations and Government Information of the House Committee on Government Operations.

ANYONE WHO HAS EVER changed jobs knows how disruptive it is to relocate oneself and one's family while mastering a new position. An incoming congressman faces extraordinary challenges, including hiring a staff, organizing his office, answering a flood of congratulatory letters and others conveying constituent requests, and getting to know hundreds of new colleagues. Generally he has almost two months to accomplish these tasks before Congress convenes and the legislative process begins. Nonetheless, a man is not likely to feel at home in the fast-moving Washington community for many more months.

A few members initially win their seats not at general elections, but at special elections held to fill a vacancy caused by the death or resignation of an incumbent. For them, because they arrive in the midst of a legislative session, there is no time for gradual orientation. Such was the challenge facing David R. Obey in the spring of 1969.

On April 1, 1969, there was a special election in Wisconsin's Seventh District to fill the seat vacated by Republican Melvin R. Laird. Laird, who enjoyed a plurality of more than 44,000 votes the previous November in winning election to his ninth term, had resigned in January to become President Nixon's Secretary of Defense. The race to succeed him fell to State Senator Walter J. Chilsen (R), 45, and Assemblyman David R. Obey (D), 30.

In an upset, Obey polled 63,567 votes to Chilsen's 59,512, becoming the first Democrat to win the seat in this century. It seemed clear in retrospect that Laird's popularity and ability outstripped his party's, and that the district was not, after all, as Republican as it had appeared. Indeed, in November, while Laird was amassing 64.1 percent of the vote, Nixon eked by with 50.1 percent. Moreover, Democratic U.S. Senator Gaylord Nelson carried the Seventh District with 58.6 percent and the losing Democratic candidate for governor, Bronson C. LaFollette, did so with 50.4 percent in the Seventh District. Obey got an election day boost from the weather, which was good enough to permit the large turnout of dairy farmers and other voters he felt he needed to win, and from the Nixon administration's Department of Agriculture, whose unpopular decision not to maintain the support price on manufacturing milk at 90 percent of parity was being broadcast that morning to those same dairy farmers.

On April 3, Obey and his wife, Joan, flew to Washington to be met at National Airport by former Vice President Hubert Humphrey. "This is the greatest thing since Coca-Cola," said Humphrey, hustling Obey over to the Capitol to be sworn in as the youngest member of the House of Representatives.

ORIENTATION TO THE HOUSE

In just two days, Dave Obey had been transformed from winning candidate into freshman congressman. A water pollution bill he knew nothing about was up for debate the next day. His office in the Longworth Building was devoid of files of any kind. There were, however, between 4,000 and 5,000 letters piled atop the desks, some of them from people with urgent problems. The letters deserved prompt handling, but he had no staff to start the processing.

Every congressman has certain basic responsibilities, among them providing service to his district, carrying out his committee assignment, and conducting himself capably on the floor of the House. The newcomer's task is to learn quickly how he can fulfill them. "In the early stages," Obey declares, "I wasn't equipped to do any of these."

The freshman faces a broad range of problems from the outset. He wants to get to know the other members of the House and the rules of its legislative road. He wants to learn about effective committee service: how committee assignments are made; what attendance, homework, and specialization they entail; and how to utilize committee staff. He wants to know how to serve and inform his constituents.

It took Obey approximately two and a half weeks to put a staff together. He interviewed about 30 applicants before hiring a head secretary, and screened another 20 to find the caseworker he wanted. During those hectic weeks the staffs of other members helped him process the most urgent cases among the thousands of unanswered letters. Obey's one advantage in coming into the House alone was visibility, which meant more members could get to know him in a short time than would normally be the case.

He missed the freshman seminar. Held at the start of every new Congress since 1963, it is presented by a bipartisan committee of House members with the co-sponsorship of the American Political Science Association and the Congressional Research Service of the Library of Congress. The seminar in January, 1969, co-chaired by Representatives Morris Udall (D., Ariz.) and Albert Quie (R., Minn.), was open to all 39 freshmen. Three titles from the seminar outline suggest the range of challenges facing a freshman congressman: "Becoming an Effective and Creative Member of the House"; "Operations and Administration of the House Office"; and "Working for the District."

In terms of his own background, Obey may have had most to gain from the seminar discussions on office administration. His experience as a state legislator prepared him very adequately for other aspects of his role as a congressman. He had been elected to the Wisconsin Assembly from Marathon County's Second District at the age of 24 and re-elected three times, becoming assistant minority leader. Obey in 1964 was named one of three outstanding freshman assemblymen by several newspaper writers, in 1966 received a legislative leadership award from the Eagleton Institute of Politics at Rutgers University, and in 1968 was named Outstanding Education Legislator in the Nation by the National Education Association's rural division.

BEGINNING TO MAKE AN IMPACT

Congressional observers often comment that a member may achieve the greatest impact within Congress through specializing in a small number of policy fields, generally within the jurisdiction of the committees and subcommittees on which he serves. While a newcomer may be aware of this need, he doubtless finds it difficult to realize, particularly during his first months in office when he confronts a baffling array of demands from within the Congress, the Washington scene, and his district. Yet it is important to make an early impact upon the people he represents, and useful to make some early, positive, and noteworthy impact upon the business of the House. The background of a member often affects his progress.

Former state legislators coming to Congress must learn to cope with greater responsibilities and probably adjust to a new legislative style. They generally are unaccustomed to working with sizeable personal and committee staffs and may find it difficult to relinquish as many chores as they should to meet the demands of their crowded congressional schedules. These are the kinds of changes of habit which were required of Obey.

Problems of office administration can be compounded by the casework load. Added to the new requests for information or bureaucratic intervention that a freshman receives are the many cases resubmitted by constituents dissatisfied with the previous member's service. The caseload thus can appear to be staggering. Unless the freshman avails himself of an experienced and efficient caseworker, he may amass a huge backlog of unprocessed cases and render inadequate constituent service.

To whatever extent any congressman must visit his district, the need for a freshman to do so is even greater. He is not likely to be well known around the district and there is a widespread curiosity to see what he looks like, hear how he sounds, and learn how he thinks. Obey, like most newcomers to Congress, found it compelling to travel, despite the substantial expense and considerable disruption and fatigue. Little more than four months after the Congressman took office, Norman Miller of the *Wall Street Journal* wrote that Obey was gaining political strength because of his travel and concluded that a member receives quick and valuable benefit in exchange for his personal expenses and his extensive efforts on behalf of constituents:

Mr. Obey flies back to Wisconsin three weekends out of four: one trip a month comes out of the Federal budget, and the others cost him about $125 each. But it's money well spent for an ambitious politician. The Congressman has no trouble finding a service club or similar forum for speechmaking, and radio-TV stations usually ask to interview him.[1]

Helping ordinary constituents solve problems is perhaps the most politically rewarding work of all. Obey or an aide frequently responds by telephone when someone back home writes for help, drawing upon the generous allotment of telephone and telegraph service which is immediately available to the new congressman.

When a person is elected to Congress, he discovers that his new position opens many free or low-cost opportunities to keep his name before the public. Obey found that the daily and weekly newspapers in his district were willing to publish a weekly column under his byline on public issues.

Several radio stations broadcast as a public service five-minute programs which he taped each week at the House recording studio. The circumstances of such media opportunities vary with the political calendar. The Federal Communications Commission holds that broadcasting a congressman's newsletter during a campaign requires that other candidates be given equal time. Recognizing the immediate need to broaden his reputation, Obey began utilizing radio opportunities shortly after taking office in anticipation of the campaign barely more than a year ahead.

Another way to make an impact on one's constituents is to seek their opinions on leading issues. The postal frank enabled Obey to mail a questionnaire free of charge to all 152,000 households in his district soliciting opinions on 18 issues, among them social security benefit increases and deployment of antiballistic missiles. A congressman derives benefits from such a poll beyond knowledge about the attitudes of his constituents. He enhances the recognition of his name. Also, the process of consulting the people conveys a sense that the congressman is truly representing them and promotes good will, often regardless of the questions asked or his eventual vote.

During his first four months in office, Obey employed all of these means of establishing personal and media communication with his constituents. Simultaneously he was trying to make an impact in the House, wrestling with the problem of speaking out without getting shut out. As Representative Richard Bolling (D., Mo.) has put it, "The seniors tend to regard new members as fraternity brothers regard pledges."[2] Tactics smacking of showmanship or aggressiveness are unwelcome. Being a freshman means ranking last on a committee roster and being last to question witnesses at committee hearings, if, indeed, having a chance to question them at all.

Each newcomer must decide for himself how to shake off his junior status and start making a difference in the national legislature. By advice or by instinct, he learns when to accept and when to challenge the restraints imposed by the seniority system. Assuming he genuinely intends to become a legislator, he learns hard work and loyalty, and develops a personal blend of speech and silence, perseverance and patience, conscience and compromise, in order to make an impact.

Obey was assigned to the Public Works Committee. The slot had potential because this committee handles legislation on water pollution control, which is a pressing problem for many small communities in his district. While Obey did not have the leverage needed to win many projects for his district, his committee assignment could help municipal officials in his district deal with the Federal bureaucracy. The assignment also made it quite natural for him to speak out on the House floor, as Obey frequently did, to demand increased Federal appropriations for water pollution control equipment.

Just two months after taking office, Obey had to decide whether to support or oppose his committee chairman on a bill to prevent demonstrators from using Federal property in the District of Columbia for camping, sleeping, sitting in or other overnight occupancy, or for erecting any temporary structure. In a maverick course, Obey joined Representative Richard D.

McCarthy (D., N.Y.) in filing minority views opposing passage of the bill. They contended in part:

> Campsites on the grounds of the Lincoln and Jefferson Memorials are a disfigurement to the landscape of this city. But, tragically, they are no more a disfigurement than poverty, hunger, and injustice, that part of our national portrait which these camp-ins are trying to bring to the attention of the Congress and the American people.[3]

The bill passed the House anyway. Meanwhile, Obey was passing the leadership's tests, whatever they were. While some members wait years for preferred committee assignments, Obey's opportunity came very early. The resignation of Representative Charles S. Joelson (D., N.J.) to accept a judicial appointment created a vacancy on the powerful Appropriations Committee, and Obey was chosen to fill it.

According to Representative Wilbur Mills (D., Ark.), Chairman of the Ways and Means Committee (whose Democratic members comprise the House Democratic Committee on Committees and hence control all of the party's committee assignments), Obey was only the third freshman of his party in this century to be appointed to Appropriations. In announcing the assignment, Mills termed it "an indication of the confidence we have in his future performance," and observed that "Obey's predecessor was on this committee and used that position to good advantage for his constituency."

Three months later, Appropriations Committee Chairman George Mahon (D., Tex.) named Obey to its District of Columbia and Interior subcommittees. The latter position offered him a good vantage point from which to oversee expenditures for the conservation of natural resources, including timber, water, minerals, oil, fish, and wildlife, major concerns of Obey's district.

Desirable though it was, the new committee assignment promised to be time-consuming. Chairman Mahon was determined to avoid a re-run of the appropriations "late show" of 1969, when fiscal 1970 money bills and their authorizations piled up on one another, and that would mean working diligently to adhere to his committee timetable for fiscal 1971. Time, alas, is even scarcer for the newcomer in his second year.

TAILORING EFFORTS TO RE-ELECTION

Quite apart from his serious and determined efforts to achieve stature within and outside of Congress, the freshman feels the relentless pressure of the impending test at the polls. While on the one hand the member must find it satisfying to run for the first time upon the basis of his own record in office, on the other hand he will inevitably find himself confined by that record. Now he is more than a challenger. No longer is he free to merely question and advocate in abstract terms; he carries with him a sense of responsibility to his office and to the Congress. He is now the defender, facing the people upon a platform of both words and actions.

Particularly in the case of a new member such as Obey, who had replaced a longtime leader of the opposition party, the realities of the political process are sometimes truly foreboding. Obey could not afford complacency. As a Democrat, his only route to a congressional career lay in convincing the voters of central Wisconsin that he merited their continued support, despite their habitual Republicanism. To meet this objective, Obey needed to consider its consequences in terms of organizing his time in Congress, giving priorities to constituency-oriented issues, sounding out public opinion, and securing favorable publicity.

Meanwhile, state and district Republican leaders were forging plans to recapture the seat. A Milwaukee newspaper reported in March of 1970 their open acknowledgement that "failure might lead to Democratic control for years to come." The newspaper article cited agreement that Obey had built an effective personal organization, and said, "The do-or-die Republican attitude suggests that the GOP will pour substantial sums into the district and perhaps even dispatch a superstar to woo the voters."[4]

Mapping the campaign becomes a more or less constant exercise, especially demanding if the freshman has not learned how to delegate responsibility. Inability to master administration of a congressional office can darken a freshman's electoral outlook, because it siphons off his very precious personal campaign time and energy. He ends up doing himself what should be delegated to others.

For example, a freshman will want to find and develop his own issues. That means extrapolating beyond the needs of his district to areas of personal interest or expertise. It isn't any easy goal to meet. His staff's capability comes into it, and whatever his staff may lack in direction or resourcefulness will devalue the freshman's time or political stock.

Obey's legislative program was fairly broad. Representing a region both urban and rural, with strong dairy interests, he introduced a bill, co-sponsored by nearly the entire Wisconsin delegation, to make indemnity payments available to dairy manufacturers as well as to milk producers when their milk has been contaminated by pesticides. The provision was incorporated into the final conference version of the 1970 farm bill. He also introduced legislation to boost Social Security benefits, and a package of bills pertaining to the environment.

Keenly interested in improved health care, and aware that the average Seventh District dairyman is 57 years old, Obey spent several months preparing a bill to provide outpatient prescription drug coverage under Medicare. It may have been the first such measure to prescribe payroll tax financing under Medicare's Part A provisions, instead of monthly premium financing under its supplementary medical insurance (Part B) provisions. He also introduced Senator Gaylord Nelson's bill to set up a national drug testing and evaluation center, and took part in the losing floor fight to add a $350 million emergency health amendment to an appropriation bill. There were other bills pertaining to mink ranchers, the shooting of animals from airplanes, speedier criminal trials, shoe and textile imports, and corporate farming.

Pursuing one's own issues means not only doing legislative homework, but dunning Federal agencies about such things as their use of DDT and their knowledge of the environmental effects of mercury compounds. It can also mean supporting the Federal Trade Commission's intention to promulgate a rule banning the issuance of unsolicited credit cards, or protesting the decision of the Civil Aeronautics Board to permit the airlines to round off passenger fares to the next higher dollar, or querying Seventh District auto dealers about manufacturers' warranties and service problems. Obey did all of these things.

As the months passed, Obey sent out postal patron news-letters on such topics as the tax reform bill, crime, and the economy. He devoted much attention to local opinion through frequent visits home and by reviewing voluminous constituent mail. He listened to local opinion, but he also tried to guide it.

In an election analysis, *Congressional Quarterly* wrote of the Seventh District race:

> The seat was perennially Republican, and Laird had consist-ently won by large margins. But Obey's strenuous campaign-ing, and the vigorous attention he has given to constituent needs, lead Wisconsin observers to call him the favorite as he seeks his first full term.[5]

This respected journal concluded that the outcome "leaned" Democratic.

On the day before the election, the *Capital Times* of Madison, Wisconsin, whose Seventh District circulation is small, noted that the *New York Times* two days earlier had ranked Wisconsin Congressmen Robert Kastenmeier, Henry Reuss and David Obey among the "most valuable members of the House." In editorially praising Kastenmeier and Reuss, the New York paper had declared, "David Obey, a freshman Democrat, gives promise of being a congressman of the same high quality." The story added that the three were among 40 House members praised by the *Times* as "outstanding because of their generally effective work or their devotion to the public interest in certain fields."

Field & Stream, a magazine of considerable interest in Obey's recreation-conscious district, rated congressmen on environmental issues in its September, 1970, issue. Obey was among the top 21 in the House who were rated as "very good," defined by the magazine as "usually can be counted on; willing to tackle tough issues."

Endorsements notwithstanding, it remained to be seen in November how well Obey had met his freshman challenges. He would be judged on how well he had fulfilled his basic responsibilities, especially service to his district, while beginning to make an impact in the House. How did the voters react to Obey's performance as a freshman?

On a wet and dreary November 3, 1970, Obey defeated his Republican opponent, Andre Le Tendre, and a third party candidate, claiming 68 percent of the vote. As a sophomore, Obey would be facing new challenges, but he would be doing so with the confidence of a second-term congressman.[6]

CONCLUSION

In summary, the challenges to a freshman congressman are to gain a good working relationship with new staff and colleagues; to widen public contact, not only by personal meeting, but also by constituent service and through the media; not least important, to become a good listener; to identify the issues in the legislative process which are of value to his district and the avenues through which to make an impact upon them; and to present a creditable record for the purpose of re-election.

The freshman term is a time of learning, generally by the time-honored approach of trial and error. For many members it represents a change in life style. Obey had met the challenges and significantly strengthened his political base. His 1970 margin of re-election attested to his effectiveness in broadening his constituency support.

Yet, in looking back at his freshman term, Obey, as all other members, could discern a number of things that he would have done differently had he had the benefit of hindsight. He would have put greater emphasis upon learning the procedures of House debate, so that he would feel more confident in his floor activities. He would have sought a better sense of legislative scheduling, in order to take greater advantage of long weekends for visits throughout his district. He would have been somewhat less combative with the press, or in other words, "rolled with the punches." And on a personal note, he would have limited his appearances at receptions and other social events and sought to spend fewer evenings working in his office, so that he could devote more time to his family. As Obey entered his second term, he took steps to fulfill these needs.

Obey's candid reflections express the extent to which a member's first years in office are a kind of "on-the-job training" experience, in which he comes to grips with the dimensions of his role and develops a personal approach to his tasks. Given the many challenges, the overall conclusion is readily apparent: the key to effectiveness in Congress is the ability to organize well within a framework of carefully selected priorities. It is not possible, however, to construct a grand master plan such that priorities and the time to be devoted to each will neatly mesh, for legislative life is subject to sudden and numerous complications. While the legislator keeps his overall objectives in mind, he establishes operational priorities in large part by political instinct.

1. Norman C. Miller, "New Congressman Finds Campaigning Is Easier Now That He's in Office, The *Wall Street Journal*, August 8, 1969, p. 1. Newcomers to the 93rd Congress received a vastly expanded Washington-to-district travel allowance of 38 round trips per Congress.

2. Richard Bolling, "The House," *Playboy* (November, 1969), p. 255.

3. U.S. Congress, House, Committee on Public Works, Report No. 283, 91st Congress, 1st Session, on H.R. 1035, June 4, 1969 (Washington: Government Printing Office, 1969).

4. James W. McCulla, "GOP Rallies to Regain Obey Seat," *Milwaukee Journal*, March 30, 1970.

5. *Congressional Quarterly Weekly Report*, XXVIII, No. 30, Part 1, July 24, 1970, p. 1882.

6. The 1970 decennial census revealed that Wisconsin's population had not grown as rapidly as the nation's and that it would have to endure the torturous political experience of eliminating one of its ten congressional seats. A reapportionment plan was enacted which broke up the Tenth District, a forested, northwestern region of dairy farmers, tourism, and economic stagnation that, while often voting Democratic, had been represented by Republican Alvin O'Konski since 1943. From Obey's adjoining Seventh District the plan stripped nine counties lying to the east and south. To the remaining six counties it appended 12 of the 17 counties comprising the Tenth District, expanding the size of the Seventh from less than 13,000 square miles to more than 18,000, one-third of the State's land area. Obey faced the necessity of building voter support in a district in which he was not well known. But O'Konski, who chose to challenge Obey in 1972 rather than to retire, confronted a constituency which seemed on the surface to be favorable to the Democrats. Indeed, Obey won 63 percent of the vote.

III | Symbiosis: Congress and the Press

DELMER D. DUNN

A congressman must work through the media to gain publicity in support of his legislation, image, and future candidacy. In turn, the media are a source of his policy ideas and information about his constituency and the activities of fellow legislators. This chapter explores the methods by which senators and representatives make news and the ways they organize their office staffs to conduct press relations.

The author, who earned a Ph.D. from the University of Wisconsin, is Associate Professor of Political Science at the University of Georgia. He is the author of Public Officials and the Press (1969) and Financing Presidential Elections (1971), the latter undertaken as a Brookings Institution Research Associate in 1969-1970. During the previous academic year, he was a Congressional Fellow of the American Political Science Association, serving in the offices of Senator Walter Mondale (D., Minn.) and Representative Frank Thompson, Jr. (D., N.J.).

IT IS DIFFICULT TO READ a newspaper or watch a national television news program these days without hearing charges of "credibility gap" or "news management" with countercharges of "slanted news" or "nonobjectivity." The intensity and persistence of such discussions suggest that both political reporters and public officials regard the relationship between the press and government as fundamental to the democratic process. Analysis of press work in congressional offices shows it to be a central element of office structure and responsibility.

COMMUNICATING THROUGH THE PRESS

To be an effective senator or representative, one generally needs to develop both skills and routines in working with the press. For several purposes it is important for legislators to make news. Of primary importance is showing constituents that their man is doing a "good job" in Washington. The most notable examples of press communications designed to fulfill this function are the many routine announcements of bills introduced and grants made by the Federal government to the benefit of the home district. Regular newsletters offering commentary on national problems also serve this function.

While not all representatives and senators are "publicity hounds," most reap satisfaction from personal publicity. This publicity, of course, can have more substantial payoffs than personal satisfaction. Senators and representatives believe that the better known they are, the greater are their chances for re-election. Publicity which emphasizes their names is a primary means of building this identity with their constituency. Senators and representatives who seek to become national political figures recognize that the press offers opportunities to communicate their policy views throughout the country. Building a reputation for policy leadership cannot be done solely through direct personal contact. The media become crucial to the success of persons seeking higher office.

Congressmen also desire to make news in order to create an image of themselves as active and concerned leaders. A government commission recently recommended such "symbolic output" in calling upon the President of the United States to better indicate his responsiveness to students by showing greater willingness to listen to them. An official's concern may be expressed entirely apart from government actions actually providing goods and services or initiating the regulation of behavior. By disseminating symbolic outputs, the media enable a legislator to respond to the full range of society's needs and wants. Through news photos and television coverage of a walking tour of a ghetto, the senator or representative can demonstrate his interest in the problems of the poor. By visiting malnourished families or scenes of disasters he can demonstrate, the press permitting, that he is actively seeking out the problems of society and attempting to alleviate them.[1]

Officials also need the assistance of the press as they seek to introduce ideas and develop support for them. The Senate has increasingly become a place where new ideas for public policy are "incubated."[2] Before there is any hope of approval for such a policy, an interested senator can introduce the idea in the form of a bill and seek public support for it. While doing so he can communicate to others throughout the country that an official is interested in their ideas and perhaps provide them some incentive or encouragement to sustain their original interest. In addition, he can introduce the policy idea to others and suggest ways of using it to solve problems. Or perhaps he may attempt to dramatize the extent of a problem. By talking about the problem and presenting possible solutions, over the years a senator can make such matters acceptable in public discourse. Ideas that may at first seem radical become familiar and less imposing, and problems that once went unnoticed gain amplification. A few years ago "busing" and "pollution" were not part of the national political vocabulary. Today they are, as an increasing number of people perceive these subjects as grave public problems. Likewise, "medicare," though popular with many citizens 25 years ago, was viewed by some as suspect, if not heretical. But it became more familiar and less suspect throughout the fifties and early sixties until finally, in 1964, it was enacted into public policy. The role of the media is crucial both in transmitting and cultivating ideas during their incubation and in the growth of their acceptance.

LEARNING FROM THE PRESS

One reason senators and representatives desire to make news is that publicity has an impact on the policy process. They learn from the media and assume that other officials do also. The media, for example, constitute a sources of ideas. When the *New York Times* executes a study of what it perceives to be a national problem, the resulting work can provide a seedbed for policy ideas. A report on the state of medical education could generate numerous policy ideas. Likewise, a dramatic television documentary, ripe with ideas for new policy initiatives concerning a public problem, might produce extensive publicity. In addition, columnists frequently offer ideas and suggestions which an official finds congenial. These suggestions, of course, have further implications. Others read the same stories or watch the same television programs, including reporters and editors, who define what is and is not news. Their future news judgments may be affected by the suggestions, as the columns and programs at least tend to heighten their interest. As a consequence, an official taking action with regard to subjects examined in the media is in a good position to have his actions accepted as news. Indeed, an official may "plant" ideas for such documentaries and feature stories in an effort to dramatize the need to act on a program in which he has long been interested.

What senators and representatives learn from the media helps them in evaluating their own activities. Success is frequently determined, in their own judgment, by the extent and character of publicity. Failure to gain publicity may result in a legislator's decision to drop an idea. However, if his proposal is well received, he is likely to increase his attention to it if he thinks it has the potential of yielding even more news.

Officials also learn from the press how to order their priorities. Events, problems, and policy proposals which receive emphasis in the media *a priori* become important. By calling attention to an item, the media elevate its importance. They cause senators and representatives to devote more interest to the matter, because legislators from experience will be certain that the policy makers with whom they will be talking will also discuss such emphasized events and activities. Moreover, constituency mail often concentrates upon the top items in media presentation. Another reason for enhanced legislator interest is that events and activities emphasized by the press may provide a clue as to which interest groups will be activated and perhaps be calling upon officials to present positions or demands.

These uses of the press are evaluative in that they help officials decide what is important and where to place emphasis. Senators and representatives also learn from the press in two additional ways that increase its importance in the policy-making process.

The press frequently transmits substantive information that senators and representatives find useful in their work. Congressmen read newspapers to discover what is occurring on the Hill itself. The myriad of committee meetings makes it impossible to keep abreast of everything. Much business in the Senate and House is conducted with few members actually present on the floor. And while the late Senator Richard Russell is reputed to have read the *Congressional Record* from cover to cover each day to keep up with floor activity, few legislators find time to do so. Summaries of lengthy presidential messages, complex bills, and commission reports which appear in daily newspapers provide a shortcut in the lives of busy men to keep abreast of many activities.

The major legislation introduced each day and the most significant proposals of outside groups generally receive press attention. Again, the condensed versions in the newspapers provide helpful time-savers in the lawmakers' personal information-gathering activities. Finally, lawmakers utilize newspapers to keep up with events back home. Involvement in Washington frequently produces a feeling of isolation from the home district which can be particularly worrisome for elected representatives. Although one may keep in touch through periodic visits and telephone calls, these means do not yield the comprehensive constituency contact that newspapers from the state or district can provide.

Lawmakers, as do their counterparts in other governmental systems, also utilize the media to gauge constituency reaction.[3] Editorial reaction, particularly in papers back home but also in those which circulate daily in Washington, provide clues as to what their constituents are thinking. Senators and representatives watch letters-to-the-editor and reports of group activity as well as editorial commentary to measure opinion and reactions to policy proposals or political events.

ELEMENTS OF THE MEDIA

The job routines of representatives and senators provide numerous opportunities to those who desire to make news. Accredited to cover the Capitol are 2,182 political reporters representing 811 newspapers, magazines, news bureaus, wire services, radio and television stations.[4] Thus there are about five reporters for each senator or representative. The structure of the lawmaker's job coupled with pluralism within the news industry dictates certain variations of making news.

The media are differentiated into the "national" media and the "local" or "regional" media. The national media consist of the radio and television networks, the wire services and the major East Coast newspapers which circulate in Washington on the day of publication, often called the "prestige press." These newspapers include the *New York Times*, the *Washington Post*, the *Washington Star-News*, the *Christian Science Monitor*, and the *Baltimore Sun*. There are several advantages in making the prestige press. Many senators, in particular, are cultivating a national constituency in order to create the possibility of generating future support for high office. If they hope to become presidential or vice presidential candidates, they must make themselves and their activities known beyond the borders of their state. The national media are, of course, crucial in fulfilling this goal. Moreover, they are important because it is through them that officials do much of their "talking" and "listening" to one another, thereby extending considerably the scope of their communication. For this reason, an official developing a policy proposal must utilize the national media to communicate the substance of his ideas to other policy elites. Even those who are not engaged in advancing policy ideas or presidential ambitions find it advantageous to receive national media publicity. In many states such exposure increases the lawmaker's prestige among his constituents. It also provides him satisfaction in knowing that his colleagues are reading about his latest activity or pronouncement as they drink their morning coffee. All of them read the national press for its domestic and foreign coverage, even if they disagree with the editorial viewpoint.

At times, of course, legislators and those who write about them are suspicious of each other's motivations, hold contrary views or develop animosities. One is reminded of the legendary exchange in which a lawmaker concluded an interview with an antagonistic reporter by asking sarcastically, "Well, is everything you are writing today the truth?" The reporter replied, "Yes, everything not enclosed in quotation marks!"

Legislators seek to develop particularly close working relations with the "regional" or "local" media serving the home state or district. Many metropolitan newspapers and stations have correspondents in Washington. Smaller newspapers often buy the services of a news bureau or participate in a pool of correspondents maintained by a newspaper chain. Regular contact between a Federal lawmaker and the local media is mutually beneficial. The senator or congressman sends a steady stream of grant announcements and other press releases of local interest to the media, enhancing his image of constituency service. The local radio and television stations and newspapers solicit his reaction to major events, for he, as their audience's voice in Washington, is a prime source of news. At times legislators are cornered in the Capitol corridors to provide spontaneous interpretation of news just then unfolding. In 1972, for example, legislators were contacted almost immediately for their comments on the attempted assassination of Governor George Wallace and President Nixon's decision to mine the harbors of North Vietnam.

Understanding congressional press relations requires differentiation not only between national and local media but also between their use by senators and representatives. While senatorial advantages are strongest with regard to the national media, they at times extend to the local or regional media as well. Senators are more interesting news targets than congressmen for several reasons. Many openly aspire to higher political office, and journalists pay close attention to potential presidential candidates because these politicians command broad public interest. In addition, the Senate generally considers questions of broad public policy more openly than the House of Representatives, whose procedures frequently structure debate rather rigidly and, some think, predispose it toward superficiality. Recently, for example, some senators have attempted to alter military and foreign policy, and the drama of their efforts has attracted extensive reporting. The Senate's greater prestige further increases media interest in its deliberations, while rules for media coverage are more flexible in the Senate than in the House. Its open committee meetings may be covered by television cameras any time. By contrast, not until 1971 were television cameras allowed to cover House committee meetings, except during brief periods when the Republicans controlled the House in 1953-1955. Even now they cannot do so without committee approval.

Although representatives, by comparison to senators, rarely make the national media, there is some reversal with regard to the local or regional media. Representatives usually have deeper roots within their constituencies than do senators. Most local media are very interested in stories with a local angle, and a representative may be in a better position to satisfy that news definition than his counterparts in the Senate. If the representative happens to live in a district with a newspaper or station large enough to have a correspondent in the capital, so much the better. He may receive attention in such media because he is a readily available source to a reporter, indeed one of the few sources about news of interest to the state or locality. But if the regional medium is also a metropolitan one, the representative is again at a disadvantage compared with other officials, including senators. Such media frequently have a state-wide audience and accordingly a greater interest in a senator and his viewpoints. They also frequently devote attention to urban politics, to mayors, councilmen, and other politicians whose business appears to have more immediate and direct impact than that transacted in the Congress. Thus a metropolitan area's several congressmen face rigorous competition from a state's two senators in securing extensive attention to their individual opinions and activities.

METHODS OF GAINING COVERAGE

Senators and representatives desiring press coverage can acquire it in a variety of ways. The most ubiquitous is the press release which the typical office on both sides of the Hill distributes several times each week. Some indicate bills which the member sponsors or co-sponsors. The subjects for most of these releases are attendance at important conferences, results of constituency polls, committee activities, letters to the President, major government grants, key votes, and general policy positions. If the member disagrees with the policy of the administration, he may utilize this means to inform his constituency or the national media of that fact. News stories indicating how various senators or representatives responded to a presidential speech, policy message, or activity, very often quote from a legislator's press release.

One variant of the press release is the weekly news column or radio or television program. In these, senators and representatives frequently develop themes—the volunteer army vs. the draft, the performance of President Nixon vs. the proposals of leading Democrats, tax reform, inflation, and the environment—discussing their view of a problem or situation and their efforts to ameliorate it with positive and progressive action.

The typical Senate and House office has automated mailing lists of newspapers in the state or district. Such lists are usually divided between daily and weekly publications, and sometimes the daily is further segmented into metropolitan and non-metropolitan papers. Most news releases go routinely to these papers through use of such a list. From time to time offices also send special news releases to papers in areas where some local interest item is emphasized. For radio stations, many offices use a "beeper." It consists of a tape recording, usually of the senator's or representative's voice. Radio stations are then called and fed the transcript, which they re-record for later transmission. Stations often present such releases as "interviews" with the member. Weekly radio or television programs are sent by tape or film directly to the stations. They are frequently professionally produced within the Senate or House itself, as both Houses maintain recording and filming studios offering services at minimal cost. Press releases designed for the national media take a different route. They are distributed to the House or Senate press galleries, to the National Press Club where many reporters have their offices, and to reporters who are known to be interested in the subject matter of the release and are considered "friendly" by the member.

Personal interviews are a second way that Washington lawmakers come into contact with the media.[5] It is the rare representative or senator who refuses to talk with a reporter. Probably no one, except perhaps large campaign contributors, enjoys better access to elected Washington officials. Such encounters range from a 60-second interview for a radio or television program to a lengthy session covering a variety of subjects. Most interviews, however, are specific. A reporter usually wants to know about a particular event occurring on the Hill or an activity in which a member is engaged. Of course he very often asks about other matters in the course of the interview and invariably provides the member with time for "free association" if he wishes.

Floor speeches[6] can also be made to generate press attention. Some observers assert that most activity on the legislative floor is "play toward the press," designed primarily for its newsmaking qualities. This is something of an exaggeration, but undoubtedly does explain much that transpires there. The lawmaker desiring to amplify remarks made on the floor can issue a press release which summarizes them, distributing it either to the papers back home or to the press represented in Washington.

Lawmakers frequently stage events to achieve publicity. The congressional investigation is one of the time-honored techniques for doing this.[7] An investigation, because it implies controversy, wrongdoing and conflict, contains many of the prime elements of news definitions. Committee hearings can have the same effect. Themes may be set, witnesses selected, and topics planned to wring the maximum news coverage out of them. When a senator or representative assumes the chairmanship of a committee or subcommittee, he gains a powerful publicity instrument. He can arrange investigations or hearings, or stage tours to demonstrate a national need for a program, thereby winning media exposure. The Senate "Hunger Committee," under the chairmanship of Senator George McGovern (D., S.D.), provides a recent dramatic example of a committee which was formed in part to educate; that is, to call attention to a problem which Senator McGovern believed needed national attention.

Finally, senators and representatives can call press conferences or briefings. Congressional party leaders do this to support or criticize the positions of the President. A group of senators or representatives sponsoring a resolution may call a conference to explain their purposes and to obtain publicity for their idea. A senator recognized as an authority in a policy area may call the press together to explain his reaction to a presidential proposal. If members can properly gauge their timing and catch an issue riding the crest of a high interest wave, they may be able to use a press conference to great advantage. These events do not occur every day. But when a railroad declares bankruptcy, a soldier is court-martialed, or a bitter military defeat is suffered, the time may be ripe for cashing in on the interest associated with this activity by introducing a bill or resolution, criticizing a President's policy, or offering an evaluation which will provide news to the media and publicity to the member.

ORGANIZING TO MAKE NEWS

The typical congressman or senator has a press secretary to marshal the lawmaker's press initiatives, to calculate the ways to increase his publicity, to answer routine reportorial inquiries, and to write the weekly newsletter for newspapers as well as the script for radio and television shows. The press secretary should have broad personal contact with reporters, know what their news needs are, be able to recognize a good story, and be aware of the possibilities of generating news for the benefit of his boss. Perhaps the most elusive of these qualities is being able to recognize a good story. An event in the office of Senator Lowell Weicker (R., Conn.) illustrates how a press secretary can sense a good news item that others might judge to be routine. A member of the Senator's staff related the story:

> A woman shipped her dog by air and found that it was dead upon arrival. She then wrote Senator Weicker to complain about airline handling of animal cargo. One of the Senator's secretaries, a lover of dogs, was about to mail a routine reply when she mentioned the situation to the press secretary, Hank Price, who spotted the possibility that the "dog letter" had news value. To get information on other such cases, he phoned the Federal Aviation Agency, the Department of Agriculture, and the Civil Aeronautics Board. The last had

recorded at least a dozen similar cases, while the Humane Society, which he also contacted, indicated that there had been more than one hundred cases. Upon presenting this information to the Senator, the press secretary next found himself drafting a bill for the purpose of authorizing the Secretary of Transportation to draft rules and regulations governing transport of animals by air, which Mr. Weicker introduced on the floor of the U.S. Senate. The story became front page news in Connecticut. It had human interest; "everybody" has a dog. Appreciative mail flowed heavily into the Senator's office. One constituent, whose letter is well remembered, wrote that he had never voted for a Republican in his life, but he loved animals and would vote for Lowell Weicker in future elections.

Senate and House offices are organized differently to handle press releases. Senate offices usually have a full-time press secretary and at least one assistant who may be titled as the assistant press secretary or the secretary to the press secretary. The "full-time" press secretary may occasionally have other duties—perhaps to write speeches or to staff a small area of legislative activities. But his primary responsibility is to handle press relations. He usually has direct access to the senator, arranges appointments with reporters for him, and discusses ideas for new publicity.

Although many House offices do have a full-time press secretary, most do not. House members' staffs are generally about half the size of senators' staffs. Frequently an administrative assistant or a legislative assistant combines his duties with routine tasks associated with press relations. As is true for most House activities, the member frequently performs his own staff work, whereas a senator normally must rely much more on his staff. Thus a representative may serve as his own press secretary. He usually knows all reporters for district newspapers from past contact in campaigning. Representatives take telephone calls much more frequently than do senators, some even answering their own telephone when in the office. Thus they often obviate the need for someone to set up appointments. Indeed, reporters may just drop in and be instantly admitted if the representative is in his office. Some congressmen have even been known to write their own press releases or weekly newsletters, something that few senators take the time to do.

CONCLUSION

Most Washington lawmakers regard press relations as very important. We have seen in this brief chapter that effective press releases determine the success of many of the legislator's other activities. The press serves almost constantly as a mechanism linking him with his larger political environment. Through it he obtains ideas, suggestions, opinions and reactions. He also uses the press to communicate to others his views and goals. If legislators cannot communicate effectively with their constituents, their re-election prospects may be threatened; losing touch is the path to defeat. For this reason, it is not surprising that reporters readily gain access to lawmakers. Regardless of occasional hostility and suspicion between them, the working relationship of newsman and legislator is fundamental to the democratic process; to be a congressman is to work with the press.

1. See Murray Edelman, *The Symbolic Uses of Politics* (Champaign-Urbana, Ill.: The University of Illinois Press, 1964), for a discussion of the symbolic output of government.

2. For an extensive discussion of the Senate's role in policy incubation, see Nelson W. Polsby, "Policy Analysis and Congress," *Public Policy*, XVIII (Fall, 1969), p. 67.

3. For an extremely valuable discussion of how foreign policy officials and others use the press, see Bernard C. Cohen, *The Press and Foreign Policy* (Princeton, N.J.: Princeton University Press, 1963), especially pp. 196-241. See also, for a discussion of utilizing the media to gauge constituency reaction, Douglas Cater, *The Fourth Branch of Government* (Boston: Houghton Mifflin, 1959), pp. 12-13, and James Reston, *The Artillery of the Press* (New York: Harper and Row, 1967), p. 63.

4. *Congressional Directory 1970*, pp. 788-818, 832-841, 844-853.

5. For a more detailed discussion of how public officials use personal contact to make the press see Delmer D. Dunn, *Public Officials and the Press* (Reading, Mass.: Addison-Wesley Publishing Company, 1969), pp. 138-141.

6. For other discussion of how officials use speeches to issue information, see Donald R. Matthews, *U.S. Senators and Their World* (Chapel Hill: University of North Carolina Press, 1960), pp. 203-204, and Cohen, p. 179.

7. For discussion of how the investigation can be used to generate publicity, see Cater, pp. 56-65, and David B. Truman, *The Governmental Process* (New York: Alfred E. Knopf, 1952), pp. 379-386.

IV | The Constituent Needs Help: Casework in the House of Representatives

T. EDWARD WESTEN

The job of a congressman encompasses a varied set of roles and tasks. This essay describes how with the aid of his staff, a congressman performs everyday constituency service. Casework is differentiated according to whether congressmen themselves must perform it or can delegate it to their staffs. The chapter concludes with a brief evaluation of the casework function.

The author is an Instructor of Political Science at the University of South Carolina. During the academic year 1968-1969 he was a Congressional Fellow of the American Political Science Association, serving in the offices of Congressman Barber Conable, Jr. (R., N.Y.) and Senator Ted Stevens (R., Alaska).

THE CONGRESSMAN'S REPRESENTATIVE function extends beyond legislating to serving as the middleman between his constituents and the Federal agencies. He must oversee the administration of the country's laws as they affect the individuals who live in his district. It is frequently the representative's task to seek redress from the Federal bureaucracy for an inequity, loss, or other damage that any of his constituents may have suffered in dealing with the government. All such work involving the processing of constituent requests for personal assistance is known as casework.

Casework is an indispensable function of a congressman. He often can be re-elected without being a creative legislator, but he cannot be re-elected without attending to the many individual problems of the people he represents. Accordingly, examining the casework process is important for understanding his role in our political system. Yet the handling of casework is little understood, generally failing to attract the attention of scholars, students, and citizens. Focusing on casework provides the best possible opportunity to examine congressional staff support: in casework the staff carries the burden even to the extent of functioning as the congressman's surrogate or alter ego.

We can divide casework into categories corresponding to the kind of constituent seeking help: individual citizen, business or civic group, and unit of local or state government. For analytic purposes we shall call casework stemming from individual requests "routine," the others "high level." Subsequent sections will distinguish procedurally between urban and rural casework as well as between high level and routine casework. This chapter emphasizes and begins with the handling of routine casework, because it is the most common type.

ROUTINE CASEWORK

Each mail delivery to a congressman's office is likely to include a number of pleas for help from constituents believing themselves to be victims of governmental excesses or inadequacies: a widowed mother of six children, living in a mobile home and working as a waitress in a diner, with one child placed in a home for retarded children, finds that the Veterans Administration is no longer sending her monthly check for child support. A father who has fallen victim to a stroke and is no longer able to run the family business is unable to obtain from the Army the early release of his son who has only six remaining months of active duty. A baker who entered this country some 20 years ago and failed to fill out the proper forms has been given 30 days to leave the country.

These problems illustrate routine casework. All members of of Congress help with such problems. Of all the areas of constituency service that congressmen perform, casework requires the most sustained individualized attention. This is not to assert that the member attends to these problems personally, nor that he should do so. John Saloma reports that, whereas casework is only the fifth most time-consuming part of the congressman's average work week, it is the single most time-consuming task confronting the staff.[1]

Context and Categories of Routine Casework

In the management of governmental services, quite often technical mistakes are made, or program administrators are unwilling to make liberal interpretations in eligibility rules lest they commit more resources than the agency is able to command, or applicants fail to submit information and/or documents required by laws or agency regulations. As in the examples cited earlier, it is easy to see that statutes and regulations often need interpretation to be applicable to individual circumstances. Some people are aggrieved by administrative interpretation. Others, occasionally, are overlooked in the administration of our laws. Both of these kinds of individuals find themselves unable to secure satisfaction from the appropriate agency. Sometimes individuals of low educational background have difficulty expressing their problems; the agency loses patience because of being unable to understand their concerns. At times even an articulate individual feels bewildered by aspects of administrative response. Many persons, some distrustful of government agencies which they feel are remote, turn instinctively to their congressman for help at the first hint of complication. Bureaucrats, moreover, are subject to the common weakness of being unable to recognize their own mistakes. These situations give rise to the bulk of the problems handled by congressional offices.

We have already indicated that casework involves a wide variety of problems. For purposes of management and filing, most congressional offices categorize cases according to functions of the executive branch. Although the titles vary from office to office, the major classifications of routine casework are veterans' affairs, draft and military, social security, immigration, and civil service. For example, a case involving the Veterans Administration usually results from a veteran being denied a benefit which he feels is rightly his, or his losing a benefit previously enjoyed.

Draft cases deal with a variety of problems from helping a young man clarify his draft status, or, in the pre-lottery period, helping him to regain a deferment lost through clerical errors in the local draft office. Military cases range from assisting a soldier to secure duty near his home at a time of family illness to ensuring that a soldier charged with a violation of the military code obtains proper legal aid. An administrative assistant described the handling of a common military case:[2]

> Anybody who wants a compassionate reassignment or compassionate discharge writes to us. The caseworker can write an enthusiastic letter in favor of a compassionate discharge or reassignment, for sometimes the people involved get a fast shuffle from the first person they talk to ... A Marine sergeant says, "None of my men chicken out and you're not going to chicken out" when the guy gives a perfectly reasonable request for his compassionate reassignment. We have one, a guy who has done two tours in Vietnam and is to get out in January. His two brothers are in the service and his

father runs a distributorship and needs his son at home to help him. The boy asked to get out early. Well, they didn't even listen to him the first time around, so we wrote a letter to the Commanding General of the Marines and said this is clearly a beautiful case and we know you will let him out. He sent it back saying let's take advantage of this case, and they will. They will give the guy a square review and let him out early.

Most social security cases involve routine concerns such as helping a constituent establish his eligibility, or intervening in the bureaucracy to hasten the search for a lost check.

Immigration cases are unusual in that they sometimes require that the congressman introduce private legislation to resolve a problem. Civil service problems are distinct in that they may require that the congressional office contact the Civil Service Commission to help a constituent appeal a ruling; they may involve the office in helping a constituent find a position in government. Until recently, a time-consuming task for congressmen of the President's party was the securing of postmasterships for faithful supporters. Although President Nixon removed these positions from the patronage process, there remain many other posts which may be filled at congressional initiative, especially at the beginning of a new administration.

There are other kinds of constituent problems that do not neatly fit into these categories. One such example concerned a divorced woman who had custody of her three girls, ages three, five, and seven. Her ex-husband, who had remarried, wanted to take the girls on a week's vacation. The woman apparently didn't trust him, so she consulted a judge, who told her that it would be all right for the father to take the children. Her apprehensions became reality when he disappeared with the girls. The woman turned to the police, the FBI, and private detectives for help, without results. Soon the woman, who was a telephone operator, was completely out of funds. A friend knew her congressman and suggested she go to him for help. By this time a year had elapsed since she had last seen her children.

The caseworker in the congressman's office explained what the office was able to do for her:

> With a few calls and some correspondence, we got his social security number. At that time the social security personnel couldn't give the last place of work unless extenuating circumstances existed. Since then it has changed and in circumstances like this they would give it to you. . . . We determined that at one time they had lived in San Juan, Puerto Rico; he had worked on ships as a radio operator and he was able to get a job easily. We also learned of relatives in the West who might know his whereabouts. The congressman had some contacts in San Juan and of course they checked for us. We gave them his social security number and all the other information we had. We found that they were there. . . . We had to get her sister to prove that the kids were hers before they would release the children, since the father had them. They were physically out of the country, so we got her a local lawyer and the children were subsequently released to her.

How Requests for Help Are Made

Requests for assistance are made in many ways. Some requests for help are made directly to the congressman when he is travelling in his district. Some constituents direct their requests to staff persons at the district offices which almost all congressmen maintain. In Washington, cases originate through personal visits, correspondence, or phone calls; some people even call "collect." Either the caseworker or the administrative assistant handles such calls. Occasionally the constituent insists upon talking to the congressman himself; however, such insistence may delay attention to the case, as other duties keep the member away from his office most of each day. Congressmen are not loath to talk with their constituents over the phone; indeed they are usually more than willing to do so. When the congressman talks to the constituent, he has to take notes and pass the information to the caseworker, whose information accordingly is secondhand. Therefore, the congressman will listen to the constituent and then most likely ask him

to repeat his problem in detail to the caseworker. He might say
something like:

> Mrs. Jones, I'm going to let you talk with Mrs. Smith in our
> office. She is our expert in these matters, and she will need to
> have all the information you have given me. She will
> probably have a few questions to ask you so we can help you
> better.

Normally, Mrs. Jones is delighted to talk with Mrs. Smith and is
pleased to have spoken with her congressman and to have found
him sympathetic.

Office Organization for Casework

When a request is received, it is immediately assigned to the
office caseworker. There is usually one caseworker in each
House office, although some offices have more than one. In the
latter circumstance, the offices divide the work in either of two
ways. The first method is simply by volume. If one person is
particularly bogged down, it is common under this system for
that person to receive fewer new cases until he or she gets
caught up. (As most caseworkers are women, we shall hereafter
say "she.")

The second basis of assignment is by topic or agency
specialization. Under this system it is common practice to assign
one caseworker to veterans affairs and military matters and
another caseworker to social security and immigration. Work
allocation is by an office manager or the administrative assistant
who reviews all incoming mail. In offices having only one
caseworker, often a second employee, who may perform a
variety of duties ranging from receptionist-typist to office
manager, does casework from time to time, thus becoming
familiar with the procedures and problems. This allows the
office to have an experienced substitute so that an illness or
vacation will not disrupt casework management.

Offices maintain a special filing system wherein current cases
are placed in a special folder and tagged for review within a
specific period of time. In this way pending material is readily

available to both the caseworker and the "backup," and the case will be automatically reviewed as progress is or is not made in the bureaucracy.

Handling a Case

Upon receiving a case, the staff immediately drafts a letter of acknowledgement. The letter usually takes the following form:

Dear Mr. Jones:

I received your letter regarding the problem you are having with your social security payments. I have asked the Social Security Administration to check into the matter. We will contact you as soon as we have anything to report.

Very truly yours,

Able Ben Congressman

ABC/tew

If the caseworker needs further information—for example, a social security number—she will request it at this time.

The same day that the caseworker drafts the reply, she will request the pertinent facts from the appropriate agency, or ask that the agency review the case. The caseworker may make a copy of the constituent's letter and attach a note of referral, commonly called a "buck slip," to the agency. She may herself write a letter outlining the problem; indeed, she must do so if the case originated by telephone. Alternatively, she may initiate the office's action with a telephone call to the agency's legislative liaison staff.

Both the letter to the constituent and the "buck slip" or letter to the agency are written over the congressman's signature. Even though congressmen delegate such responsibilities to their office staffs, it is important to remember that the office staffs have authority and influence only from the members for whom they work. At the end of a representative's day, it is customary for him to spend an hour or longer at his desk signing the mail. He skims the constituent letters to which the staff has responded during the day and monitors the replies they have drafted. In this way the representative does not have to go through the bulk of the mail as it comes in and decide what he wants done with each letter, yet he is still able to see the constituents' letters and get a feel for what they are writing about. In this manner he is also able to ensure that the staff is responding in a manner that he feels is appropriate.

Congressmen new to their office sometimes want to see the mail as it arrives, reply to some of it themselves and assign the remainder of it to staff members. After a man has been in Congress for a while, he probably finds this too time-consuming, and he is not able to justify the double handling of his mail—first, when he reads it and second, when he reviews and signs it. It is interesting to note that the longer a man serves in Congress the less time he is able or willing to spend on the mail; paradoxically, his mail may get better attention. A corollary to this proposition is that the longer a congressman has served, the better the staff becomes at answering mail in a manner of which he approves. When a new member arrives he does not have a staff experienced in doing things the way he wants them done; thus, he has to spend more time with the mail if only to train his staff. Many new members attempt to hire seasoned caseworkers because of this need for expertise. Beginners tend to learn from other offices about procedures and expedient ways to get things done. As the staff and files grow, there is ready reference to how the congressman wants to do things. Accordingly, he does not have to spend as much time with the mail as he did at the start of his congressional career.

Resolving the Case

The caseworker does not just wait for something to happen with the case after contacting the agency. She will pull the whole file from the "pending file" if the agency has not replied within a specified period of time, placing a call to the agency to find out what has happened to the letter. Generally the agencies are quick to reply, doing so within a few days, and no reminder is necessary. If the agency acknowledges administrative error, the problem will already have been corrected. At this juncture the caseworker drafts a letter to the constituent informing him that he can expect the agency to contact him and rectify the mistake. The agency will simultaneously be drafting a letter to the constituent, to arrive shortly after the congressman's.

At other times, when the agency does not see the error of its ways, the caseworker will compare the agency report with the information supplied by the constituent. She may need to contact the constituent for additional information. This second contact is by phone, more often than not, for the caseworker may need to pursue a line of questioning or may need to be able to explain her needs to the constituent; a letter is not always an efficient way to get such information. With both sets of information, the good caseworker can usually ascertain the root of the problem. Often it is a matter of supplying the agency with a specific document or presenting the constituent's problem in terms that are more compatible with the agency's interpretation of similar cases.

Matters of Discretion

In some instances the caseworker and his principal, the congressman, enter into a case that is a matter of discretion within the agency. In these cases the congressional office will point out the area of interpretation and ask the agency to reconsider the dimensions and implications of its statutory authority. Perhaps the agency had never had a similar request and wants to avoid the risk of establishing precedents. A rather firm phone call between a member himself and the head of the agency may be required to achieve a favorable decision.

Illustrating such decision-making is the story in which a caseworker told of a veteran who had contracted multiple sclerosis. A doctor had told the constituent that he needed therapy and that a swimming pool would be a good place for him to get physical exercise. The caseworker recalled: "Never before had anyone tried to get a pool for a veteran, but we tried. We got it, the V.A. approved it, he had his pool installed, and he was happy."

62

The Role of the Congressman in Casework

Cases in which congressmen actually intervene are not common. If all cases received personal attention from the congressman and he were actually to make the phone calls and write the letters, he would not have time for much else. Furthermore, if agencies were accustomed to dealing with the congressman on a routine basis, his personal inquiry on behalf of a constituent would begin to lose its effectiveness. As it is, any display of interest by the congressman takes on special significance and the agency feels compelled to take a very careful look at the problem.

Aside from reserving the congressman to "bring up the big guns," there is the added constraint that some congressmen don't want to be active in personally handling constituent problems. One staff member reported that his congressman did not get involved in casework any more than necessary:

> It absolutely bores him to tears and takes a lot out of him. And, I don't blame him because it bores me too, although it is very important to us both politically. Every once in a while you have to get the congressman on the phone to tell people what we want or ask them for something; it just works better to use him when we really need him. He does it reluctantly and minimizes those times. He is not very interested in spending his time on casework. He is more interested in issues.

This is not to say that this particular congressman would not want the task performed. Indeed, most offices operate under the premise that they are there to serve the people in their congressional district. One staff member asserted that the major function of the congressional office is "to serve the constituents, because we really don't work on legislation in this office, so it is mainly to fill requests of the constituents and answer their mail and keep in touch with them." This is the office of a quite senior member who has all the access to committee personnel for legislative work that he could want. Emphasis on constituent service, of which casework is the backbone, is typical of even those offices where the member's staff must do all the preparation for his legislative work.

Another staff member of a senior congressman made a quite caustic observation when asked what the major task or function of the office is:

> The major function of this office is to assist the congressman in the performance of his duty, which is, of course, to legislate. I suppose you have noticed that congressional offices are becoming sort of errand boys to their constituents. But I think the main function of the congressman is to legislate, and in turn the responsibility of the staff is to provide him with all possible assistance. At the same time, we certainly don't ignore all these other things because we work on a theory around here that when a person writes, regardless of how picky it may seem to us, it is important to him, and we treat it in that manner. We try to get the answer back the same day.

Yet, this lawmaker gets involved in some casework. When asked about the level of the congressman's participation in casework, the aide remarked:

> Yes, he does handle casework from time to time. Someone calling from the district always wants to talk to the congressman. . . . He happens to get involved in some of these cases. In fact, there was one particular case, a military case, in which he personally walked down to the Army liaison office in our building instead of turning it over to me or the caseworker.

Some members of Congress actually find it very satisfying to help constituents personally, but they just don't have enough time in the day to meet the demand. As one member stated:

> After all, my people sent me here, and it is my job to do what they want. The government has gotten too big and any degree of compassion and humility that we can bring to it all the better. Some of these bureaucrats think government jobs were created just for them, and they forget that they are to serve the people. I guess we are the last true servants that the people can turn to.

Although this congressman seemed to have a personal vendetta against the bureaucracy, still other representatives derive genuine satisfaction from helping people. As one caseworker described her boss:

> This man has a real heart for people, and he'll do anything he can to help, and everyone knows this and they come to him. This is why we have such a heavy case load all the time, even when we're out of session. People don't write unless they have a problem, and then they expect you to work a small miracle. If they have a legitimate request, we see what we can do, and usually they get what they want.

Not every request results in constituent satisfaction. All congressional offices will help anyone with a legitimate problem or complaint. Since most caseworkers have several years of experience, they know where to turn and how to proceed. The constituent has a better than even chance of getting an equitable solution to his problem. But offices do not hesitate to tell a constituent, as tactfully as possible, when they can't help.

URBAN AND RURAL INTERPRETATIONS OF CASEWORK

Our discussion to this point has centered on a conception of casework limited to assisting citizens' relations with the Federal government. Conceived more broadly, however, the concept extends to processing all types of constituent requests, including some that are unrelated to Federal agencies. Virtually all members of Congress who maintain offices in their congressional districts receive requests for help with problems related to state and local governmental functions and services. To the extent that the district staffs refer these people to the proper state or local unit of government, they are performing non-Federally related constituent services. All offices at least assist a constituent to identify the state or local agency that will be able to help with his problem. However, congressional offices in cities containing two or more congressional districts go much further and actually complete casework tasks related to state and local government. One staff member from a large city put it this way:

> There are districts in New York and other places where the congressional office is run to be sort of an ombudsman. They help with anything, e.g., potholes, curbs falling down, sidewalks broken, anything like that is done in those offices. They do it by having a lot of referrals to local government. That comes from a certain type of district and certain types of problems, and from people who don't know where else to turn. If you make it clear that no matter what your problem, you can come to the congressman, then he becomes the guy who handles everything.

A brief look at staffing patterns confirms that there is a distinction in the place where constituent problems are handled. Using the *Congressional Staff Directory*, a privately published personnel guide, to look at the breakdown of the staff between the Washington and district offices, one finds that big-city congressmen tend to assign more staff people to the district office than do members from other kinds of constituencies. These district offices do not just become local problem centers, for they do resolve constituents' problems with the national government. A staff member for one metropolitan congressman described the routing of casework:

> Case problems that can be handled at the district level are done there. For one thing, we have many regional offices in our city where the matters can be handled more quickly than here. Anything that has to be handled at the Washington level is sent here. I don't make a cut and dried situation of it. For instance, if a veteran case comes in by mail, I'll handle it rather than refer it back to the city, but if it is a social security problem, knowing that the files are there in the district, I'll send it back to the district office. The military problems are handled here because we have the liaison, unless they are emergency cases of people stationed in the district. Of course, we get a lot of problems unrelated to Federal areas—street lights, garbage pick-up, etc., so the office maintains liaison with city, county and other local agencies in working on those problems. So, this is generally how we handle constituent problems, fifty-fifty.

66

Rural congressional districts are large, often encompassing several counties or an entire state. All congressmen are allowed up to 16 full-time employees,[3] and given the essential responsibilities of the Washington office, normally can allocate only a small portion of their staff to field offices. These aides must travel extensively to service the needs of the scattered population. Because of sporadic contact, they are not available for much local government consultation; however, rural people tend to know their county and town officials and to address their local concerns to them.

The big-city constituency exhibits characteristics which are the opposite of those just described. It is possible for an urban congressman to place a large office staff in one district office and perform all of his constituency service functions in that one location. An extreme example of a congressman putting most of his personal resources into the district office is the late Congressman William L. Dawson from Chicago. Representative Dawson employed only one staff member in his Capitol Hill office. His Washington staff worker described the situation by saying "he keeps a one-man staff here because we have a full office in Chicago, and that is where most of the work is done, unless it is something that has to be handled here." In cities the single office is highly accessible to constituents because of district geographic compactness. The increasing number and complexity of links between cities and the Federal government further burden the urban congressmen's district staffs.

Another reason why urban offices engage in state and local casework is that urban congressmen are more closely tied to city and county political parties than are non-city congressmen. A tightly-knit city party structure may control a congressional district lying within the city's boundaries, but rural parties are not likely to identify with or dominate the politics of a far-reaching congressional district. Metropolitan congressional campaigns will be an integral part of the local party's effort during the campaign. The seat itself may be a reward to a loyal party worker for long and faithful service. Since the seat is wholly within a local party's geographic boundaries, there is also the potential opportunity to utilize the staff positions as patronage. Also, the congressional seat can be an integral part of the local political-governmental machinery. Because of the greater local party interest in the seat, because the winner of the election has experience in local government, and because he has worked closely with the local officials who are probably of the same party, the big-city congressman naturally falls into the role of continuing to serve the constituency he has served in the past. Being elected to Congress merely increases the volume and diversity of constituent services, of which casework is the most important part, that a big-city congressman has performed throughout his public career.

HIGH-LEVEL CASEWORK

Not all constituency problems called to the attention of congressmen originate with individuals. Indeed, businesses, civic groups, and state and local units of government seek their congressman's aid in resolving their problems with the Federal government. A small metropolitan area may find that its application for Federal assistance from the Urban Mass Transportation Administration was misplaced in files and accordingly not given proper consideration by that agency; a sparsely populated community may find that it is having difficulty getting information about the status of its application for Federal funds to aid in the construction of its sewage treatment plant; onion farmers suddenly find that the price that the Army is paying them for onions is lower than that paid in another part of the country; a specialized manufacturing concern in a rural community finds that the renegotiation of its contract means that continuing to do business with the government will cause it to suffer a loss, and it needs help in locating other markets for its product; a ghetto resident who wants to start a business needs help in applying for a small business loan.

These kinds of problems illustrate an area of casework that staff personnel in members' offices call "high-level" casework.

Such casework differs from the individual constituent help we have been discussing because casework involving units of government, businesses, and civic groups affects greater numbers of people. High-level casework can be differentiated from routine casework by the fact that the congressman and his staff are working with those individuals in their constituency who are highly politically motivated and active. Accordingly, the kind of political delicacy that is needed in handling these problems requires that the person working with the cases be able to see policy implications and react to political realities.

Unlike routine casework, the bulk of high-level cases is initiated by telephone or personal contact with the congressman. The people who initiate these cases—business executives, state and local government officials, and community leaders—are highly articulate and well educated. Moreover, they are accustomed to picking up the phone to get things done. Unlike the average constituent, these people are known by the office staff, with the consequence that when they call, they are immediately put through to the congressman or his administrative assistant. From the beginning of such a case, the congressman and his administrative assistant are drawn into it with continuing personal attention. While it is not uncommon for a caseworker or other staff aide to make initial inquiries and gather information, their work is closely supervised and coordinated, usually by the administrative assistant. It is more common, however, for the administrative assistant to call a fairly high-level civil servant in the agency concerned. Again, unlike routine casework, the congressman is kept constantly apprised of the progress in these cases. This is done for two reasons. First, it is highly likely that the congressman would have extensive contact with the individual involved. Secondly, the congressman, in his daily contact with other congressmen, committee staffs, and government officials, may be able to gather additional information, run across a similar case, or even find a solution to the problem. Once sufficient information has been gathered to make an assessment of the case, the congressman is given a complete summary of what is available, and he personally calls the district to inform the individuals concerned of the progress or solution. The most important high-level casework involves supporting a local government's application for Federal assistance. Initially, the office may collect the necessary information and forward it to the local authorities, who will proceed with the application. Several months to a year later the local unit of government may experience some difficulty with an application procedure or a deadline and will again contact the congressman for help. Quite often the congressional office may coordinate the projects' progress through the bureaucracy. One administrative assistant, whose congressman represented a district with a high level of unemployment, handled a case that involved the loss of a Federal facility:

> We got wind that the Department of _____ was going to shut down operations in our district. The congressman told me to see what I could find out. After a few calls I talked with their bureau chief who told me it wasn't public knowledge yet, but they were faced with some budgetary problems that forced them to close up shop. Well, there wasn't much we could do about their leaving, so we started scouting around and found that another agency was going to locate a new facility in our section of the country. I contacted their division chief and the departmental budget section and talked up our city. We brought the mayor and a representative from the state's department of labor to talk up the savings they could realize by using the other department's buildings and even labor. Before we finished lobbying them, which was a switch, we had the congressman "camping out" on the secretary's front door. Several months later when the department announced that it was closing its facility in our district, we were able to announce in the same news release that the other department would be opening their new operation in the very buildings that the first department had been using. That was a coup!

This example demonstrates that some high-level casework may be done without submission of a request. Indeed, anticipatory cases are not at all unusual.

70

EVALUATION

This discussion would be incomplete without raising two questions. First, do congressmen need to provide this service to their constituents? And, second, do they do a good job with casework?

We have observed that the casework function is one of the more time-consuming activities within congressional offices, yet is only indirectly related to the job of making laws for the country. In answering our first question we can say that casework is not totally separate from legislating, for casework allows the Congress to review the administration of laws. A second relationship between casework and legislative work stems from the assumption that diligent performance of casework leads satisfied constituents to re-elect their congressman. The fact that tenure in Washington increases a representative's impact upon policy-making offers substantial justification for his service as, in effect, a "Federal Department of Complaints," or to use the word adopted from the Swedish language, an ombudsman. Furthermore, congressional offices fundamentally view their job as one of constituency service. Given these premises, congressional performance of casework makes good sense. There is, however, some sentiment favoring removal of the casework function to an independent office of ombudsman. In each of the past few Congresses, members who feel for one reason or another that the job would best be done outside of their offices have introduced legislation to establish this procedure.

In attempting to determine whether congressional offices are doing a good job with casework, one can point to substantial evidence that when a constituent writes to his congressman for help, he will get it. The many women on Capitol Hill who are caseworkers put their hearts into the job, and it is a job that they know how to do.

It is important to remember that Federal agencies are dependent upon appropriations from Congress and operate

71

within the constraints placed upon those agencies by legislation. If for no other reason than that Congress controls the purse strings, heads of Federal agencies are responsive to individual congressmen, particularly to senior members of committees overseeing their work. However, the need for agency responsiveness transcends mere monetary considerations. To the extent that the agency selects priorities within the limits of its authority, it makes highly political decisions. The conduct of casework provides every congressman unique insight into the operating policies of Federal administrators. Just as casework enhances a congressman's understanding of administration, political realities encourage agency responsiveness to congressional inquiries.

1. John Saloma, *Congress and the New Politics* (Boston: Little, Brown, 1969), pp. 184-185.

2. All the staff members cited in this essay were interviewed during July and August, 1970. They will not be identified because they were promised anonymity in exchange for their cooperation.

3. The Clerk of the House allots to each member $185,168 per year for staff employment. Only one employee may receive the maximum salary of $32,175.

V | The Clubs in Congress: The House Wednesday Group

SVEN GROENNINGS

Many congressmen belong to informal groups which provide both a relaxed social atmosphere and a means of sharing information. The Wednesday Group, a House organization of 29 Republicans, also maintains a staff to help its members formulate policy ideas. This chapter describes and explains its development and operation during both Democratic and Republican Presidencies. Emphasizing the communications and policy innovation functions, it concludes by discussing the conditions under which informal groups can be effective.

The author directs the Policy Planning Staff, Bureau of European Affairs, Department of State. Beginning as a Congressional Fellow of the American Political Science Association in 1968-1969, he served two years as Staff Director of the Wednesday Group in the House of Representatives. After earning a Ph.D. at Stanford University in 1962, he taught six years at Indiana University, where he won the 1964 Brown Derby teaching award as the university's most popular professor. His books are The Study of Coalition Behavior *(1970) and* Scandinavia in Social Science Literature *(1970).*

IN LEGISLATIVE COMMUNITIES, just as in residential communities, small informal groups of friends and close associates meet socially, exchange information and sometimes undertake projects together. In the House of Representatives, most of these groups are almost entirely unobtrusive and keep knowledge of their membership quite private.

Among House Republicans, there are the Chowder and Marching Club (1949-), S.O.S. (1953-), Acorns (1957-), and the Wednesday Group (1963-). Largest and best known is the Democratic Study Group (DSG, 1959-). The Wednesday Group and DSG are distinct in having independent staffs for policy research and innovation.

Each Republican group has a membership numbering in the upper teens to mid twenties and meets weekly on a rotating basis in various members' offices, where the legislators exchange information in an informal manner. President Nixon characterized them all when he said of his own group, "The Chowder and Marching Society is the most disorderly, badly organized organization I know. It has no charter, no by-laws and no president."[1] The Wednesday Group is exceptional only to the extent that there is an officer for liaison and administrative control of the staff.

Additionally there are class clubs which operate similarly. Each freshman class of legislators organizes two, one for every party, but usually such clubs fade away after the early period of shared socialization. However, nearly all informal groups have emerged from a class club core. President Nixon remarked: "I thought of what brought us together 20 years ago. All of us were young, all of us were new members of Congress. All of us were veterans of World War II. We were concerned about the strength of the United States, and we were concerned about how we could help secure peace."[2] Congressman H. Allen Smith recalled the beginning of Acorns in the 87th Club: "One night I took a bunch of the guys out to dinner. There were 15 or 20 of us Republican freshmen that year . . . we went out to my house and sat around batting the breeze and we decided to organize a club of our own."[3] The S.O.S. core was in the 83rd Club.

There are more Republican than Democratic informal groups. That this is so is probably attributable to the great size of the DSG, to which approximately half of the Democrats belong and in which there is activity within sub-groups. The DSG is too large, and its sub-groups are too specialized, to permit communications in the manner of the Republican groups. Nevertheless, its members generally do not wish to take the time to belong to a second group. Moreover, membership in the DSG is open, whereas membership in Republican groups is by invitation. Because of the Democratic Party's success in the 1964 elections, the DSG became so strong that there was little more to be gained by forming additional liberal groups; given this success, any new group would be overshadowed.[4] On the Republican side, however, there developed a tradition of small groups, so that it is quite natural to form new ones.

The impact of informal groups upon the legislative system is largely subtle. Informal groups are mechanisms for the development of close rapport, confidence in one another's political judgment, and mutual support. Some groups develop patterns of cue-giving and cue-taking, and it is normal that members help one another with problems. Collectively they serve as a quiet communications network, with some overlapping of membership. Selective in membership, the Republican clubs tend to recruit those men who are particularly able or promising as well as compatible.

That clubs can be important vehicles of promotion to positions of leadership is suggested by the membership of Richard Nixon, Melvin Laird, Rogers Morton, Kenneth Keating and Gerald Ford in the Chowder and Marching Club. The name S.O.S. reflects a spirit of mutual help, and the adoption of the name Acorns stems from the notion that "Tall oaks from little acorns grow." While these names may be conceived in humor, and while there is no factionalism, competition, or aggressiveness among Republican groups, there is indeed impact, however quiet. Subtle also is their policy significance, which depends mainly upon the closely related factors of membership, legitimacy, and resources.

WHY THEY EXIST

While it is a function of every legislative system to present and discuss ideas and a function of legislators to contribute to these activities, no other system relies so heavily on informal groups as the American. The sheer size of the House, with 435 members, gives many a sense of isolation and anonymity, even within their own party. While most members have but two committee assignments, and the others only one, they often have great interest in what occurs in other committees. Because state delegations may consist of one member or more than 20 with personal rivalries or differences of philosophy, these delegations have limited usefulness. Moreover, because our parties are decentralized and therefore are ideologically eclectic aggregations lacking strong discipline, members have a latitude and often constituency pressure to act independently of their leadership. It is in these circumstances that legislators create informal groups to improve their communications.

The Wednesday Group and DSG staff operations are associated with additional problems of legislative structure. When a party controls the Presidency, it thereby has a large centralized policy staff. When it does not, its policy initiatives are left almost entirely to the congressional party, wherein the committee chairmen or ranking minority members exert overwhelming influence, with the result that newer members feel less effective in shaping policy. When a party is in the majority, that party controls most of the committee staff positions; consequently the minority is badly disadvantaged.[5]

Both the DSG and the Wednesday Group developed from desire for constructive opposition. The DSG began operations in 1959, toward the end of the Eisenhower administration, with thoughts of developing policy positions prior to the 1960 elections, translating the Democratic national platform into legislative programs, and countering the roadblocks to progressive legislation erected by the conservatives in both parties.

The Wednesday Group, founded in 1963 as an informal discussion group, acquired staff in 1965. The Republican Party at that time not only lacked the benefits of the White House but moreover was the minority party in both House and Senate, had disastrously lost a presidential election, and seemed forced into the position of saying either "no" or "me-too" to Democratic initiatives, some of which came from the DSG. In this situation there was need for an entity to develop "constructive alternatives."

It was expected, given certain other House features, that the formation of the Wednesday Group would have additional advantages. Members could become involved systematically in policy areas beyond their own committees. They might consider in overview policy problems diffused across various formal committees. They might set forth their ideal positions without concern for as much compromise as would be expected within any of the task forces organized by the House Republican Conference after 1965. In summary, through an independent staff, Wednesday Group members would be able to undertake projects of national consequence which would be beyond the capacity of any individual member's staff.

Since the advent of the New Deal in the Franklin Roosevelt administration, initiative had flowed mainly from the executive branch. In the face of executive ascendancy, however, there was concern about the implications of the constitutional doctrine of separation of powers. From changing circumstances one could deduce a constitutional need for the legislature also to expand its creative thrust, to prepare alternatives independently of executive processes. In the words of one legislator, "The responsibility of the legislative branch is to legislate, not sit back to await initiatives from downtown." Informal groups might contribute toward redressing the imbalance.

Buttressing these considerations were three fundamental assumptions about politics: that knowledge is a form of power;

that it is most usefully developed through informal exchanges; and that research toward knowledgeable statements, reasoned judgments, and constructive alternatives would yield legislative performance commending re-election.

By way of comparison, the Senate, whose members regard their entire body as a club, has not developed similar groups. The structural conditions are such that there has been little demand for such groups. As the Senate is far smaller, its members tend to know one another. Senators serve on several committees and have staffs large enough to allow some innovative specialization. In European parliaments, by way of further contrast, there is far greater party discipline; in· their multi-party systems many of the legislative parties are no larger than an informal group in the Congress. Only in the very largest European parties might one look for a functional equivalent. The British Conservative Party, for example, has the Bow Group, "PEST," and the Monday Club. While they, however, include members of Parliament, they are in large part extra-parliamentary and therefore structurally more like the Republican Ripon Society than the informal groups in the House of Representatives. Accordingly, the American lower house, with its system of informal groups, is a unique national legislature.

This chapter, with some comparison to the DSG, will focus on the Wednesday Group's performance of two functions: communicating and elaborating policy ideas. Because the Wednesday Group has developed a policy process, however inconspicuous, it has become an actor in the legislative system. An assessment of its impact enables one to posit the conditions of such groups' effectiveness.

ORGANIZATION OF THE WEDNESDAY GROUP

The Wednesday Group is the most liberal of Republican legislative organizations. With 29 members, it is also the largest.

It acquired staff after functioning more than two years as the one Republican informal group whose orientation was "activist."

The group was formed in January, 1963, on a Wednesday afternoon in the office of F. Bradford Morse. Six others were present and became co-founders, namely Robert Ellsworth, John Lindsay, Charles McC. Mathias, Abner Sibal, Robert Stafford, and Stanley Tupper. These men joined in an informal group because they shared similar experiences and perspectives. Most of them had developed a sense of comradeship by voting, against the overwhelming majority of Republicans, to expand the Rules Committee. All but Ellsworth had established voting records well to the left of most of their party, and all except Lindsay had been freshmen together, having entered Congress in 1961. These men were issue-oriented and wished to combat the frequent negativism of the Republican Party in its role of opposition. It was Sibal's suggestion, that first day, that they call themselves the Wednesday Group.

The first purpose, as in all other informal groups, was to broaden communications. In expanding the membership, the group's progressive ideological bias was clear and dominant but never narrowly rigid. There was no intention of becoming a faction, operating as a unified and bargaining bloc of all the party's liberals.[6] To the contrary, it was assumed that effectiveness in communicating within and contributing constructively to the Republican Party would be sharply constricted by holding exclusively to the left. Moreover, some ideologically sympathetic but pragmatic legislators would not want to be associated with any entity representing only a minority wing of the party.

The original seven doubled their numbers in the year and a half prior to the 1964 elections, adding not only more liberals but also some friends who were moderately conservative. The group had little chance to develop norms or settled methods of operation before conflict developed. Most members opposed the presidential nomination of Barry Goldwater, three disassociated themselves from his campaign, and the Wednesday Group name was linked with anti-Goldwater statements. The most conservative members, asserting that party unity was of primary importance, stopped attending meetings. At the end of the year, the remaining active members joined in calling for the resignation of Dean Burch as Chairman of the Republican National Committee.

In the wake of the Goldwater defeat came the related House Republican leadership contests in January, 1965. The majority of Wednesday Group members were very leary of the group's involvement, and in the main contest between Gerald Ford and Charles Halleck there was no group position. When John Lindsay unilaterally attempted to bargain with Halleck for Wednesday Group support, his action led to renewed internal conflict. Most of the members supported Ford, who was calling for constructive Republican alternative proposals. Two were in the nucleus of Ford's campaign and several others campaigned for him.

Overwhelmingly, the members felt that the incumbent Chairman of the House Republican Conference, Melvin Laird, had become objectionable because of his role as Chairman of the 1964 Platform Committee. At first hesitant to act, group members on the night before the elections finally decided to present a candidate. While their first choice was Robert Stafford, they thought they had a better chance by supporting Peter Frelinghuysen, a new affiliate whose membership in the group was not yet widely known and therefore was not likely to be a basis for conservative attack. Frelinghuysen lost by only seven votes and, given a few more hours, might have won. The closeness encouraged the group's activists to think favorably of its potential impact.

At the end of its first two years, the Wednesday Group's condition was that of a badly divided informal group which had not yet settled upon a long-term role. It did not again become intensely involved in a leadership struggle, although two members later won office in the legislative party. It did, however, enter a second phase of its development, a phase which was to change its image.

The members, seeing the necessity for Republican policy alternatives, hoped that the group could become a catalyst for party change. The activists proposed hiring a research staff to develop new ideas for the group to contribute. Concern that the group might develop an ideologically divisive output again led to dispute, with the result that in early 1965 the chief promoters of staffing proceeded to hire a researcher for themselves. The person selected, Dr. Douglas Bailey, was to play a major role in establishing the Wednesday Group as the first Republican legislative organization of its kind. Bailey gained wide acceptability and support, and the staff soon grew to three plus a secretary, its present size.

As staff director, Bailey developed members' ideas into position papers and contributed his own topic suggestions. Short pieces critical of the Johnson administration were frequent, but the main effort was concentrated upon long-term projects. The results were well-founded and well-reasoned statements before the Congress which were endorsed by several or even as many as 40 members of Congress. Several presentations gained wide press coverage. As the development and discussion of research papers became a principal activity, it became customary that the staff director attend the organization's weekly meetings.

Two of the founders, Brad Morse and Robert Stafford, were co-leaders until very recently. Morse served as the principal innovator and enthusiastic energizer at every stage of the group's institutionalization and expansion until, in mid-1972, he left Congress to become Under-Secretary-General of the United Nations. The principal originator of research topics, he was central in every decision concerning the group's structure and functions.

When Morse and Bailey concluded that the Wednesday Group needed an executive committee, it was natural that Stafford would become its permanent member, a position renewed without contest and by acclamation until his departure to the Senate in late 1971. He represented a central position among the members both in his voting record and in his view of the group's functions. A former governor, broadly respected in the party, even-tempered and conciliatory, Stafford handled administrative problems and made statements "for the good of the order" at meetings. As the group's executive, he devoted the most time to its operation.

The membership expanded steadily, reaching 20 in 1965, 26 by the end of 1967, and 28 in 1970. Growth has the advantage of broadening communications, the range of viewpoints presented, and the potential support for research. It has had the effect also of weakening the activist impulse, as it became more difficult to approach consensus with greater numbers. The early activist pressure declined for additional reasons; namely, the passing of the leadership contests, the departure of John Lindsay to seek the mayoralty of New York City, and the belief that activism had been costly in terms of cohesion. The residual activist taint for many months caused difficulty in gaining breadth of sponsorship for the research papers. However, by the end of 1966 half the membership consisted of men who had joined the Wednesday Group after the activist period had passed and the research period had begun.

A recurring issue is the relationship of group size to the communications function. Some members have expressed concern that individual participation in discussion and therefore attendance at meetings would decline as numbers increase. Another factor is that further growth would make it impossible to gather in members' offices. Accordingly, there is consensus that the organization should grow no larger. Whenever there has been a decision to expand or to fill a vacancy, the membership committee offers a detailed appraisal of the group's needs and the corresponding attractiveness of possible candidates.

The membership criteria vary. Recent concerns have included gaining representation from particular committees, so as to gain breadth of information; from the freshman and sophomore classes, in order also to prevent ossification; and from various geographic areas, in order to broaden the range of viewpoint. While these have been the initial guiding criteria, others have been controlling—above all, the candidate's intellectual abilities, his inclination to be among the party's moderates or liberals, and his ability to mix well with other members. It has happened, after great care to consider criteria objectively, that the majority have bent the guidelines by voting for those they know or like the best.

In analyzing 93rd Congress membership in terms of these criteria, one finds that, of the 29, 13 are from the East, 9 from the Midwest, 6 are from the West, and, beginning in 1971, 1 from the South. While there are no more than 4 from any state, there are at least 3 each from California, Michigan, Ohio, and Pennsylvania. No Wednesday Group member serves on the Rules Committee, but the group does have representatives on all of the other 20 standing committees except Agriculture, Public Works, Internal Security, and Standards of Official Conduct. There have been 4 or more members on the Appropriations, Education and Labor, Foreign Affairs, and Merchant Marine and Fisheries Committees. In 1973, at the beginning of the 93rd Congress, 4 Wednesday Group members had attained sufficient seniority to become the ranking minority members on their committees.

While the members originally were young newcomers their average age now corresponds closely to that of the legislative party as a whole. Ranging from freshmen through eleventh-termers, the median member is in his tenth year in Congress. More intellectually oriented than the party generally, the Group has included five former professors and the majority hold graduate degrees.

Wednesday Group members largely represent districts which are suburban or have an urban-suburban or suburban-rural mix. The constituency-determinism hypothesis would lead one to expect voting records more liberal than those of most Republicans since the party generally is slightly more rural.

Additionally, the ambition for higher office which is common to many group members suggests a tendency to be more liberal than could be deduced from district analysis. Moreover, there is certainly some independent impact of conviction upon voting behavior. On the *Congressional Quarterly's* conservative coalition scores for the 90th Congress, the average support among House Republicans was 65 percent and among Northern Democrats, 13 percent. For the Wednesday Group the average was 49 percent. For 1968, the group's range on the ADA "liberal quotient" was 0-83 percent, with an average of 36 percent, whereas the range on the ACA "consistency index" was 9-82 percent, with an average of 47 percent.[7] Although the group's liberal image is particularly fitting with regard to civil rights and within the Republican context, one may conclude that the generalization "moderate to liberal" is more appropriate. A still more accurate generalization is that the ideological cement is the willingness to explore and promote new ideas and new approaches to solving problems.

Probably most members have been attracted to the group primarily by the opportunity to communicate, often with like-minded men, and secondly by its problem-solving research. However, both functions are generally valued, and for some the research is the more important. Consequently some members are mainly social members, while others are the mainstays of the research efforts. For virtually all, committee work is more important than Wednesday Group activity, and many consider state delegations or class clubs of greater importance. However, Wednesday Group members have close rapport and tend very much to value and enjoy their association. It follows, nevertheless, that there are different kinds and levels of involvement and contribution.

Leftist position in the group's ideological spectrum correlates positively with taking initiatives toward "research activism" and with study group involvement. However, the more conservative are just as likely to attend meetings regularly and to contribute office space, equipment, and supplies. They are also as willing, whenever it is possible, to hire staff members for the joint effort, as is common practice in the DSG and House Republican Conference. The payroll slots become available somewhat irregularly, particularly in election years, and do not fulfill payroll requirements.

At the time the group acquired staff, it established the Committee for Republican Research, largely for the purpose of paying Doug Bailey. Friends of some core members helped raise a few thousand dollars, and Republicans for Progress provided the financial base until it ceased non-campaign activity in 1967. The following year the group began a low-key and very selective annual mail solicitation, enclosing some Wednesday Group products which had appeared in the *Congressional Record*. The formation of the legislative party's Republican Research Committee in mid-1969 led Minority Leader Ford to request that, to avoid confusion, the Wednesday Group change the name of its funding affiliate. It thereafter became the Institute for Republican Studies.

The Wednesday Group, never well financed, operated with deficits in the campaign years 1966 and 1968, when there were other demands upon potential contributors. There were no major donors. With rare exception, contributions range from $100–$500. While not involved in campaigning or lobbying, the funding organization has always submitted full financial statements to the Clerk of the House in order to be entirely "above board." Each member receives a list of all solicitation-letter recipients. There are no membership fees or dues. In contrast, the DSG, in addition to its solicitations, assesses its members $100 per session. With four to six times the Wednesday Group's membership, it has twice the Wednesday Group's budget for staff operations and twice as many staff members.

It has been difficult to raise money for an anonymous and little understood research organization, inconspicuous among the many party organizations. Consequently donors are few. However, there have been some letters indicating appreciation of the group's efforts, as indicated by remarks such as "applaud the approach," "thoroughly in sympathy," and particularly the following excerpts from two letters:

> While naturally no one will agree with everything that the Wednesday Group has produced, the fact that its members are engaged in systematic forward-looking research is a highly constructive development which I am glad to assist.

> It has done excellent work under a Democratic administration and I hope it will not relax under a Republican one. . . . I have a high opinion of the general calibre of people in the Government but stimulation with good ideas from the Hill are both needed and well received.

The Wednesday Group, then, has broad membership, a staff and very limited financial resources. It seeks to enhance communication among its members and create policy alternatives. We turn now to how it operates.

OPERATIONS

Communication among members is enhanced by means of weekly meetings held on Wednesday afternoons in members' offices. The members rotate as hosts, in as close to alphabetical order as the staff director can arrange. The host chairs the meeting, calling upon each member to report on whatever may be of interest from his committee or from the world of politics generally. Each usually makes a three-or four-minute "nutshell" presentation; occasionally reports extend to twenty minutes. It is characteristic of such legislative groups that the tone of their meetings is informal and relaxed, while the members achieve orderly and effective communication. There are procedural norms. For example, in all such groups it is customary that when a member wishes to question or comment, he asks "Will you yield?" or "Would the gentleman yield?" Given the various committee specializations and ranges of experience, it is natural that some subtle cue-giving and cue-taking develop which have consequences in individuals' behavior beyond the meeting.

A regular feature is statements or questions pertaining to "the good of the order." Members frequently suggest research topics at the meetings. However, for two reasons the discussion of research is brief, consisting mainly of summary progress reports. The primary purpose of the meetings is to focus upon what is happening in the House. Moreover, the members consider the staff's research papers by another process, to be described shortly. On occasion distinguished visitors are invited to speak and join in discussions, but there is a general ban against interest group spokesmen on grounds that the group's purpose is not to facilitate being propagandized. Attendance is almost always from 13 to 18 and has been as high as 24. It tends to decline as legislative activity declines, because members are often out-of-town when the schedule is very light and because there is then little of urgency about which to communicate.

The group has no equivalent of the DSG whip system for handling communications regarding action on the floor of the House. Whereas the DSG, ranging from 115-145 members, has floor power, the Wednesday Group lacks the basis for conceiving of itself in parallel manner; floor power is not among its basic purposes. Because of its great size, the DSG necessarily does much of its communicating by mimeographing;[8] it distributes great numbers of papers which offer analyses of bills.[9] The Wednesday Group wishes not to become so large as to require change from the present pattern of informal gatherings to that mode of communication.

The Wednesday Group carries out its research function by a well-established process. Members are the primary source of initiatives, but the staff, which has always enjoyed the freedom of a semi-academic association, often develops its own ideas. Among many agencies and private groups in Washington, the Wednesday Group has gained a reputation for openness and for developing concepts, with the result that outsiders often bring ideas directly to the group office. Accordingly, policy ideas may have many roots. It is not necessary to gain the support of all or even many of the members to undertake a project.

On most large projects, one or more members with the staff director judge the feasibility of the project based on the breadth of potential interest within the group, the possible impact, the requirements of time, the staff's technical capability, and other criteria. While the organization concentrates mainly on projects too large for any single member's office to undertake, it avoids such broad fields as tax reform on grounds of excessive technicality, scope, and competition. Policy problems which overlap formal committees, such as drug abuse, on which the Judiciary Committee may have one perspective and the Education and Labor Committee another, are often ideal. The group tends to avoid issues which will be ideologically divisive, preferring such projects as its study of air safety. To preserve spirit and cohesion, the members favor involving the greatest possible number in various projects; accordingly they prefer not to concentrate a year's effort exclusively on two or three giant undertakings. Research has been divided almost equally between domestic and foreign policy topics.

On projects likely to be greater than thirty pages in length, it is customary to circulate a prospectus for critiquing. Upon completion of the staff's final draft, a four- or five-member study group considers the product.[10] Membership on a particular House committee may or may not be a criterion in selecting study group members. Attempts are made to achieve some breadth of geographic and ideological representation when possible and to involve as many members as practicable in such study groups in the course of a Congress. Selection to the study group has usually become formalized by invitation from the Wednesday Group leader.

A study group may hold several meetings, and occasionally its members prepare written critiques and suggested wording. Members' administrative or legislative assistants participate in the final stages and occasionally have joined the study group sessions. Its chairman may be the initiator of the project, or someone else may emerge as leader during the sessions. Because he will serve as the principal spokesman, he and the staff draft the final product in his style.

At this point a decision must be reached as to the form of release. Twice the members have published books, but in most instances the chairman presents the study to the Congress on the floor. Often there are follow-up procedures to keep the Congress and public attentive to the subject. These may include a press conference, committee testimony, speeches, or additional insertions in the *Congressional Record*. In each case, the Wednesday Group staff drafts the releases. If there is to be legislation, the staff director consults the House's office of Legislative Counsel for drafting assistance.

Sponsorship of the finished study paper is open to all group members and selected Republican non-members who may be interested in the topic. In presenting the paper to the Congress, the study group chairman usually makes a statement like the following:

> Mr. X: Mr. Speaker, it is my privilege as chairman of an informal study group to announce completion of an intensive examination of . . .
>
> . . . I would like to cite three other members who joined me as sponsors of this study group . . .
>
> The following members of Congress have joined the study group in encouraging, through the release of this paper, a re-examination of . . .

In this presentation the Wednesday Group name is never mentioned. Its explicit use would inhibit endorsement by non-members, thereby limiting the group's impact. Moreover, if the membership were generally known, members might find themselves being associated even with those projects which they did not wish to sponsor. Because members and non-members endorsing the products vary, few in or out of Congress would recognize the work as the Wednesday Group's. Indeed, some legislators do not know of the group, whose anonymity is enhanced by its unmarked office door. This anonymity extends to answering the phones by extension number. The staff acts in the name of individual members for such practical purposes as ordering materials from the Library of Congress and gaining information from agencies. Yet in one sense the preservation of anonymity is somewhat surprising: since 1965 more than 20 study groups have issued approximately 50 releases endorsed by 6 to 55 congressmen.

The preponderance of the staff's research is done by the two staff research associates, who draft most of the long-term papers and occasional FYI's on aspects of issues before the House. While the staff director does some of the research, he mainly assists in conceptualizing, directing and editing the research of others, serves as a point of contact within and outside the group, and takes charge of scheduling, negotiating payroll support, and gaining endorsements for the research products. Thus the staff functions are not only research but also administrative and coordinative.

ADAPTATION TO A REPUBLICAN ADMINISTRATION

Following Richard Nixon's election to the Presidency, members discussed the future of the Wednesday Group under a Republican administration. No member advocated phasing out in the manner of the National Committee's Republican Coordinating Committee.[11] The communications function would remain important, and there was consensus that the administration would need the assistance of constructive legislative groups. The group increased its membership and maintained the research staff at full strength. With the election of two of its members, Charles McC. Mathias and Richard Schweiker, to the Senate in 1968, a few members entertained a fleeting thought of bicameralization. In the Chowder and Marching Club, for example, Senate members occasionally host meetings. However, this possibility, which would have involved a reconceptualization of the Wednesday Group, was impractical for most communicative needs, as the two Houses do not consider bills simultaneously and problems of disruption by floor action would be compounded. It was not seriously considered for the function of producing research.

The group would proceed as before, but with prudence and courtesy in complimenting the administration where appropriate, in sending the White House and the departments copies of its research products prior to release, and in eliminating the kinds of attack pieces released during the Johnson Presidency. For the first time, invitations to discussions at Wednesday Group meetings occasionally were extended to members of the administration; on such occasions the group meeting served as a channel for new directions in communications.

There was a complete turnover of staff as first Doug Bailey and thereafter his collaborators departed, to be replaced by the author of this essay and new teams. The personal role of Bailey became a more institutionalized staff director's role. Procedures and arrangements which had been uniquely his became subject to greater record-keeping, in part because of the accumulation and extension of financial efforts.

With the broadening of contacts accompanying the change of administration came two developments in the Congress which further extended discussion and research channels beyond the group. When Brad Morse succeeded former Senator Joseph Clark (D., Pa.) as chairman of Members of Congress for Peace through Law (MCPL), several other Wednesday Group members joined in its activities, especially its study groups. MCPL, organized in 1966 with a small staff, is the only group which is both bicameral and bipartisan.[12] Also, Wednesday Group members became increasingly involved in the task forces of the House Republican Research Committee after one of its members, Robert Taft, Jr., was elected to its chairmanship.[13] Although these pursuits diffused some members' energies, interest in the Wednesday Group's research remained very keen.

Although the long-term research continued, this dispersion of energy diverted leaders from directing preparation of short pieces for quick punch. Because the paths to quick publicity had been more obvious when the party was in opposition, it subsequently required more direction to gain commensurate coverage. In March, 1970, at Morse's suggestion the group created a research committee, its most recent structural innovation, to regain occasional quick impact. At the end of that year the staff began circulating a weekly "Legislative Summary" outlining the salient points in leading bills. Parallel to the DSG's, it has been very useful to members and their staffs.

Some dilemmas inhered in the new situation. The staff helps to create a voice for the members, but there has been some uncertainty regarding the kind of voice that is most feasible and appropriate. No dilemma existed during the Democratic administration, for no question of party loyalty was involved. There are subsequent predicaments, however: if the group focuses on an issue which immediately concerns the administration, it is likely to be without impact because the latter can probably do the work more quickly and with greater expertise; if it selects a project not considered by the administration, it may in effect be criticizing it for ignoring a problem which the group thinks important. These considerations compound the old problem that if the group selects a project within a field of great popularity, such as pollution, the work of others in the field will detract from the group's potential impact. These are other reasons for adding the research committee to provide the greater guidance needed in determining which topics have greatest potential.

EFFECTIVENESS

That the Wednesday Group is perceived as effective in its communications function may be deduced from the generally good attendance at the weekly meetings. This conclusion is supported also by the fact that the first two members elected to the Senate, Mathias and Schweiker, were instrumental in organizing the Wednesday luncheon gathering which has become known as the Senate "Wednesday Group." It is clear from observation that the House meetings provide not only information but also mutual support and confidence. Effectiveness in the research function is more difficult to measure. One tends to be leery, as Sir Lester Pearson once said, that "the road to nowhere is paved with good reports—and some not so good."

The record, however, permits a more favorable interpretation. The press has reacted positively to many of the Wednesday Group's releases, many praising the careful research and problem-solving intention. Columnists have commented, and the *New York Times* and *Washington Post* have carried non-editorial first-page stories. Among the foreign policy studies, a 1967 booklet by nine members, "Parallel Steps to Peace in Vietnam," which outlined a plan for staged de-escalation of American bombing, received editorial comment from more than 80 newspapers. While proof of impact is difficult to obtain, it appears to have been instrumental in the Secretary of Defense's decision to order a study of a two-stage bombing reduction; it was the formula with which President Johnson finally drew the North Vietnamese into negotiations. "CBW and National Security" (1969), a theoretical evaluation of the strategic and tactical purposes served by chemical and biological weapons and sponsored by 16 members, was acclaimed on the floor of the Senate by the Chairman of the Foreign Relations Committee. Minimally, to employ a football metaphor used in the group, it was "a nice downfield block" which broadened congressional receptivity to President Nixon's subsequent ban upon biological weapons.

Sometimes the Wednesday Group undertakes studies which it realizes may be ahead of their time. The purpose is in part educative, to provide "lead legislation" which will stimulate debate. A 1967 book on *How to End the Draft: The Case for an All-Volunteer Army*, with 5 authors and an endorsing introduction by 15 others, was such an effort. It led to the appointment of the principal Wednesday Group research associate to President Nixon's Commission on an All-Volunteer Armed Force. Portions of "Crisis in Urban Education" (1968), in which 11 members advocated massive Federal assistance, were quoted with agreement by HEW Secretary Robert Finch, who hired the group's researcher as special assistant to the Department's corresponding commission.

Legislation has been a purpose of several projects. "Crisis in Urban Education" resulted in introducing a "Federal Urban Education Act." "A Study of Air Safety" (1969), a comprehensive systems approach endorsed by 30 legislators, similarly led to legislative drafting. "Organized Crime and the Urban Poor," bearing 23 endorsements in 1967, culminated in nine bills, including the act which outlaws loan-sharking. It also contributed to making crime a major facet of the Republican campaign against the Johnson administration. A major 1971 effort resulted in a bill on nationwide transportation strikes which had the bipartisan support of 55 congressmen.

One of the group's basic goals has been to add to the capacity of the Republican Party to solve problems. There are some Republican members of the Congress, non-members of the group, who hold the Wednesday Group's work in high regard. The impact upon the legislative party, however, has been minor. The Wednesday Group is generally little understood or misunderstood, and some have regarded it as a collection of incorrigible liberals, marginally Republican and best to be ignored.[14] While for three years it seemed isolated from, and even competitive with, the legislative party's task forces, this isolation is yielding to proportionate integration as well as occasional staff consultation.

The Wednesday Group is gradually gaining in the breadth of its legitimacy within the legislative party. Its work has been useful beyond the group, its "Young Turk" image has receded with both time and changes in membership, and its integration has been increased through both its many overlapping memberships in informal groups and its members' greater involvement in party-wide task forces. Stafford served during the 92nd Congress as Vice Chairman of the party's caucus, the House Republican Conference. Gains in legitimacy and communications, plus advances in seniority, may result in increased influence. Substantial limits will remain, however, because the

Wednesday Group's main thrust will remain to the left of the Republican middle.

It is not enough to analyze the effectiveness of the group upon policy and party. One needs also to consider its impact upon the members themselves. The research operations broaden their expertise, gain favorable publicity, and provide the support of co-sponsors. By helping to build constructive records, the research helps the members achieve re-election. While it is impossible to measure this contribution, there is some evidence to support the contention. In the five elections since the Wednesday Group's formation, only three members have lost their bids for re-election, and one of them ran far ahead of his party's presidential candidate at the time. Unlike the DSG, the Wednesday Group does not prepare campaign literature and does not engage in campaign fund-raising. However, several members have employed Wednesday Group research papers extensively in their campaigns.[15] They support the staff because they believe that it increases their effectiveness in contributing ideas and that it can help their party to be constructive and innovative. Ultimately, they feel, a party is as good as its ideas.

CONCLUSION

Informal legislative groups have much in common. At least on the Republican side, they fulfill their communications or information-sharing function in the same way. One may posit, on the basis of the detailed examination of the Wednesday Group and a cursory knowledge of the others, the conditions of their effectiveness in communications. There seem to be four: that the members represent most of the formal legislative committees; that they report perceptively on committee activities; that they are reasonably consistent in attending group meetings; and that ideological and social compatibility are sufficient for the development of rapport. Adding breadth in the representation of classes and regions further enhances a group's informational value.

To be effective in fulfilling a research function, informal congressional groups must satisfy additional conditions. There are certainly six: that the staff be professional; that the members contribute ideas and direction; that their unanimous agreement not be required at any stage; that a product be reviewed and endorsed by a study group prior to its submission to the full membership; that the staff have a good working relationship with the individual members' staffs; and that there be sufficient financial means to sustain operations.

1. *Washington Post* (March 21, 1969), p. B-3.

2. *Ibid.*

3. *New York Times* (March 23, 1969).

4. In 1971, 18 members of the DSG formed The Group, without staff support. The most liberal of all informal groups, it has adhered to the pattern of holding weekly meetings.

   In 1973, southern Democrats began planning to organize a smaller, conservative counterpart to the DSG, with staff, office facilities, and regular meetings. In the new 93rd Congress, the southerners found themselves without a representative of their region in any of the top three House Democratic leadership posts for the first time in this century, and the conservative southerners failed in their bid to fill the vacancy in the Rules Committee after Chairman William Colmer of Mississippi retired. Organizing to maximize impact became the purpose of a core group hoping to compensate for declining influence among the party's leadership. Said one southerner: "The leadership seems to understand groups. The liberals have the DSG. The blacks have the Black Caucus. Maybe if we organize, the leadership will listen to us a little bit. They're not listening to us now." *Washington Post* (February 15, 1973), p. G1.

5. Figures are not available for all years. However, in 1962 only 43 of the 504 House committee staff members were minority staff. For elaboration, see James D. Cochrane, "Partisan Aspects of Congressional Committee Staffing," *Western Political Quarterly* (June, 1964), pp. 338-348.

6. Whereas the Wednesday Group has no intention of engaging in bargaining, the DSG has intended to do so from the time of its founding. Eugene Eidenberg and Roy D. Morey, in *An Act of Congress* (New York: Norton, 1969), p. 36, point out that "In fact, the DSG was organized to give some organizational drive to the liberals' dream of enacting legislation under conditions where they lacked a working majority. They hoped to develop enough organizational strength to force the leadership to negotiate with them on the same terms as the leadership had negotiated with the conservative coalition of Southern Democrats and Republicans."

7. *Congressional Quarterly Weekly Report*, XXVI (November 1 and 15, 1968), pp. 2983-2989 and pp. 3152-3153.

8. The DSG holds a monthly plenary session characterized by relaxed discussions. An executive committee of eleven deliberates separately on questions of public policy. The three-man Wednesday Group executive committee has no function beyond considering the group's own administrative problems; it meets so rarely that its composition occasionally is forgotten. Neither group takes formal stands on issues.

   The DSG is not so close an association as the Wednesday Group. Its membership is open, varies, and is so loosely defined as to include some people who do not pay dues. Membership is kept secret to protect those who would suffer in their districts from known affiliation with a liberal organization.

9. Three of the eight to ten members of the DSG staff are legislative aides; the Wednesday Group has no equivalent designation. It is a DSG goal to draft a legislative program at the beginning of each session; the Wednesday Group has no such aspiration.

10. While Wednesday Group study groups are *ad hoc* and there is rarely more than one in operation at a time, the DSG has appointed so many task forces and committees that its structure has come to resemble that of the House.

11. A few conservative non-members questioned whether the Wednesday Group had outlived its usefulness; their rationale was that whereas the group's purpose was to provide alternatives to Democratic policy, such services would be handled by Republicans in the White House.

12. In 1973, the 25 New England House members created a bipartisan organization with staff. Their primary purpose is to promote Federal action to ameliorate the region's economic difficulties. The members hope that, once they have demonstrated the utility of their effort, the region's senators will join the group.

13. Taft's candidacy did not begin as a Wednesday Group project but was supported by most of the members, some of whom campaigned on his behalf. Soon after his election, Taft "temporarily resigned" from the group in order to avoid conflict of research interest.

14. Wednesday Group members have been among the most consistent supporters of Nixon administration bills, although many of the members have not been supportive on a few of the most controversial. The reasons for alignment go beyond the desire to help a Republican President. Most group members belong to what may be regarded as the presidential wing of the party generally, in that they tend to advocate a strong Federal role in providing direction to the country. For this reason many were also among those Republicans who most frequently supported President Johnson's proposals. For the latter support the Wednesday Group was denounced by conservative Republican John Ashbrook in his *The Democratic Margin of Victory: How Liberal Republicans Provide the Winning Margin for Democratic Legislative Programs* (Washington: American Conservative Union, 1967). On Ashbrook's list of Republicans who on 24 occasions between 1961 and 1967 provided the "Democratic Margin of Victory (DMV)," Wednesday Group members are 10 of the 15 regarded as the worst offenders. It was not recognized in this study that 6 members had better records by his standards than did the Minority Leader. Since the Nixon administration has come to office, the majority of Wednesday Group members have had higher rates of voting alignment with the party position than the majority of those who had never contributed to the ACU's objectionable DMV.

15. By way of example, in Mathias' 1968 senatorial campaign approximately one-third of the releases concerned Maryland, one-third the candidates, and one-third national issues. In the last category, perhaps as many as half the releases were on subjects related to Wednesday Group projects. Doug Bailey left the Wednesday Group to become a partner in Campaign Systems, Inc., now Bailey, Deardourff and Eyre, Inc., which has worked with Republican candidates for a variety of offices. While most of the campaigns handled by this firm have not involved Wednesday Group members, it has worked on three members' winning re-election campaigns and managed two members' successful campaigns for higher office: Schweiker's 1968 bid for the Senate and William Cahill's 1969 campaign to become governor of New Jersey.

VI | Committees and the Politics of Assignments

ROBERT HEALY

At the center of a congressman's activities are the committees in which he participates. By gaining assignment to a committee whose work is both interesting to him and relevant to his district, a member maximizes his opportunity for useful service. This chapter examines the structure and functions of committees, and describes the process through which a member seeks the posts he prefers, as well as the criteria employed by those who make assignments. It concludes with guidelines for evaluating committee member effectiveness.

The author is Legislative Assistant to Senator Hubert H. Humphrey (D., Minn.) and a Ph.D. candidate in political science at the University of Pittsburgh. During the academic year 1970-1971, he was a Congressional Fellow of the American Political Science Association, serving in the offices of Congressman William Green (D., Pa.) and Senator Humphrey.

A NEW MEMBER OF CONGRESS encounters a system of committees, each of which possesses a continuity of membership, a firmly established jurisdiction, and distinct operational characteristics. These committees, whose history extends back to the first years of the republic, provide mechanisms for rationalizing the tremendous workload of the legislative branch. Standing committees were in their infancy at the turn of the nineteenth century, when the 6th Congress considered only 161 bills and resolutions. Today, when dependence upon committees is considerably greater, a Congress processes approximately 20,000 such items of legislation.

There are three general types of committees: standing committees, select or special committees, and joint committees. The last of these, of which the most prominent are the Joint Economic Committee and the Joint Committee on Atomic Energy, are essentially organizations which study specific matters of public policy requiring maximum coordination between the two Houses. The purpose of a select committee, created for a temporary need, is to examine a particular public problem and to report its finding to the Congress. Some select committees, such as the current Select Committee on Nutrition and Human Needs chaired by Senator George McGovern, attract considerable publicity to their activities and leaders.

Most important are the 21 standing committees, which are a permanent feature of congressional organization. Their members serve throughout their careers unless they choose to change assignments. With the exception of the Joint Committee on Atomic Energy, only standing committees have authority to report bills and resolutions to the floor of the House and Senate for possible enactment. Their significance stems from the expertise and power which they achieve in their respective policy fields. Since 1795, for example, the prestigious House Ways and Means Committee has processed complex and vital legislation pertaining to taxation and tariffs, and in more recent years has acquired jurisdiction over bills pertaining to social security, welfare, and trust funds.

Another highly important standing committee having financial responsibilities is the House Appropriations Committee, which oversees all Federal expenditures. Each year, after the President's budget is presented to the Congress, its subcommittees hold hearings and evaluate the dollar requests pertinent to each department and agency of the government.

Unlike these financial committees and the Rules Committee, which performs the highly powerful role of scheduling legislation for House floor action, most standing committees are primarily concerned with the development of programs which later will be implemented by the executive branch. Each such committee reviews legislation referred to it by the Speaker, either choosing to take no action on particular proposals or to recommend them to the House for passage. Such recommendations often include amendments to the original bill which the committee feels should be made. These committees are commonly referred to as "authorizing committees" because their principal task is to evaluate legislation which would establish, or, in legislative language, "authorize," specific programs. For example, the Public Works Committee evaluates programs for attacking the national problem of water pollution.

Just as Congress rationalizes its workload by assigning legislation to committees, most committees similarly distribute bills referred to them among subcommittees of either permanent or temporary duration, whose members are appointed from the full committee rosters by the chairman and ranking minority member. At the start of the 93rd Congress there were 128 subcommittees in the House alone. While there are many examples of their impact upon the Congress and the policy process, a traditional one is the 12-man House Military Appropriations Subcommittee's domination of defense budgeting.

Increasingly, subcommittee chairmen have achieved powerful independence, particularly when committee chairmen have permitted them to hire and direct staff personnel. During the 92nd Congress, the House Foreign Affairs Committee sprang from its seemingly lethargic past, displaying unusual vigor in its oversight of the administration's foreign policies. The change in character was commonly attributed to Chairman Thomas E. Morgan's decision to permit young and ambitious subcommittee chairmen to employ staff people and to develop their own programs.

The tendency toward subcommittee permanency and autonomy was underscored rather sarcastically by the late Senator Allen J. Ellender (D., La.), a persistent foe of subcommittee proliferation. Among his official papers aides found this scribbled comment: "If there is a life hereafter, I want to come back as a standing subcommittee in the Senate, because they never fade out."

A few committee chairmen have managed to block this dispersal of power by resisting subcommittee specialization. By designating subcommittees numerically rather than by fields of policy, a chairman retains the flexibility to assign legislation to a subcommittee likely to dispose of it in the manner he prefers.

Perhaps the most visible consequence of the committee system is fragmentation of authority. Concerned that the committee framework and jurisdictions which were established in the Legislative Reorganization Act of 1946 were no longer suitable to the policy-making responsibilities of Congress and that the proliferation of subcommittees had simply destroyed the integration which that law had sought, Speaker Carl Albert proposed a new study of the committee system at the opening of the 93rd Congress.

At his request, Congressmen Richard Bolling (D., Mo.) and David T. Martin (R., Neb.) introduced a resolution to establish a Select Committee to Study House Rules X and XI (Rule X sets forth the committees of the House and XI describes their powers and duties). The resolution was noteworthy in several respects. It established the first comprehensive study of the House committee system in 26 years. Second, it provided for equal numbers of members from the two parties and equal shares of the $1,500,000 budget, both sharp contrasts to the customary majority party dominance of committee composition and finance. Finally, the new committee was to be established despite the existence of the Joint Committee on Congressional Operations, formed in the 91st Congress to evaluate the institution continuously. While some House members preferred that the Joint Committee perform this task, in part for the economy of avoiding duplication, the leadership of both parties pushed for the formation of the select committee because it would be nonpartisan and isolated from Senate influence.

The new study must be regarded as an important effort to strengthen the capacity of the House, and thus to reverse the gradual erosion of Congress' power as perceived by members and the public. The goal, as Representative Martin stated, was "a more efficient operation of the committees of the House which are the heart and soul of the legislative process."

THE CONGRESSMAN IN COMMITTEE

One of the greatest demands upon a congressman's time is his committee activity. His committees are his principal avenues for shaping legislation. Here he listens to testimony from government officials, interest group representatives, fellow members, and various experts. The committee is often his most promising arena for advancing the interests of his constituents and congressional associates. By his advocacies, bargaining, and voting in committees, a member shapes much of his legislative reputation.

Hearings, generally conducted by subcommittees, usually begin around 10 a.m. in a chamber resembling a courtroom. Congressmen sit behind a dais with the chairman of the committee in the middle. Republicans sit on his left and Democrats on his right, with committee members arranged according to seniority. Staff personnel are close at hand, while the witnesses, stenographer, and reporters sit at tables in front of and usually below the members.

The chairman normally opens with a short statement welcoming the participants, announcing the subject of the hearings, and conveying his perspective on the issue. The lead-off witness then presents his testimony. As most committees require submission of prepared texts, the witness may choose to summarize his view.

The congressmen question the witness, may try to get him to agree with their point of view, to clarify points of contention, or to provide additional data for the hearing record. Spirited debate may occur. Throughout the session, members interact, watching each other, making judgments about the quality of their colleagues' performances, and attempting to substantiate or undercut one another's positions.

During these encounters congressmen explore legislative proposals and alternatives in depth. If members of a committee get along amiably and in a spirit of bipartisanship, their approach to hearings will be cooperative rather than conflictual. At the hearing stage, many issues are more technical than they are partisan. Members seek information and understanding. However, hostility among members, sometimes directed toward the chairman, pervades some sessions. The dialogue may feature sharp encounters among colleagues and witnesses. Appearances by administration spokesmen frequently trigger partisan exchanges.

Hearings also allow the congressman to perform his function of legislative oversight. He asks about the implementation of existing law, often seeking to discern the impact of administrative regulations upon congressional intent. He frequently seeks information concerning the financial support of a program. He will want to know whether congressional appropriations are matching its authorization, and whether the Office of Management and Budget in the Executive Office of the President is approving such expenditures. He will want to know where money is being spent and whether it is being spent properly. He will ask for and receive progress reports, as he will want to become familiar with the problems an agency is encountering.

104

At the conclusion of hearings, congressmen sharpen consideration of legislation in "mark up" sessions. When the committees were holding organizational sessions at the beginning of the 93rd Congress, several committees broke with tradition to permit the public to attend all meetings including mark ups, except in extraordinary circumstances. The prevailing practice has been to hold executive sessions for this purpose, with only members and staff personnel present. At this nitty-gritty stage the members consider the bill line by line, discussing their contentions and offering amendments.

After a subcommittee acts favorably on a bill, its leaders seek consideration of the legislation by the full committee. Here amendments may be offered and the bill passed or killed. If the committee votes to send the measure to the floor, it must prepare a report explaining the legislation's purpose and the amendments which have been incorporated. The members rely heavily upon the staff in this task. A member wishing to offer additional views or a dissenting opinion may draft comments for publication as a part of the committee report. The chairman, sometimes joined by other committee members, may introduce a new bill embodying the terms as reported.

After a committee reports a bill to the House, its leaders go before the Rules Committee to obtain a rule permitting the legislation to be considered on the floor. The rule, which itself must first be adopted by the House, structures the length and format of debate.

Members from the majority and minority sides of the committee reporting the bill are active participants in the floor debate. The chairmen and ranking minority members of the full committee and subcommittee take leading roles, supported by other committee members who are assigned individual portions of the legislation. Speaking from large tables near the well of the House, they defend the committee's version against amendments to which the committee is opposed. Committees generally prefer to go to the floor in cohesive fashion, Democrats and Republicans working together to seek passage of their product. If the majority of the committee has accurately gauged the will of the House, the bill will survive the test of floor voting without major change. Nonetheless, amendments commonly are adopted, and occasionally a bill is virtually gutted. In some instances committee members who have opposed the bill as reported will lead efforts to win major floor amendments.

COMMITTEE ASSIGNMENTS

The importance of committee assignments stems from their effect both upon the careers of individual members and upon the performance of the committees themselves. The "right" committee can help a congressman survive election challenges and determine his impact upon public policy. Thus, to a congressman from western Kansas, with all of that area's wheatland, an assignment to the Agriculture Committee not only allows him to keep a protective eye over legislation of importance to his state but also is a strong asset for re-election.

A challenging committee assignment strengthens one's motivation to remain in Congress. Moreover, as a member accumulates seniority on a committee, he gains the satisfaction of exercising increasing power over policy. A congressman who sees his House term as a stepping-stone to another office may reap considerable benefit from a "visible" assignment fostering his expertise and public recognition.

The legislative system functions optimally when members are happy with their assignments and their personal interest leads to diligence. Assignment can make a further systemic difference in those cases in which appointments can shift the balance of power toward a more liberal or conservative policy orientation. One of the most consequential appointments in recent years was the selection of a moderate member to the Rules Committee when that body was expanded in 1961.[1] Because this committee was balanced between liberals and conservatives, the moderate newcomer, occupying a pivotal position, enabled House liberals to secure some favorable committee decisions. His selection was highly significant, given the Rules

106

Committee's role in generally determining which bills will reach the floor and under what conditions they will be considered.

Assignment of Members to Committees

As with almost all aspects of legislative procedure, formal and informal features mark the assigning of members to committees. Formally, the House meets to elect members to the committees. In reality, the House is faced with a *fait accompli*; barring extraordinary circumstances, it approves lists presented by party committees. The real power lies with those who prepare the lists.

Since 1911, each party has utilized a Committee on Committees to make assignments. The parties use their committees somewhat differently. This chapter will concentrate on the Democrats.[2]

The Democratic members of the Committee on Ways and Means, elected by the Democratic caucus, together with their floor leader, caucus chairman, and, if in the majority, the Speaker, constitute the Democratic Committee on Committees. Each of the 15 Ways and Means members represents a geographic zone composed of an approximately equal number of House Democrats.

The zone man, however much he may be influenced by others, is the primary key to assignment. Until 1971, the power to nominate was exclusively his. To provide candidates with some protection against the biases of zone men, the caucus then changed its rules to permit nominations by home state delegations. This alternative approach is likely to be pursued reluctantly, as the zone man remains central to the process by virtue of his own assignment and is likely to be displeased by any action which in effect would challenge his judgment and fairness.

A congressman seeking assignment normally consults with the dean of his state delegation concerning his chances for successful pursuit of various assignments. After weighing the advice of the dean and others whose counsel he respects, he submits a letter to his zone man stating his top three choices. He may also visit or send letters to other Committee on Committees members stating his reasons for pursuing a post and his qualifications. He may consult party leaders, get supporting documents from the dean of his state delegation, inform the desired committee's chairman of his interest, and continually remind his zone man of his objective.

While reliance upon the zone man is sufficient for assignment to committees of lesser importance, it is a basic first step in all cases. If a member is seeking a seat which his state's delegation traditionally has controlled, he may find it expedient to seek unanimous backing from these colleagues in support of his application.

A member seeking an especially coveted assignment may bid for the support of his party's House leaders in return for his previous loyalty. Bargaining is often an important element in gaining a key slot. At a time of lively competition among delegations and individual members for several attractive posts, the maneuvers can be quite complex. When a contest for a leadership post is in progress, an aspirant to a committee seat may decide to lend his support to a candidate in hope of gaining favor with the victor. If the right man wins, the new leader may be instrumental on his behalf within the Committee on Committees.

A few candidates place considerable emphasis upon support from pressure groups such as labor or business organizations. But a member who, for example, asks a Chamber of Commerce or AFL/CIO lobbyist to intervene for him does so at considerable risk, because assignments are customarily regarded by members as an in-house process. For outside groups to tamper with internal congressional procedures may be dysfunctional both for the member seeking a committee seat and for the pressure group's general objectives.

Committee on Committees meetings are held at the beginning of every new Congress or whenever a committee vacancy occurs. Speaking in order of seniority, the committee members propose candidates for the various slots open on House committees. Each man speaks for the interests of the members from his zone. After the nominations, Committee on Committee members vote, ten votes currently being required for assignment. The outcome, a culmination of intricate negotiations between the November elections and the organization of the new Congress in January, is awaited anxiously because of its great impact upon the focus of one's congressional activity.

A member who is extremely dissatisfied may appeal his assignment when the nominations are presented to the caucus for approval. There have been only a few such appeals, and they tend to be memorable. At the opening of the 92nd Congress, freshman Herman Badillo (D., N.Y.) was assigned to the Agriculture Committee by the Committee on Committees. Complaining bitterly, Badillo took his case to his caucus, which reassigned him to the Committee on Education and Labor. Going to caucus is a reluctant step involving departure from normal bounds of custom and tradition. It clearly marks one as a maverick. New congressmen, incumbents, and returning members do so gingerly, ever mindful that their future effectiveness within the House may be impaired.

Thus the process of seeking assignment can be intricate. It blends personal initiatives with customs and norms and the influence of party leaders. While it culminates in selections of some members for highly coveted assignments, other members generally must accept posts which are less prestigious or less politically rewarding.

Criteria for Assignment

Six factors are of primary influence upon the committee assignment process: interpersonal relations, geography, re-election needs, seniority, ideology, and expertise.[3] A number of interviews suggested that one's personality and stature in the eyes of colleagues can have a decisive impact upon chances of securing the assignment desired. Congressmen who sit on the Committee on Committees make many judgments about their associates, ranging from their personal feelings about them in terms of their desire to socialize and work with them to more complex notions such as political benefits to be derived from appointing a colleague to a particular committee.

The applicant quickly makes impressions upon his zone man, delegation dean, and committee chairman. In a narrow time frame, before substantive reputations are formed, personality characteristics and impressions of compatibility can be especially significant in determining their opinions. Any of them or a member of the Committee on Committees may say, "I like that new congressman, and I want to help him," while of another he may say, "I think we should put him in his place now by denying his request." Chairmen sometimes request by letter or less formal means that particular freshmen be assigned to their committees. In turn, the zone man may recall that a particular candidate for a post has good relations with a committee chairman whose support is vital to his own legislative interests.

There are many arenas in which congressmen form impressions of colleagues, most of them informal: the cloakrooms, the gymnasium, the dining room and social gatherings throughout Washington, as well as the committee rooms and the floor of the House. Of particular consequence are a member's relations to those who have power, to those who must make decisions about other members, and to those who can aid a member both legislatively and politically when assistance is required. This is not to say that members who fail to curry the favor of the powerful are automatically excluded from power. But it does suggest that obstreperousness and legislative nonsense detract from one's chances of securing preferred posts.

As one congressman crudely but succinctly put it: "What matters is what those guys [Committee on Committee members and committee chairmen] think of you." Or as another member said: "It is not a question of just making waves, but making prudent waves." More than anything else, the interpersonal relations among members set the tone for the decisions

110

which result when imperfect men judge and allocate power to other imperfect men.

Members of the Committee on Committees regard the more objective criterion of geography as an appropriate guide in making assignments. This criterion is applied variously to committees. However, the patterns are so strong that they have resulted in norms. It is generally understood that such committees as Ways and Means and Appropriations, whose concerns equally affect all parts of the country, shall have balanced geographic membership.

In contrast, some committees are characterized by geographic imbalance. Western congressmen have had a propensity to request and receive assignments to Interior and Insular Affairs, a committee whose jurisdiction over public lands and natural resources gives it disproportionately great impact upon the West. Two-thirds of the Committee's members in the 93rd Congress are from districts west from the Mississippi River. Said one member, "Take Congressman X: he comes from a western state and is interested in its public lands; this is a cardinal fact to him; and with Congressman Y leaving the Committee, we needed to find someone from the region to represent that interest." Similarly, congressmen from farm areas normally seek and usually attain membership on the Committee on Agriculture.

Relevant also is whether a committee assignment will help a member's chances for re-election. If it will, the Committee on Committees strives to be accommodating. If there is any unifying thread among all congressmen, it is the desire to be re-elected. Understanding this common drive, congressmen are inclined, whenever possible, to aid one another in the fight for electoral survival. Attempting to maximize the advantages of incumbency, the parties' assignment committees seek to give their members opportunities for the kinds of impact most appreciated in their districts. A party's desire to retain control of a marginal seat can be a consideration. It is not uncommon for an assignment request letter to end with the statement, "This committee assignment will help my chances for reelection." By the same token, a freshman may be discouraged from seeking a committee whose controversial legislation might jeopardize his seat.

To report that seniority is a factor in the assignment process is to say what all assume. Exactly how seniority influences selection is not so obvious. Assignments to the most prominent committees such as Ways and Means, Rules, and Appropriations are normally governed by seniority. As with other legislative norms, however, exceptions occur. Most extraordinary was the assignment of freshman Clem Rogers McSpadden (D., Okla.) to the Rules Committee in the 93rd Congress.

Seniority can be as much an excuse as an aid. The reason the Committee on Committees did not select a member for a position might well have been adverse interpersonal relations, but congressional gossip will suggest that he did not make it because he lacked seniority. As one member said, "Congressman X has been around here a long time, but no chairman wants him. In fact, I wish we could get him off ours. He talks all the time, asks stupid questions, and seldom contributes anything. He just rubs people the wrong way."

A member of Ways and Means notes: "We often encourage members to reapply for the top committees next time around. For example, we wanted to give ___ Appropriations, but one influential member said to wait until next session when he will have more seasoning."

Ideology is important when a committee chairman attaches high priority to keeping his committee ideologically compatible. Chairman F. Edward Hébert of the House Armed Services Committee reportedly worked against the 1970 appointment of liberal Michael Harrington of Massachusetts. Harrington was a doctrinaire liberal, "a left-leaning member who," as one member noted, "would not be in the thinking of a majority of the Committee. He would be a troublemaker and cause Hébert sleepless nights." Hébert approached the leadership, lobbied the

Committee on Committees and threatened to challenge Harrington's assignment in caucus. Although he failed to keep Harrington from the Committee, he managed to maintain his committee's ideological bias by enlarging it and securing the appointment of additional conservatives.

Ideology was also central in the 1973 assignments to the Rules Committee. The retirement of conservative William Colmer resulted in the elevation of liberal Ray Madden to the chairmanship. To maintain their influence, southern conservatives made strong bids to fill at least one of the three vacancies. It was in this new Congress, however, that liberal forces had managed to add the three members of the Democratic leadership to the Committee on Committees as voting members in order to strengthen the party's leadership. The prevailing bias was that the Speaker should be assured the Rules Committee's cooperation in advancing legislation. Thus the Committee on Committees filled all three slots with moderate-to-liberal members expected to be loyal to Speaker Albert's leadership.

The politics of committee assignments relegates the criterion of expertise to a subordinate position. Indeed, Committee on Committees members tend to be more impressed by elements conducive to the development of expertise than by subject-matter knowledge. For example, they may note such characteristics as quickness of mind and sharpness in questioning. However, the element of character to which they are especially alert is diligence. What counts is how hard, how doggedly, one works. The qualities that are important are doing one's homework and knowing details. A congressman gains esteem if he is a "driver," a "real go-getter," a "prodder." These are the values that become expertise values. Other things being equal, they may be the determining element in the assignment process.

The Context of Assignments

The dominance of various criteria in making assignments depends upon the context in which assignment occurs. This section will discuss the importance of the committee, the traditional interests associated with a vacancy or reasons underlying the creation of an additional seat, and the tenure of applicants.

First, the factors involved in a particular assignment depend a great deal upon the committee's importance. Following the precedent established by Lyndon Johnson as Senate Majority Leader, House Democrats in the 93rd Congress voted to assure all freshmen Democrats assignment to a "major" committee. Committees so designated were Agriculture, Armed Services, Banking and Currency, Education and Labor, Foreign Affairs, Interstate and Foreign Commerce, Judiciary, and Public Works. The caucus continued to recognize the extraordinary importance of the committees on Appropriations, Ways and Means, and Rules by prohibiting their members from serving on any other committees.

For assignment to one of the three "exclusive" committees, the most critical factor is the interpersonal one; the ability of the potential member to get along, to be flexible and personally acceptable to other members of the Committee. For these committees, the chairman and the House party leadership have a major influence, and that influence is tempered by their personal relations with the applicant. The power of the chairman is so great with regard to assignment to these committees that few members whom they oppose on personal grounds would be slated for these seats. Chairman Wilbur Mills of Ways and Means is reported to have commented that "No one has been appointed to Ways and Means without my approval."

Consider, for example, the 1971 fight over filling a vacant Ways and Means seat. Joe D. Waggonner, a southern conservative, was opposed by Donald M. Fraser, a Minnesotan with a solid reputation as a liberal bellwether, a hard-working, personable but outspoken legislator. The Committee on Committees, after much internal division, slated Waggonner for the seat. Fraser carried his fight to the Democratic caucus, thereby providing another example of not playing by the unwritten rules. Waggonner won the seat. Fraser lost in a secret ballot of all Democratic members, the liberals again witnessing the power of chairmen, party leaders, and conservative strength.

Both Majority Leader Hale Boggs and Speaker Carl Albert supported Waggonner. So did Chairman Mills. Other Ways and Means members let it be known that Waggonner was "more compatible" with the interests of the Committee. Moreover, the addition of 1 more liberal would have meant that among the 15 Democratic members, conservative and moderate strength would have been reduced to the bare majority of 8. Waggonner's appointment, on the other hand, would add to the already dominant conservative majority.

In occasionally sharp contrast are assignments to non-exclusive committees. Some of them have few applicants, and, as one Committee on Committees member said, "We usually end up drafting someone for these slots. No one wants them. Seniority does not matter, chairman views do not matter; what matters is finding someone who will take them." Because of defeats and retirements, the Democratic composition of the District of Columbia Committee faced a major overhaul as the 93rd Congress convened. Chairman Mills reportedly commented that he had received many letters from members asking not to be assigned to that committee, and few from persons seeking it.

A second contextual element is the association of traditional interests with a vacancy. Democratic seats on the Committee on Education and Labor are filled with highly partisan Democrats. As a congressman said, "This committee really takes members who enjoy the cry to battle: the legislation is partisan and the politics is bitter." Furthermore, the Democrats always have added one other criterion; namely, that the member must be favorable to organized labor. This committee handles much labor legislation including, for example, bills involving the minimum wage and occupational safety. For labor, it is important to have "their people" sitting on this committee.

In other cases, the traditional interest is geographic. In 1969, when a seat on the Ways and Means Committee became vacant

115

by the retirement of Pennsylvanian George Rhodes, the seat remained a Pennsylvania seat. The political play was entirely within the state's delegation, with little or no outside influence. The appointment went to Philadelphia Democrat William J. Green. It is noteworthy that Green was selected for the post with less than three terms' seniority. The salient factor in appointment was that the seat was Pennsylvania's by tradition and custom. He had only to win the backing of his 14 state Democratic colleagues.

The creation of additional seats on a committee can determine the pattern of appointment. As previously discussed, the appointment of Michael Harrington to the Armed Services Committee coincided with the Committee's expansion and led to the appointment of a member of countervailing political philosophy. At the time, two seats on Armed Services were vacant. One was a "regional seat" belonging to New England. Harrington, in the face of opposition from Hébert, waged an active campaign for it. He won the backing of his New England delegation and was duly nominated. Liberal Les Aspin of Wisconsin was nominated for the other seat, reportedly because his vote for the leadership contest had been for the winning Hale Boggs, who had argued for Aspin's Armed Services assignment. Faced with the prospect of the addition of two Democratic liberals to his ranks, Chairman Hébert promptly created two more positions on the Committee. Hébert gained the support of the members of the Committee on Committees, and secured the appointment of two conservatives to these new posts, thereby preserving the character of the Committee's majority.

The remaining contextual element affecting the dominance of assignment criteria is the tenure of applicants. The circumstances of freshmen, incumbents wishing re-assignment, and former members returning to the House are quite different.

In assigning freshmen, the Committee on Committee members, lacking ample observation of interpersonal relations, must rely heavily on the applicant's letter and the advice of his delegation's dean. Typically the letters they review emphasize the significance of the assignment for constituency service and re-election. Thus, as the 92nd Congress convened in 1971, William Cotter of Hartford, Connecticut, requested assignment to the Banking and Currency Committee in order best to represent his insurance community; Cotter could present himself as a man of relevant experience, as he had been a state insurance commissioner. Both James Abourezk of South Dakota and Alaska's Nicholas Begich sought to join Interior and Insular Affairs because of the great impact of Federal land use policies upon their constituencies.[4] Given such self-serving statements from applicants they most likely barely know, the assigners rely greatly upon the evaluation of the zone man or dean, whom they know well.

In considering requests from incumbents, the assigners can balance the full range of objective criteria with their personal appraisal of the applicant. They may meet requests for re-assignment with such phrases as, in the words of one congressman, "they have served their time, and now we should promote them." Other reasons for granting re-assignment include their observation that the applicant has become respected and well-liked. In some cases their favorable decision stems from delegation support for succession to the "Ohio seat" or "Michigan seat." It is noteworthy that the non-freshman normally does not submit three choices, but rather only one. His investment in existing assignments tends to narrow his choice of preferences quite sharply. He might prefer only one other assignment to the one he has, and that might be to an exclusive committee for which he has only a marginal chance. In part because of this narrowing, non-freshmen tend to be less successful than freshmen in pursuing their top choices.

On the occasion of a former member's return to the House, the Committee on Committees makes a special effort to renew the previous assignment if the member wants it and a vacancy exists.

The entire process of assigning seats is particularly fascinating after the retirement of many senior members, as in 1973, or when defeats of incumbents create an abnormally large number of both committee vacancies and congressional newcomers.

BEING AN EFFECTIVE COMMITTEE MEMBER

A discussion of committee member effectiveness must begin with the recognition that each congressman has a unique conception of his role which varies with his political values, professional and social background, associations with other members, and his political environment. The importance each member attaches to his committee work depends upon his assignment, constituency, and opportunities within the committee.

Because some members find that their assignments offer only marginal political benefit, they devote little time to committee activities, instead emphasizing other congressional responsibilities and concerns. But because the committees are central to the legislative process and have great potential impact upon legislative careers, most members place considerable importance upon their committee activities. Committees often provide an opportunity for influencing policy and for advancing constituency interests, as well as occasional platforms for political exposure. A member associates his effectiveness in committee with his success in pursuing such objectives.

A member who defines effectiveness as meaning "making detailed, substantive contributions to legislation," must invest his time in careful preparation and in arduous committee sessions; moreover, he must use his staff supportively, question witnesses rigorously and precisely, and remain alert for opportunities for influence. He acquires specialized expertise, performs consistently as well as regularly, and is generally attentive to his committee's procedural norms.

A member seeking to be an effective voice for a geographic, ideological, or ethnic grouping is likely to place emphasis on his visibility as spokesman, utilizing his committee as a forum and

118

judging his effectiveness in these terms. He may publicize grand ideas, lament general policy directions, and otherwise seek to educate the public.

Effectiveness is related not only to goals but also to committee situations. It is likely to be enhanced where the chairman promotes participation, and where one has an advantage in expertise. The opportunity is generally related to seniority. Attendance at any particular session can also be a factor. As Senator Hubert Humphrey has stated on numerous occasions, "The influence and effectiveness of a senator is in inverse proportion to the number showing up at the meeting." Even a member with great seniority has little impact when absent.

Assessments of effectiveness are as diverse as the goals of the members and the viewpoints of the observers. It may or may not be equated with public acclaim. Political interest groups and Federal agencies may have vastly different understandings and appreciation of a member's committee contribution. But from the viewpoint of the congressman himself, the opportunity for effective action is directly related to the value he attaches to his committee assignments.

1. See Milton C. Cummings and Robert L. Peabody, "The Decision to Enlarge the Committee on Rules: An Analysis of the 1961 Vote," in Peabody and Nelson W. Polsby, eds. *New Perspectives on the House of Representatives*, 2nd ed. (Chicago: Rand McNally, 1969), pp. 253-281.

2. A Republican seeking assignment to a committee would pursue a course similar to that described here for Democrats. However, it must be emphasized that the composition and voting patterns of the GOP Committee on Committees are markedly different. Each state having Republican representation in the House is entitled to one seat. There are a total of 45 members in the 93rd Congress, appointed according to seniority by Minority Leader Gerald R. Ford. Most of the work is performed by the 16-member Executive Committee, presided over by the Minority Leader, who is not a voting member. Each state having 7 or more Republicans in the House has 1 seat. Ford selects someone to represent all states having 6 Republicans, someone else to represent those having 5, and so forth down to a representative for states having 1 GOP congressman. Each member of the Executive Committee votes in proportion to the number of Republicans in his own state's delegation. In the 93rd Congress, the representatives of California, New York, Ohio, Illinois, Michigan, and Pennsylvania had the greatest number of votes.

3.   The seminal work on assignments, Nicholas A. Masters, "Committee Assignments in the House of Representatives," *American Political Science Review*, LV (June, 1961), pp. 345-357, asserts that the single most important criterion for assignment is "legislative responsibility." Thus, according to him, seats on major committees go to those members "whose ability, attitudes, and relationships . . . serve to enhance the prestige and importance of the House of Representatives." However, in all the interviews for this chapter, respondents said little about "legislative responsibility." While there is some overlap between his concept and my concept of "interpersonal relations," there is clearly a basic difference of thrust which goes beyond mere refinement. For a recent treatment of both Democratic and Republican assignments, see "Politics of House Committees: The Path to Power," *Congressional Quarterly Weekly Report*, (February 10, 1973), pp. 279-283.

4.   In the 1972 elections, Abourezk won a seat in the Senate, where he again gained an Interior Committee assignment. During that fall, the crash of Begich's campaign plane in Alaska resulted in the death of both Begich and House Majority Leader Hale Boggs.

120

VII | Seniority and Committee Leadership: The Emergence of Choice

JONATHAN P. HAWLEY

No other single feature of Congress so greatly has affected the individual and collective experiences of members as the seniority system. Legislators find that longevity of service, particularly within committees, essentially determines their power. Focusing on the seniority system's continuing evolution, the essay examines its impact within and outside Congress, the criticisms directed at seniority, and arguments offered in its defense. The achievements of the 91st, 92nd, and 93rd Congresses' reform movement receive major attention.

The author is Legislative Assistant to Congressman Guy Vander Jagt (R., Mich.). A graduate of Park College, he received his M.A. and Ph.D. from the University of Missouri, Columbia. He is on leave of absence from the University of Tulsa, where he holds the rank of Associate Professor of Political Science, and has served as head of his department. In 1968-1969, he was a Congressional Fellow of the American Political Science Association, serving in the offices of Senator Frank E. Moss (D., Utah), and Representative Vander Jagt.

121

ALMOST 50 YEARS AGO, Professor James K. Pollock, a distinguished political scientist, described the seniority system's significance in words relevant even today:

> Congresses may come and go, but the seniority rule stays on indefinitely . . . after men have been in Congress for several years they realize that they are only units of the four hundred and thirty-five atoms which make up the House, and that their influence is *nil* unless they have secured preferment by being appointed to the chairmanship of some major committee.[1]

Personal power in Congress principally stems from one's tenure on a committee. Prior to recent procedural modifications, the longest-serving majority party member automatically was its chairman; his counterpart within the opposition party became the ranking minority member and assumed the chairmanship if his party won a congressional majority.

The durability of the seniority hierarchy has contributed to its becoming, next to the committee structure, Congress' most conspicuous organizational characteristic. It has affected the consideration and passage of statutes for nearly a century, and has influenced the careers of thousands of our politicians. Seniority's impact has been so pervasive for so long that today an observer may almost feel its presence when walking through the stately corridors of Capitol Hill. And seniority is something that each member of Congress deeply understands in working alongside and amidst his colleagues to fulfill his portion of their collective responsibility of representation. According to folklore, when one first comes to Congress, he can find no merit whatsoever in the seniority system, yet the longer he stays the greater wisdom he finds in it.

Although the role of seniority is quite apparent to persons directly concerned with Congress, there is disagreement as to its value. While critics for decades have decried the system as "senility rule," other commentators persistently have risen to seniority's defense, emphasizing its capacity to provide experienced, stable leadership within our complex national legislature.

Seniority extends throughout congressional life, affecting even the process of office selection. A congressman retains his office space as long as he desires. As retirements, deaths, and defeats create vacancies, members in order of their seniority may move to more spacious or elaborate quarters. Newly elected congressmen draw by lot for the offices which are unoccupied.

Seniority also affects the control of Capitol Hill patronage, frequently plays a role in the assignment or reassignment of members to committees, and influences the distribution of responsibilities and staff resources within committees. It affects a member's role in committee sessions and shapes the composition of conference committees appointed by the presiding officers of the House and Senate to resolve differences in legislation passed by the two Houses.

To a considerable extent, seniority conditions personal relationships among members. Members of Congress are generally deferential toward their senior colleagues, and occasionally markedly intimidated by them. Looking back to the time when he first entered the House, former Speaker Joseph Martin wrote:

> The men who were loaded with the coin of seniority were rather more aloof in those days than they are now. They were less reticent about letting a newcomer know that they were running the show. The large round table . . . in the House restaurant was reserved for the Speaker, the Chairmen of the various committees, and perhaps a few senior members of the Rules Committee. Anyone serving his first term would have been completely out of place. I had been in Congress three years before I dared pull up a chair.[2]

As Martin implied, newcomers are no longer so reluctant to mingle with the power brokers of the House and Senate. But a new member rarely feels completely at ease in his initial associations with senior members.

Attendance at a few congressional hearings enables an observer quickly to perceive the manifestations of seniority. The members sit according to party affiliation and seniority. All of the Democrats sit on one side of the chairman, who is at the center, the newest members of the committee sitting farthest away. The ranking minority member sits alongside the chairman, with his colleagues arranged in similar order of committee tenure. After making introductory comments about the purpose of the hearing and inviting the witness to present his statement, the chairman begins the questioning. He may raise the most pertinent and provocative questions himself, or give a senior colleague an early opportunity to do so. Questioning proceeds in order of seniority. While a time limitation sometimes is imposed, in other instances this is not done, leaving the newer members to sit in frustration awaiting an opportunity to enter the dialogue before it is terminated by luncheon recess, a quorum call, or recorded vote.

Newcomers commonly receive little staff assistance during hearings other than a few whispered remarks as to the issue at hand when they enter the room. The committee staff personnel devote most of their attention to the chairman and ranking minority member, who determine subjects to be emphasized in the hearings and direct other preparations. The reporters tend also to focus upon the most influential members, according almost no attention to the others.

The nature of a committee's business as well as the style and personality of its chairman establish the tone of its proceedings. A chairman and senior members, supported by close staff relationships, commonly dominate inquiries into complex issues. The younger members, lacking other means to achieve recognition within Congress and desiring to participate in its central workings, nonetheless attend hearings, learning and waiting. Gradually they too become enmeshed in the system.

It should be no surprise that observers, in expressing their concern over the responsiveness of our governmental machinery, often have asserted that the seniority system is dysfunctional. Yet, they then have confronted a fundamental dilemma: How could Congress reconcile its responsibility to represent all people equally with its obvious need for internal organization and leadership?

THE HISTORY OF SENIORITY

The power structure of the contemporary Congress differs markedly from its ancestry. Neil MacNeil offers this contrast:

> In the House that Henry Clay first entered in 1811, the centers of power were controlled by young men. Clay, at thirty-four, led an assembly in which many of the most powerful members were so young as he . . . Charles Ingersoll was thirty-one years old when he first became chairman of the Judiciary Committee. A century and a half later, the chairman of the Judiciary Committee was Emanuel Celler of New York, seventy-three years old and a veteran of thirty-eight years' service in the House . . . The House had become, obviously, a citadel of power for the men of seniority, men tested and proven over long years of partisan battling in the House committees and on the floor. And the change altered the nature of the men who most influenced the House's decisions.[3]

A principal distinction between the House of the nineteenth century and today is the increased stability of its membership. In the old days, when average tenure in the House was about four years, seniority was of minimal importance. Indeed, many congressional districts in that period seemed to practice the principle of rotation in office. An example is Abraham Lincoln, who had been elected to the House in 1846, and wanted to run again two years later. He was denied the opportunity, however, because someone else in the constituency wanted the job.[4]

MacNeil suggests that an early indication of representatives' deference to institutional seniority was their practice of calling attention to their most senior colleague by designating him "Father of the House."[5] These dignitaries typically were men of about 40 years of age. In 1972 the "Dean," as the most senior member commonly is known, was 84 year-old Emanuel Celler (D., N.Y.), first elected to the House 50 years earlier. When Celler left in 1973, he was succeeded by Wright Patman (D., Tex.), who was beginning his 44th year of service.

The increased tenure in Congress may be a reflection of several factors, including the considerable extension of life expectancy. One might speculate that the ease of travel today makes it more attractive to remain in Congress, and even makes possible the tenure of men not robust enough to have survived nineteenth-century transportation. Similarly, the era of mass communications, enabling a well-known incumbent to rely less upon personal appearances, has reduced the strain of campaigning. In recent years, moreover, the salary and retirement benefits have become very attractive. Not least, some members eventually become motivated toward a congressional career by the prospect of power to be gained by seniority.

Prior to 1910, the Speaker of the House appointed members to the standing committees and determined the chairmen. While seniority offered one means of choice, the Speaker frequently disregarded it for political or personal reasons.

Resentment over the increasing dominance of the House by the Speaker reached a peak in 1910, when liberal Republican congressmen teamed with the Democratic minority to alter the rules of the House. The Speaker was deprived of much of his appointive power; party committees on committees assumed the power, with ratification by the full House, of assigning members to standing committees and designating their leaders.

Seniority gradually increased in importance as the basis of advancement within committees, reaching its peak after World War II. Since that time seniority in the House has been virtually inviolate.

In the absence of a powerful presiding officer, seniority appeared earlier in the Senate. During the late 1840's and throughout the 1850's, seniority had a significant effect upon Democratic committee advancement. However, between the outbreak of the Civil War and the late 1870's, the Republicans so outnumbered the Democrats that the Republican leaders could be highly subjective in selecting chairmen. Even if they offended some colleagues by displaying personal favoritism, they were assured of legislative success.

After 1877, revived Democratic strength forced the Republican leaders to avoid alienating their members, and automatic reliance upon seniority in committee advancement became characteristic of the Republicans. Seniority gained favor with Democratic senators as their numbers grew during the 1880's. By the use of the practical concept of seniority, they too could avoid intra-party struggles and the alienation of their own ranks.[6]

The custom of seniority became deeply rooted within each legislative party. While not a part of the formal rules of Congress, it is nonetheless so durable as to be regarded as a permanent element of organization. Being external to the legal framework, the seniority system lay beyond the reach of the major Legislative Reorganization Act of 1946, which greatly reduced the number of committees in each House. The Reorganization Act of 1970, described in detail later in this essay, similarly failed to modify the system. In the early 1970's, when the element of choice began to enter the processes of committee leadership selection, it occurred within the individual party caucuses.

The seniority system has tended to be self-perpetuating. As Professor Pollock explained almost 50 years ago, "It is only natural, when senators have waited many long years to gain preferment, that they should object to any modification of the rule that might cause their displacement."[7]

As a member begins to accrue seniority on a committee or perhaps even a subcommittee, he recognizes that a change in assignment can be disruptive to the development of his expertise and influence. Hence, the seniority system acts as a stabilizing influence upon the composition of standing committees. As former Senator Joseph Clark, one of the most persistent advocates of reform, wrote, "once a member is appointed to a major committee he tends to dig his feet in and wait for death, defeat, or resignation of his seniors to bring him out at the top of the list."[8]

THE EFFECTS OF SENIORITY

Secure in their seats by virtue of constituency stability and in their committee leadership posts by seniority, chairmen have become highly independent factors in the policy-making process. Possessing awesome power over the course of their committee functions, chairmen grow apart from the leaders of the congressional parties and other elements of the policy system, reigning in individual styles over sectors of public policy.

Subcommittee chairmanships, now nearly as coveted as the chairmanships of full committees, commonly are determined by seniority. While narrower in jurisdiction and controlled in varying degrees by committee chairmen, subcommittees provide specialized leadership opportunities to many more members than would otherwise have such roles. But it is not unusual for a representative or senator to wait many years for even a subcommittee chairmanship, particularly within major committees led by chairmen who adhere to the order of seniority in designating these leaders. Achievement of a subcommittee chairmanship would give him new opportunities in the policy process. He would be able to follow through on policy initiatives, not only in the subcommittee's field, but, through bargaining, in other fields as well. A subcommittee chairmanship also imparts prestige to a legislator, strengthening his credentials and attracting news coverage.

A member of a senator's staff once remarked that ten years' work in that office became worthwhile when the senator received his first subcommittee chairmanship. The staffer relished the knowledge that his senator finally was in a position to lead colleagues and to advance policy with institutional clout. He also knew that the senator's chance of surviving an anticipated tough re-election battle had been greatly enhanced. It could be assumed that the staffer gained corresponding advantages.

In addition to these individual consequences, seniority has had great effect upon Congress itself. The traditional geographic

128

patterns of party strength have produced disproportionate numbers of chairmen from certain areas of the nation. The best example is the South which, to paraphrase a popular observation, may have lost at Appomattox but won a major victory in the Congress. Since the Depression the Democrats have controlled the Congress for all but four years; during that time seniority has enabled the South to maintain possession of most of the major chairmanships. Despite Republican inroads into "Dixie" in the last two decades, many seats remain safely Democratic; their occupants have amassed seniority on major committees.

The results of a single year's election can greatly increase the impact of seniority. Only recently have the more liberal Democrats of the North recovered from the 1946 congressional elections, which produced a Republican majority. The GOP victories in previously Democratic districts occurred primarily in northern and western states, thereby advancing the seniority of the southern conservative Democrats. Liberal Democrats elected thereafter confronted committee leadership dominated by conservative colleagues.

The southern orientation of many chairmen contributed to a struggle between Congress and the White House in the post-World War II years, especially during the administrations of liberal Democratic Presidents. While recent reapportionments have strengthened urban representation, the higher echelons of the standing committees have been only gradually affected by this trend. The death, primary election defeat, or resignation of one southern chairman has often resulted in the ascension of a man of similar background, who had labored for many years at the side of the departed member, and who had a great likelihood of maintaining a steady conservative course. Liberal Democrats have found this pattern particularly frustrating. One of the seniority system's most vocal critics, Congressman Richard Bolling (D., Mo.) wrote:

It is, of course, gratifying to the Republicans to see the Democrats put conservative foxes in charge of the liberal chicken coops, appointing to high committee posts members who reflect Republican rather than Democratic views on great national issues.[9]

After two decades, time itself has begun to erode the South's position. We are on the verge of a new era to be shaped by the accruing seniority of liberal members. In several Senate committees, younger liberals are just a notch below aging southern colleagues. At the opening of the 93rd Congress, liberals not only occupied all the House Democratic floor leadership posts, but also gained control of the critically important Rules Committee.

THE THEMES OF DEBATE

In his provocative commentary on the Senate, *Citadel*, journalist William S. White wrote, "A Senate committee is an imperious force; its chairman, unless he be a weak and irresolute man, is emperor."[10] All emperors are controversial. Congressional committee chairmen have been no exception, and the system by which they have come to power has been the object of persistent attacks.

The seniority system has been commonly criticized for perpetuating elderly men in the most vital posts. While committee seniority has no direct correlation to members' ages, older and even elderly men are likely to be at the helm of committees. At the age of 80, very few men are running corporations or banks or even holding down full-time jobs. But in Congress, because of the seniority tradition, a man of that age may just be attaining a leadership role. At 80, Ray Madden (D., Ind.) became chairman of the Rules Committee in 1973. While some men, such as he, are vigorous in body and mind at that stage in life, few have the stamina needed for aggressive leadership. Automatic advancement by seniority has permitted no evaluation of individuals.

Moreover, the traditional system gave committee members no leverage by which to pressure arbitrary and abusive chairmen toward responsiveness. Because chairmen had no fear of losing their status, they did not have to adjust to criticisms of their styles or decisions.

Another major criticism of the traditional system has been its tendency to perpetuate committee control by members from one-party congressional districts. Inversely, constituencies having sharp party competition are less likely to be represented by men of seniority. Many observers regard it as fundamentally undemocratic to punish the areas of most vigorous partisan competition by giving them less clout within Congress.

Geographic imbalances among chairmen have also led to charges of inequitable legislative response to national needs. For example, early in the 92nd Congress the citizens' organization Common Cause expressed concern that 12 men whom it believed to be among the most powerful in Congress, namely the subcommittee chairmen of the House Appropriations Committee, were elected from only a few states. Of the dozen, 3 were from the Northeast, 1 from the Northwest, and the remaining 8 from the South. In the words of the *Washington Post*, "The result is an outrageous concentration of power over government spending within a few states that are not representative of the nation as a whole."[11]

Some idealists have criticized seniority because it has discouraged the development of greater party discipline over legislators' voting. The absence of national party influence in the selection of committee leaders has symbolized the weakness of parties in the policy process.

On the level of the individual member, critics have viewed seniority as creating unevenness in members' capacities to represent their constituencies. In a House conceived as a mirror of changing citizen sentiment, it seems inconsistent to encourage members to campaign for re-election on the theme of having the seniority to function effectively.

Finally, it is said that the system discourages talented, ambitious men from seeking congressional office. An advancement system which accords no credit for relevant experience offers little encouragement to unusually qualified persons considering candidacy. If a former Cabinet officer were elected to the Senate and managed to obtain a seat on a committee having jurisdiction in his administrative field, he would receive the lowest position on the ladder, farthest away from a leadership opportunity. Yet, his background might enable him to contribute more to the committee's work than any other member. Also damaging to the recruitment of highly competent candidates, say the opponents of seniority, have been senile or disinterested chairmen perpetuated in power.

Despite the vigor of their appeals, the critics of seniority made no progress until the 1970's. As Professor Pollock had noted in 1925, "when a group of congressional insurgents cry, 'The seniority system must go!,' their cry [did] not bring forth a popular demonstration to support them."[12]

Every threat to the seniority system has provoked its defenders to action, voicing their belief in its many benefits. The foremost among their arguments is that seniority fosters congressional expertise. Seniority's advocates suggest that only through a member's long service on a committee, during which he undergoes an apprenticeship which prepares him to assume a leadership role, can a member acquire the understanding which will enable him to fulfill greater responsibility.

Supporters of the seniority system argue that it provides protection against interests which seek to influence legislation. As chairmen are secure in their seats, they have no need to curry favor with vested interests. In a "Dear Colleague" letter to members of the House early in the 93rd Congress, Representative Burt L. Talcott (R., Calif.), previously a participant in a GOP task force on reform, warned for this reason against vitiation of the seniority system:

> Elections or appointments of any kind would invite and continuously breed "politicking," "wheeling and dealing," trading, and bartering that would precipitate chaos and corruption not only in the selection of Committee Chairmen (or ranking minority Members), but also in the Congress. Few, except those representing powerful, monied or political

special interest groups, favor elections even if "secret." There are no "secret" elections around the House. The campaigners are too experienced at poll taking and "nose counting," particularly in continuous campaigns among small groups.

The independence of chairmen extends not only to pressure groups but also to party leaders and to the President, whose wishes they frequently ignore. Political scientist Alfred de Grazia found particular strength in this characteristic:

> The selection of committee chairmen is accomplished by procedures far more complicated and defensive than are generally understood, and the seniority principle that plays a large part in the selection should not be put aside for any other method that directly or indirectly would increase presidential or political-party control of Congress.[13]

Another common argument has been that seniority avoids disruptive competition among committee members for the chairmanship or ranking minorityship. Such competition would waste time, destroy the comraderie necessary for legislative bargaining, and undermine the likelihood of members' taking independent positions on sensitive public policy questions.

Defenders of seniority often have argued that critics are attacking the wrong target. They have emphasized that committees always have possessed the power to out-vote a domineering chairmen, even if that power has been difficult to muster. Some spokesmen have suggested that the reform movement should be refocused. An example is provided by the "Dear Colleague" letter which Congressman Ben Blackburn (R., Ga.) distributed in January, 1973, inviting co-sponsorship of a bill to expand minority committee staffing, outlaw proxy voting in committee, provide a procedure for bringing up a bill for consideration to which the chairman is opposed, and other changes in committee processes. Blackburn wrote:

> At the beginning of each Congress, a great deal of talk is heard about the need to abolish the seniority system in the selection of Committee Chairmen. I have long felt that no legitimate quarrel exists in the recognition of seniority as a device for locating office spaces, for choosing parking places

among members, or the selection of the person who should act as Chairman of our Committees. I think it is entirely appropriate that the senior man of the majority party should be the Chairman of the Committee.

Where I do feel that considerable evil is done is in granting to the Chairman such broad discretionary power that he can be unresponsive to the will of the Congress or even to the will of a majority of his own Committee.

Throughout the years, debate has focused as much upon potential alternatives to seniority as upon its strengths and weaknesses. While some idealists have campaigned to eliminate the seniority system entirely, most reformers have sought to moderate its impact.

Frequently suggested has been the majority caucus' election of chairmen from among each standing committee's three most senior colleagues. This procedure would continue the selection of men of experience while introducing the element of choice. It would have the tactical advantage of appealing not only to the second and third ranking members but also to the fourth and fifth ranking, who similarly could anticipate an opportunity to bid for power.

Some members have suggested that the choice be made not by the caucus but by the majority members of the individual committees, either from among the three most senior members or from their entire majority membership. This concept is central to the reform adopted by Senate Republicans in 1973. The rationale is that those who serve on a committee are best qualified to judge the potential for leadership within their own group.

Another proposal has been to nominate chairmen in the Committees on Committees, subject to approval either by the caucuses or by the majority members of the respective standing committees. Such an approach would broaden the involvement of rank-and-file members while retaining the influence of those who make assignments. As will be described later, the House parties have taken steps toward this type of reform since 1970.

Virtually every proposal envisions selection of the ranking minority members in a similar manner. Indeed, the concept of the ranking member as titular chairman seems to be universally accepted.

All of these proposals have received support from critics of seniority, who would have been pleased by almost any procedure embodying an element of choice. Yet none of the proposals has been acceptable to the defenders of seniority, despite the fact that probably few of them have regarded traditional procedures as entirely satisfactory. The opinion has prevailed that while there are many proposals, there is no single alternative significantly preferable to the seniority system, particularly from the perspective of current chairmen. They occasionally have dismissed the reformers' appeals as expressions of frustration inevitably present among ambitious politicians.

At the heart of the issue has been a "chicken and egg" dilemma. The young, newer members of Congress have asserted that men should be elevated to committee leadership posts by virtue of their achievements, and that such a system would maximize congressional impact upon national needs. Chairmen and senior colleagues have replied that their experience is vital to Congress' capacity to meet its responsibilities, and that their performances repeatedly have been approved by their constituents. Debate has been unceasing, both within and beyond the walls of Congress. But one thing has been clear: any change would have to be made by the members themselves, working within the existing power structure and the congressional parties.

THE POLITICS AND ACHIEVEMENT OF
SENIORITY REFORM

As debate over seniority increased during the 1960's, it became clear that opponents of the existing system had two basic motivations. Liberal members of the House and Senate, embittered by committee obstruction of progressive legislative proposals, sought to break the impact of the "conservative coalition" by changing the leadership selection system. Most committee chairmen were personifications of this coalition of conservative Democrats and Republicans.

Augmenting their interest was the viewpoint of many newer members, conservatives as well as liberals, who were impatient and frustrated over procedural obstacles to active policy-making roles. However symbolic it may seem to some, these reformers were ultimately successful in achieving modifications. Their fight, which continued across three Congresses with increasing momentum, reveals many aspects of the politics of congressional seniority.

The 91st Congress

The first visible hint of this reform drive occurred in a mild revolt in early 1969 against Speaker John W. McCormack's re-election to that office. Arizona's Morris K. Udall, who represented the hopes of many members of the Democratic Study Group (DSG), opposed the elderly Massachusetts congressman for his party's nomination for Speaker. Although the Speakership is not determined by seniority, that custom was an underlying point of contention. McCormack's critics believed that he provided inadequate leadership, particularly by leaving conservative chairmen free to exercise autonomous power. The Speaker's opponents sought a successor who would exert greater pressure upon chairmen to move liberal legislation. Udall's bid fell short, as the Speaker was renominated by a caucus vote of 178 to 58. Nonetheless, the campaign indicated the presence of reformers within Democratic ranks who would not retreat.

Throughout 1969, the Speaker's standing with liberal Democratic members deteriorated. To their belief in his weakness was added an element of public uncertainty about his fitness for heavy responsibilities following the disclosure of alleged improprieties by a member of his staff. Meanwhile, the aged McCormack announced that he planned to run once again for

136

the House in 1970, and to be a candidate for Speaker, an intention disturbing to Democratic members who had supported him in the fight with Udall in the belief that he was then seeking his final term as presiding officer.

Unsuccessful in their effort to block McCormack, dissident Democrats turned their attention more specifically to the seniority system. The battlefield was the party caucus. After Jerome R. Waldie (Calif.) lost a "no confidence" attempt against McCormack in 1970, a group of reformers presented a resolution calling for establishment of a party-sponsored study of the seniority system. This resolution had been developed by the DSG as an expression of its desire to enhance the responsiveness of committee chairmen to both the caucus and the party leadership. Subsequent reports indicated that some reformers were dismayed by Waldie's effort to discredit the Speaker personally, fearing that his tactic had offended members and weakened chances for passage of their reform resolution. Indicative of their sensitivity to this delicate situation was the deletion of language critical of conservative chairmen, in order to win greater support for their study. The reformers also hoped that their tactfulness would encourage Carl Albert (Okla.), then the Majority Leader, to support their cause.

The liberals hoped that the study would keep the issue of seniority alive throughout the year and lead to implementation of a revised system of committee advancement at the opening caucus of the 92nd Congress. But true to tradition, the party's conservatives sought to block the seniority study, threatening to run a candidate of their own against Speaker McCormack if he assisted the liberals in their cause.

In March, 1970, the Democratic caucus established an 11-man committee to study the merits of the seniority system and to report the following January. Some liberals favoring speedier completion of the study threatened to break with their party and join Republicans in the election of the Speaker. At least one liberal called on reform-minded Democrats to nominate liberal colleagues from the floor of the House in opposition to some chairmen in the event the party's caucus failed to produce changes in the seniority system. These reformers signed a statement expressing opposition to the January reporting date, complaining that because it followed the general election, the voting public would be going to the polls uncertain of the nature of Democratic committee leadership.

In mid-summer, 1970, the House began floor debate on the proposed Legislative Reorganization Act, which contained no modifications to the selection of chairmen by seniority. The House defeated an attempt on the floor to dilute the power of chairmen. An amendment offered by Dante B. Fascell (D., Fla.) provided for the election of a temporary chairman by a majority of a committee if they determined that the chairman was physically or otherwise unable to carry out his duties. Fascell acknowledged that his amendment created the possibility that a chairman could be removed by his committee members for any reason. A considerable number of reforms, many by DSG members, were accepted on the House floor. But final voting on the modified legislation was deferred.

Weeks passed without any activity. House liberals complained that conservatives were trying to stall for time, in hopes of killing the bill or of sending it to the Senate with insufficient time remaining in the session for its consideration. Some members charged that the leadership was bowing to conservative sentiment, but Majority Leader Albert pledged that the reorganization bill would come up for final debate and a vote in mid-September. When debate was resumed at that time, the House defeated an amendment by Jonathan B. Bingham (D., N.Y.) to limit the tenure of committee chairmen to four terms unless the House made an individual exception by two-thirds vote.

Passed 326-19, the Act had no direct effect upon the seniority rule. Nonetheless, southern conservatives, notably chairmen, strongly opposed it. Three chairmen actually voted against it. Two of them, Wilbur Mills (Ways and Means) and Olin Teague (Veterans' Affairs) were southerners. Nine other chairmen, six of whom were from southern or border states, refrained from voting.

Following House action, the struggle shifted to the Senate, where passage occurred on October 6, 1970. The Senate rejected a number of amendments which would have modified its own seniority system. By 23-44, it defeated Robert Packwood's (R., Ore.) amendment to provide for election of committee chairmen by a vote of all of the majority members. The Senate also rejected a Packwood amendment to have chairmen elected by each committee's majority party members. Among those voting against both of Packwood's amendments were the southern senators. By a vote of 59-5, the Senate passed the Legislative Reorganization Act in essentially the same form as it had cleared the House, without any provisions pertaining to seniority. While the reformers were pleased with their accomplishments, they remained determined to achieve change in seniority by other means.

The 92nd Congress

The battle over the seniority system was resumed in January, 1971, when both House caucuses received reports of study groups. The Democratic Committee on Organization Study and Review, headed by Julia Butler Hansen (Wash.), recommended changes in the process of selecting chairmen. The proposed system was to operate as follows: the Committee on Committees would recommend to the caucus the composition of each committee and the chairman, if the party was in power, without necessarily following seniority. At the request of 10 or more members, a nomination for chairman would be debated and the challenge resolved by majority vote. In the event that the nominee was defeated, the Committee on Committees would submit another name for consideration.

During the previous year, House Republicans had established their own extensive study of the seniority system under a task force led by Barber B. Conable, Jr., of New York. Being in the minority and facing a less sensitive situation, Republicans felt somewhat freer to press for reform. Moreover, they foresaw considerable political advantage in achieving the breakthrough. The task force recommended a system incorporating a greater departure from traditional practices than that proposed in the Democratic caucus. The Republican Committee on Committees would nominate someone for the post of ranking Republican (chairman in the event the party held a majority) of each committee, again without necessarily respecting seniority. Each nomination would be approved by the Conference, as the House Republican caucus is formally known. The Committee on Committees would replace any rejected nominee.

It should be emphasized that neither party's proposal sought to eliminate the seniority system. Nominating bodies could select members having highest seniority for the top committee posts, and in the case of the Democrats, a vote on a nomination could be secured only at the demand of 10 or more members. Republicans would vote on all nominations. Nonetheless, while the possibility existed for seniority to rule by consent, the proposals opened the door for relief from some of the most disturbing consequences of traditional procedure.

On January 20, 1971, the House Democrats adopted the Hansen Committee's recommendations for the selection of chairmen. They also accepted a proposal that no member could be chairman of more than one legislative subcommittee, thus opening subcommittee chairmanships to more members. The action came the day after the caucus had defeated a challenge by John Conyers of Michigan to eliminate the seniority rights of the Mississippi delegation. He had argued that the five Mississippi members had no right to Democratic seniority because they had run for re-election without associating themselves with the racially integrated ticket recognized by the national Democratic party. In voting 111-55 against his appeal, the Democrats bowed to the viewpoint expressed by Mississippi's Jamie Whitten, who said that the delegation had been duly elected and that the party caucus had no authority to intervene in the public's decisions.

On the same day, the Republican Conference adopted the recommendations of the Conable Committee. Before the final vote, the Conference defeated an amendment offered by freshman Congressman Peter A. Peyser of New York empowering the Republican members of each standing committee to formally nominate one of their colleagues for the Committee on Committees' consideration.

During the same week, the Senate parties also took less conclusive actions. Earlier, two reform-minded senators, Democrat Fred R. Harris (Okla.) and Republican Charles McC. Mathias, Jr. (Md.), had scheduled two days of hearings on the seniority system in the Senate. Both parties considered certain seniority questions in their caucuses. The Senate Republicans accepted Mathias' proposal that senators be limited to one ranking committee position. The Republicans also established a special committee to study further modification of the seniority system. The Democrats accepted a proposal that the party caucus be empowered to consider and approve appointments to chairmanships and other committee positions suggested by the Steering Committee. But the caucus defeated Harris' proposal that each chairmanship nomination automatically be subjected to a separate caucus vote. The Democrats also authorized three colleagues, Harris, Hubert H. Humphrey, and Herman E. Talmadge, to offer recommendations on seniority and other problems of committee memberships and advancement.

In February, 1971, House Democrats met in caucus to receive nominations for chairmen and to test the procedure for the first time. The Committee on Committees nominated the same individuals who would have received the posts strictly upon the basis of seniority. But a group led by Brock Adams (Wash.), a member of the District of Columbia Committee, attempted to defeat the choice of John L. McMillan to continue as chairman of that committee. Adams described his efforts as

141

arising from the manner in which McMillan had directed the committee, rather than from his age or southern orientation. After a bitter fight, Adams' attack fell short, the caucus voting 126-96 to retain McMillan. The first attempt to reject a nominee for chairman was thereby defeated. But the action within the caucus made clear that the new procedures legitimized a challenge.

Challenging the premise that committee advancement was solely an internal party matter, several House Democrats then carried the issue of McMillan's selection to the House floor. Although House rules since 1910 had provided for the formal election of chairmen and committee members, the voting had been routine. The House had abided by the custom that each party determined its committee memberships and their ranking.

Led by Waldie, opponents to McMillan's continuation as District of Columbia Committee Chairman sought his defeat. Unlike Adams, Waldie believed that a member's philosophical orientation should be evaluated in assessing his suitability for a particular chairmanship. He argued that McMillan's views were "inconsistent with the responsibility that is his as committee chairman to govern the District of Columbia."[14] He blamed McMillan personally for what he asserted was a deplorable condition of the District.

A unique aspect of Waldie's campaign was his invitation to Republican members to join in evaluating McMillan's fitness for the post:

> I offer my colleagues on the other side, in the minority party, the opportunity, by following the rules of this House, to participate in that decision. And I suggest to them that their great concern for the inviolability of the seniority system can now be evidenced by this action.

Waldie's approach brought forth a spirited House debate. The late Representative James G. Fulton (R., Pa.) labelled Waldie's tactics objectionable in that they disrupted the traditional understanding between the parties in organizing the Congress. Waldie answered, "To the extent that comity and courtesy or

142

the lack thereof as a result of the decision which has been made, results in disadvantages to the national interest, it should be disregarded."

Minority Leader Gerald R. Ford sought to dissuade his colleagues from accepting Waldie's invitation:

> Mr. Speaker, I think this factual situation clearly sets forth the issue that is before us. The Democratic caucus made a decision on committee chairmen. Whether we on our side agree with it or not, by precedent that is a matter within the ranks and prerogatives of the majority party. The Democratic Party was chosen to be the majority part in the 92nd Congress by the American people. I do not happen to think that that was necessarily the right decision, but that was the judgment of the American people last November, and if they are to carry out as they see fit the mandate given them, the Democratic party in the House of Representatives ought to have the right in a democratic process to choose the individual on each of the standing committees who should serve as the chairman of those committees. By precedent and otherwise, we on our side should not get into the procedures and prerogatives of the majority party.

In contrast, maverick Republican Donald Riegle[15] congratulated Waldie on his decision to bring the question before the whole House. A four-year member of the District of Columbia Committee, Riegle said that in his opinion the committee had not been responsive to the needs of capital city residents. He reiterated that the Democratic caucus had not examined the committee's performance under McMillan, and said that the Congress owed the people of the District such a review.

When the vote came, 32 members supported Waldie's effort and 258 opposed it. Perhaps more significant were the 42 "present" votes and the 100 votes not cast. That so many members did not vote and others merely indicated their presence, revealed considerable uneasiness over Waldie's decision to take the issue to the floor and its long-term implications. Republican Guy Vander Jagt, critical of the seniority system yet respectful of the majority's traditional control of its own committee assignments, followed the debate closely. When the vote came, he first voted to support the challenge to McMillan, then changed to "present," thereby expressing both his objection to seniority and his reluctance to intrude into Democratic decision-making.

Waldie's defeat brought to a halt efforts in the 92nd Congress to reform the seniority system. Nonetheless, House foes of seniority had broken the system's automation in selecting committee chairmen. As indicated by the selections of the 92nd Congress, their procedural progress did not ensure that persons chosen for these crucial posts would be newer or younger members. But a legitimate opportunity for contesting the choices for chairmanships and ranking memberships within the party caucuses had been secured. And the possibility remained that caucus decisions might be taken to the House floor for debate, as Waldie had demonstrated. Moreover, reform-minded senators were pushing forward, seeking to overcome the rigidity of the seniority system in the upper House.

The 93rd Congress

Reform forces re-emerged following the November, 1972, election, and sought to make further progress as the 93rd Congress was organized. By late November the DSG was leading a new effort to require the election of all committee chairmen. Working alongside this internal group was Common Cause, which had made seniority reform one of its major goals in grass-roots work throughout the country. The Americans for Democratic Action reportedly was lining up members to bring nominations for chairmen to a caucus vote in the event the procedural reform movement failed.

The Democratic leadership referred the reform proposals to the Hansen Committee which after debate unanimously reported a proposal to require a vote on each nominee. The recommendation did not provide for secret balloting.

Caucusing in late January, 1973, House Democrats opened debate on the Hansen Committee proposal, as well as on one by

144

Frank E. Evans (Colo.) providing for a separate, secret vote on each nominee for a chairmanship. Subsequently, Chet Holifield (Calif.) offered a third alternative, a recorded, open vote on chairmen. The Holifield approach, which might have resulted in intimidation of rank-and-file members by chairmen, was defeated first, followed by the Evans proposal. Thereafter, the Hansen Committee proposal, which did not specify the manner of voting, was passed overwhelmingly. A major victory for the reformers came on a motion by the new Majority Leader, Thomas P. O'Neill, Jr., (Mass.) to make voting on chairmen subject to the secret ballot at the request of 20 percent of the caucus. This move greatly strengthened the reform, as it was assumed that a secret ballot would become routine.

The caucus next met with the intention of considering the designees for the 93rd Congress. But Samuel P. Stratton (N.Y.) moved at the outset to reconsider all reforms that had been adopted the previous day. Speaker Albert immediately offered a motion to table the Stratton maneuver, and Albert's motion passed by a decisive voice vote. Albert's action was seen by the reformers as a significant assertion of liberal party leadership. Democratic procedures for selecting House chairmen thus had been further opened to conform closely to the procedure adopted by the House Republicans in the previous Congress.

After resolving the procedural issue, the caucus took up the designees for chairmen in alphabetical order of committees. After 48 votes were cast against W.R. Poage of Texas to continue as chairman of the Agriculture Committee, the secret ballot procedure was employed throughout the voting.

Although all of the nominees for chairmanships drew opposition, ranging from 2 to 49 negative votes, perhaps the most significant approval was that extended to Holifield, chosen to continue as leader of the Committee on Government Operations. A week before, Representative Benjamin Rosenthal (N.Y.) had announced that he would lead a campaign to defeat Holifield on the grounds that he had provided weak leadership in consumer protection legislation and other matters. Holifield replied to the criticism with a strong caucus speech and gained approval by a margin of 172-46.

The recommendations for chairmanships, in every instance the same as seniority would have produced, were thus approved. But sizeable numbers of votes cast against several incumbent chairmen revealed some dissatisfaction. And the open challenge to Holifield established a significant precedent within the Democratic caucus.

As House Republicans organized for the 93rd Congress, they experienced the first test of the reform they had instituted two years earlier. Because of a retirement, the ranking minority position on the Government Operations Committee was vacant. Next in line by seniority was Frank Horton (N.Y.). Following him was the more conservative John N. Erlenborn (Ill.), who announced that he, like Horton, was a candidate for the post. Both men pointed to considerable involvement in the committee's legislative and oversight activities, and both campaigned openly for their colleagues' support. The Committee on Committees and its Executive Committee backed Horton, along with other Republicans having greatest seniority on their respective committees. However, the party leaders did display a willingness to ignore seniority in special cases, depriving Leslie C. Arends (Ill.) of the leading position on Armed Services because he held the party's Whip post, and John B. Anderson (Ill.) the top post on Rules because he was Chairman of the House Republican Conference.

The Conference followed the recommendations of the nominators, approving Horton by a vote of 100-36. It is also noteworthy that while Erlenborn's bid was the only open challenge to any man of seniority, all but 6 of the 21 designees drew negative votes. In displaying a continuing deference to seniority, House Republicans of the 93rd Congress nonetheless revealed that their selection procedure was something more than a *pro forma* exercise.

Efforts to reform the Senate seniority system began shortly after the November elections, as Senators Mathias and Adlai E.

146

Stevenson III (D., Ill.) convened public hearings on seniority and other reform objectives. Interest was widespread despite the fact that Senate chairmen, because of the absence of a rule of germaneness governing amendments, have a weaker command over legislation than their House counterparts. John Gardner, Chairman of Common Cause, led outside critics in the hearings, while Senator Robert Taft, Jr. (R., Ohio) spoke on behalf of the internal reform effort. Taft advised, "If representative government is to work, committee leadership should reflect ability, public sentiment and party sentiment."[16]

Senate Democrats made their 93rd Congress assignments and named chairmen essentially in accordance with seniority. Majority Leader Mansfield previously had assured his colleagues that a vote on a chairman could be obtained by any dissenter. However, reform-minded senators sought to establish a new mechanism that would downgrade the impact of seniority upon committee advancement.

It was within the Republican ranks, however, that the major action occurred. After convening, they began to debate the issue and various alternative procedures. Senators Taft and Packwood proposed that a seven-man steering committee should recommend committee assignments and ranking memberships. Opposition by a single member would secure a vote by secret ballot. The proposal extended the protection of "grandfather rights" to ranking members of the 93rd Congress. Senator Mark Hatfield (Ore.) opposed both steering committee roles on the grounds that liberals would suffer at the hands of the more numerous conservatives and that committees would be plagued by internal politicking and external influences.

Senator Howard Baker (Tenn.) proposed a different approach, permitting each committee's GOP members to determine their leader and to employ recorded rather than secret voting on assignments. Jacob K. Javits (N.Y.) argued in favor of voting on top-ranking committeemen upon demand of three members. Some members such as James L. Buckley (N.Y.) called in vain for retention of the seniority system.

The Taft-Packwood proposal was a first but narrow victim of Conference voting. Subsequently, the GOP senators adopted a Baker proposal to permit the Republicans on each committee to name their leader, subject to Conference ratifications, and to utilize recorded voting in both committee and Conference voting on these selections. Those members who already held ranking member posts were exempt from consideration, so the new procedure applied to only five positions in the 93rd Congress.

Thus, Senate Republicans adopted a significant procedural reform which opened the door, if only gradually, to challenges against leadership by seniority.

CONCLUSION

Throughout decades of debate, members of Congress commonly have related the seniority system to the effectiveness of their institution. Some legislators have justified its use on the basis of the experienced leaders it has produced for the standing committees. In growing numbers, others have criticized advancement by seniority alone as undemocratic, harmful to Congress' reputation, inconducive to recruitment of persons having exceptional ability or experience, frustrating to new and younger members, and erosive of the power of the legislative branch vis-a-vis the executive.

During a five-year period culminating at the time of this publication, a reform drive succeeded in modifying the seniority system to introduce the possibility of choice in selecting committee leaders. The reform movement has functioned through the medium of the party caucuses in the House and Senate. Its successes have been incremental rather than sweeping and thus far have yielded no revolutionary upheavals in the congressional power structure. The reforms made no change in the custom of automatically ranking all other members of committees by seniority. Further change is likely to be similarly gradual.

The establishment of party rules providing an element of democracy in the designation of committee chairmen and ranking minority members is a vital achievement. If seniority continues to dominate leadership selection, at least it will be by consent of the party caucuses.

No longer will chairmen rule without fear of retaliation by rank-and-file members. A new responsiveness to colleagues' concerns should follow these reforms. Fragmentation in policy-making and obstruction of the majority will decrease as a result of requiring approval of committee leaders at the opening of each Congress. Congress should become better equipped to cope with complex issues, and a greater public confidence in the national legislature may emerge.

1. James K. Pollock, Jr., "Seniority Rule in Congress," *North American Review* (December, 1925), p. 235.

2. Joe Martin, *My First Fifty Years in Politics* (New York: McGraw-Hill, 1960), p. 47.

3. Neil MacNeil, *Forge of Democracy: The House of Representatives* (New York: David McKay and Co., 1963), pp. 126-127.

4. *Ibid.*, p. 124.

5. *Ibid.*, p. 126.

6. Randall B. Ripley, *Power in the Senate* (New York: St. Martin's Press, 1969), pp. 42-49.

7. Pollock, *op. cit.*, p. 237.

8. Joseph S. Clark, *Congress: The Sapless Branch*, Rev. ed. (New York: Harper & Row, 1965), p. 178.

9. Richard Bolling, *House Out of Order* (New York: E.P. Dutton & Co., 1966), p. 224.

10. William S. White, *Citadel: The Story of the U.S. Senate* (New York: Harper & Brothers, 1956), p. 180.

11. Editorial in the *Washington Post*, "Sweep out the Seniority System," January 19, 1971.

12. Pollock, *op. cit.*, p. 235.

13. Alfred de Grazia, "Toward a New Model of Congress," in de Grazia, *et. al.*, *Congress: The First Branch of Government* (Washington, D.C.: The American Enterprise Institute for Public Policy Research, 1966), p. 20.

14. This and subsequent 1971 quotations are from House debate on the election of members to standing committees, as reported in *Congressional Record* (February 4, 1971), pp. H428-434.

15. Riegle shifted his affiliation to the Democratic Party in February, 1973.

16. *Washington Post* (December 2, 1972), p. 2.

VIII The Politics of Hunger: Forming a Senate Select Committee

BERTRAM G. WATERS III

The focus of a select committee, in either the House or the Senate, is on a single great issue. This chapter examines the formation of the Senate Select Committee on Nutrition and Human Needs, led by George McGovern. It illustrates the purpose and prominence of select committees, the personal opportunity which leadership of committees extends to lawmakers, and especially the intensity of internal congressional conflict which often underlies their creation and funding.

The author is Executive Director of the Associated Foundation of Greater Boston, Inc., a private, non-profit organization promoting cooperation among charitable foundations and corporations. A graduate of Harvard University in English literature, he worked five years as an education and urban affairs reporter for the Boston Globe. In 1968-1969 he was a Congressional Fellow of the American Political Science Association, serving first with the Senate Select Committee on Nutrition and Human Needs and thereafter on the staff of Congressman Allard K. Lowenstein (D., N.Y.).

TO BE A CONGRESSMAN is to have an opportunity to participate in the resolution of great issues. Success requires attention to matters of both substance and strategy, including selection of the most advantageous arena in which to pursue objectives. Occasionally the traditional focus, leadership, or membership of a standing committee is not conducive to resolving a particular issue. Congressmen may respond to such a situation by seeking to form a select committee.

Select committees can be spectacularly dramatic and command national attention. Examples are the Truman Committee, which investigated waste and inefficiency during World War II, and the 1950-1951 Kefauver Special Committee to Investigate Organized Crime in Interstate Commerce. Such committees do not report legislation, but conduct hearings and submit findings and recommendations to the House or Senate. Select committees are few, normally only three or four per Congress.[1] Their life-span is often two or more Congresses, but as in the case of the House Internal Security Committee, they ultimately may be incorporated in the rules as standing committees. For some young legislators they are especially attractive as means to circumvent the effects of seniority and as opportunities to assume leadership. They can be springboards to candidacy for higher office.

This chapter will focus on the factors leading to the creation of such a committee, on the processes of forming the committee and assembling its staff, and on a practical aspect rarely mentioned in the scholarly literature: the process of gaining an appropriation permitting the committee to perform its function.

BEGINNINGS OF SENATE CONCERN

It was in the mid-1960's that hunger in America began to attract widespread public attention. In his landmark exposé, published several years before the Senate Select Committee on Nutrition and Human Needs began its work, Michael Harrington wrote: "There are enough poor people in the United States to constitute a subculture of misery, but not enough to challenge the conscience and the imagination of the nation."[2]

Yet, food programs were not new in the United States. The Department of Agriculture had operated a variety of school lunch programs since 1936. Beginning in 1961 it administered a program whereby poor persons could purchase food stamps which were redeemable in participating grocery stores for foods of greater value than the stamps cost them. Under the 1949 Agricultural Act, the department made available to some local governments surplus foods from Federal stockpiles which could be donated to the poor. Food assistance programs of all kinds were costing the taxpayers more than $900 million a year by 1968.

Despite these activities, Agriculture Department records showed in 1967 that more than seven hundred of the nation's 3,100 counties had no food program whatsoever, and that no county permitted both food stamps and free surpluses to be made available. While debate raged over the accuracy of estimates, one authority asserted that only 6 million of the nation's 27 million poor received Federal food benefits.[3]

Certain inadequacies stemmed from the fact that states rather than the Federal government were responsible for food programs and administered them in markedly different ways. For example, in Connecticut, a family of four could earn up to $345 per month and still be eligible for food stamps; in Arkansas, the income ceiling for such a family's eligibility was only $190. The 470,000 persons enrolled in Mississippi food programs constituted nearly 10 percent of the national total.

Many observers believed that the fundamental weakness in the Federal food programs lay in the traditional motivation of the Agriculture Department and congressional agriculture committees. All of the programs which these authorities had devised shared the basic purpose of making use of farm surpluses and thereby protecting the marketplace interests of farmers.

The farm lobby, representing all of the nation's three million farmers and many other persons in rural America, often in alliance with other major pressure groups, was one of the most potent forces on Capitol Hill. In contrast, as Michael Harrington pointed out, the poor and hungry "are without lobbies of their own; they put forward no legislative program. As a group, they are atomized: they have no face, they have no voice."[4]

Against the conservative entrepreneurial philosophy prevalent in agriculture, there developed in the society as a whole a concern for the interest of the consumer. As advocates of the new consumerism, labor, welfare, and other liberal spokesmen argued that the needs of the hungry poor warranted attention quite apart from any consideration of the problem of farm surpluses.

In this spirit, two Senate liberals in April, 1967, launched a national movement to combat hunger in America. Joseph Clark (D., Pa.) and Robert F. Kennedy (D., N.Y.) members of the Subcommittee on Employment, Manpower, and Poverty, aroused the national conscience by visiting the shacks of the Mississippi Delta counties. Upon returning from their extensively publicized trip, Subcommittee Chairman Clark wrote President Lyndon B. Johnson on April 27:

> The Committee heard testimony and observed first-hand, conditions of malnutrition and widespread hunger in the Delta Counties of Mississippi that can only be described as shocking and which we believe constitute an emergency.

Their urgency arose from the estimate that 40,000 to 60,000 citizens of the Delta would be entirely or almost without cash income during the coming summer.

The administration responded by sending staff personnel from the Agriculture Department to corroborate Clark's Mississippi findings. While these officials acknowledged the existence of desperate conditions, the Department took no immediate action.

But the liberal voices were not to be silenced. The plight of the poor—rural, urban, black, Indian, Mexican-American, white—which had been exposed in the struggle for civil rights and in the "War on Poverty" initiated by the Johnson administration in 1965, was indelibly etched upon the nation's conscience. A team of physicians supported by the Field Foundation published *Children in Mississippi* in June, 1967, providing evidence of malnutrition. The following month Dr. William H. Stewart, Surgeon General of the United States, testified before the Clark Subcommittee that no government agency knew the extent of hunger or malnutrition in America and that none had been assigned to this research.

A dramatic television documentary and two major studies which attracted widespread press coverage brought public awareness to new heights in the spring of 1968. The Committee on School Lunch Participation, an ecumenical women's coalition, conducted 1,500 interviews across the nation and concluded that the school lunch program was grossly inadequate. A few days later, The Citizens Board of Inquiry into Hunger and Malnutrition in the United States, which had been formed at the instigation of national labor leader Walter Reuther, severely criticized all of the food programs. The Board reported that more than three hundred of the poorest counties in the country were without any food assistance, and that at least ten million Americans were grievously underfed. In May, the Columbia Broadcasting System produced "Hunger in America," a one-hour television documentary about the food problems of poor whites, blacks, Spanish-Americans, and American Indians. The public raised such an outcry over these continuing revelations of malnutrition that the Agriculture Committees of both Houses of Congress initiated "hunger hearings."

In June the House Committee issued a "Hunger Study" which relied upon the statements of county officials to conclude that there was very little actual hunger in the country but rather malnutrition stemming from public ignorance of the components of a balanced diet. The report left no doubt in the minds of congressional liberals that the traditional agriculture policy-makers had little inclination toward becoming consumer advocates. Agriculture Secretary Orville Freeman's repeated statements in defense of existing programs served to convince the reformers that traditional political institutions were not responsive. An increasing number of senators became convinced that the creation of a select committee to ascertain the dimensions of hunger in America had become imperative.

ESTABLISHING THE SELECT COMMITTEE

Creating a select committee requires the passage of a resolution. On April 26, 1968, Agriculture Committee member George McGovern and a bipartisan group of 38 other liberal and moderate senators introduced Senate Resolution 281, to create a Senate Select Committee on Nutrition and Human Needs. The resolution was referred to the Committee on Labor and Public Welfare, whose Subcommittee on Employment, Manpower and Poverty had initiated the investigation into hunger.

The Subcommittee solicited the views of 43 people who substantiated the existence of a major national problem and the inadequacy of the Federal government's response to it, thereby confirming the need for a national legislative inquiry. Among the spokesmen were medical and nutritional authorities, teachers and school administrators, officials from various government agencies, and 15 of the hungry.

The Committee on Labor and Public Welfare favorably reported the resolution to the Senate, recommending only minor procedural modifications. On July 30, a day which began with testimonials to the late Robert F. Kennedy, Senator Clark obtained Senate consideration of S. Res. 281. In asserting the need for the proposal, Clark said:

> Senate Resolution 281 calls upon the executive branch to immediately meet the food, medical, and related basic needs of the Nation's poor to the fullest extent. Testimony demonstrated that the executive branch, were it to use its existing powers in an imaginative and bold manner, could accomplish much of this goal. Since executive restraints are inferred from past congressional actions and testimony, the House and the Senate need to clarify the determination of this country to eliminate widespread and chronic hunger and malnutrition.[5]

Having presented the case for the establishment of the Select Committee, Clark yielded the floor to Senator Paul Fannin (R., Ariz.), who, emphasizing that no select committee is empowered to propose legislation, sought to amend the resolution to stipulate that the new committee would submit recommendations to the appropriate standing committees for their consideration. The Senate readily concurred with the Fannin amendment, and moments later, by a perfunctory voice vote, passed the resolution to establish the Select Committee.

The new committee had a virtually unlimited mandate, subpoena powers, and the momentum of months of public education to propel it. Its structure had been outlined in the final paragraph of S. Res. 281:

> *Resolved*, That there is established a select committee of the Senate composed of three majority and two minority members of the Committee on Labor and Public Welfare, three majority and two minority members of the Committee on Agriculture and Forestry, and two majority and one minority members of the Senate appointed by the President of the Senate from other committees, to study the food, medical, and other related basic needs among the people of the United States and to report back to the appropriate committees of the Senate and terminate its activities not later than June 30, 1969.

By the method described in the mandate, the following senators, mainly liberals, were appointed. Democrats Ralph Yarborough, Joseph Clark, and Gaylord Nelson, and Republicans Jacob Javits and Winston Prouty were selected from the membership of the Labor and Public Welfare Committee. From Agriculture and Forestry came Democrats Allen Ellender, Herman Talmadge, and George McGovern, plus Republicans Caleb Boggs and Mark Hatfield. Others appointed were Democrats Philip Hart and Walter Mondale, and Republican Charles Percy.

To be their chairman, the committee members elected the resolution's author, George McGovern. He was a man ideally suited to the task of leading an examination of the hunger issue.

A professor of history by training, he began his public career in 1957 by service in the House of Representatives. In 1961, President Kennedy chose him to head the first Food for Peace Program. Having gained stature in this administrative role, he returned to South Dakota in the fall of 1962 and successfully campaigned for the Senate. His ability to attract attention to the work of the Select Committee was to be greatly enhanced by his week-long foray into 1968 presidential politics following the assassination of Senator Robert F. Kennedy. The public seemed to regard his candidacy more as a tribute to a martyred colleague than as fulfillment of personal ambition. His gentle nature reinforced his effectiveness as a moralizing leader of a national crusade against hunger.

In recommending the establishment of the Select Committee, the Labor and Public Welfare Committee had proposed that the new committee, after organizing itself and electing a chairman, determine its staff and budget needs and make appropriate requests to the Senate. McGovern chose as chief counsel William P. Smith, who had served in a similar capacity with Clark's Subcommittee on Employment, Manpower and Poverty. He had taken the Delta trip 20 months earlier with Clark and Robert Kennedy, and had become impressed with the need for further inquiry into the conditions of hunger.

On behalf of the Select Committee, McGovern submitted budgetary requests for a total of $115,000 to cover activities during the final four months of the 90th Congress. The Senate Committee on Rules and Administration, recognizing the limited time remaining in the session, granted less than a fourth of this amount, $25,000.

Though he then had a fledgling staff and budget, McGovern was unable to undertake committee action because the nation and its politicians were in the midst of the presidential and congressional campaigns. The ensuing election not only turned his party out of the White House but resulted in the defeat of one of the most prominent and potentially active members of the Select Committee, Joseph Clark.

In the wake of the disruptions, Chief Counsel William P. Smith convinced McGovern that he should begin immediately to rebuild the hunger constituency by holding hearings. In mid-December, the Committee heard testimony by the renowned anthropologist, Margaret Mead. Offering one of her typical virtuoso performances, Miss Mead took Senator McGovern and a few spectators on a rambling trip through the memories of the Great Depression, indicting President Franklin Roosevelt and others whom she felt might have solved the hunger problem. She substantiated her charges with a plethora of scientific data, and McGovern, personally relieved and revitalized, had ample grounds for believing that the moral issue was revived. The Washington press corps, tired of discussing the election, dramatized the session, thus reawakening public interest in the hunger issue.

When the 91st Congress convened in January, there occurred the usual jockeying for committee assignments which follows each congressional election, with the result that the Nutrition Committee had to be reconstituted. The Select Committee lost Nelson, Boggs, Prouty, and Hatfield, who pursued other assignments more promising to them. The replacements were Democrats Edward Kennedy and Claiborne Pell, and Republicans Peter Dominick, Marlow Cook, and Robert Dole. With his new members, McGovern then faced a crucial hurdle: securing sufficient funds for the Select Committee to undertake its objectives on a broad scale.

WINNING COMMITTEE APPROPRIATIONS

One of the chief purposes of a select committee is to establish sufficient congressional and public recognition of a problem to stimulate governmental response. Whereas a traditional committee such as Agriculture has a durable relationship to a segment of the public, a new select committee must have funding adequate to attract a large audience and shape public opinion.

Control of committee budgets rests with the Committee on Rules and Administration, then chaired by Senator B. Everett

Jordan (D., N.C.), a southern conservative. It seemed unlikely, from his political philosophy and his Senate record, that he would be a strong advocate of extensive activities by the McGovern Committee. While Margaret Mead and a series of prominent physicians had intrigued the press and made brief newspaper headlines, they were unlikely to sway Jordan.

Recognizing the need for agreement among the members of his committee, McGovern convened a closed-door meeting to prepare a finance request for submission to the Jordan Committee. Eight of the thirteen members attended, four from each party, with the remainder sending proxy votes.

McGovern and his chief counsel came prepared to defend a figure of $250,000 to cover a one-year period beginning January 31, 1969. Though they did not attempt to itemize expected expenses, they indicated their intention to visit several cities and call numerous witnesses to the Capitol in the early months. McGovern also included approximately $90,000 for consultants, an amount irritating to Allen Ellender (D., La.) who, as Chairman of the Senate Agriculture Committee and long-time spokesman for traditional agriculture interests, questioned the necessity of this allocation. Ellender suggested that expert witnesses were available for the price of an airplane ticket. McGovern felt that to maintain continuity while tapping experts, the committee would need consultants as well as the testimony of witnesses.

After failing to arouse opposition to consultant fees, Ellender focused his attack in the name of economy upon the proposed salary for Smith. Brushing aside Smith's training and nine years of experience, the Louisianan asserted that the annual salary of $26,000 was too high. McGovern defended the figure, which was among the highest salaries paid to staff personnel on Capitol Hill. Ellender countered with the observation that Senator Jacob Javits, the ranking Republican, had managed to find a minority staff assistant for $9,000 less. Javits explained that his man had had no experience on Capitol Hill, and added that Smith's salary should not be considered excessive as it corresponded to salaries paid to top Senate staff.

Unable to arouse support for his economy moves, Ellender relented. Senators Percy and Javits then quickly proposed that the life of the committee be cut back by one month, to end in December, 1969, in order to demonstrate that constraints could be imposed upon the politically ambitious chairman. They succeeded because McGovern had no time to organize resistance. In order to make clear that the committee's function would then be terminated, Ellender stipulated that an interim report would be issued in June and a final report at the year's end.

The $250,000 proposal passed, 11-2, with Ellender voting against it and adding the Talmadge proxy. McGovern recognized that he might ultimately need to fight on the Senate floor for his full budget request, given the likelihood that the southern, farmer-oriented Rules Committee members would attempt to cut it. To emphasize the support for Senate Resolution 68 to extend his committee's duration with a $250,000 appropriation, he sought co-sponsorship by the bipartisan group of ten who had voted with him in committee. McGovern and Javits, to strengthen the case, appeared jointly before the Rules Committee to urge full funding.

Within the Rules Committee, conservative members moved to cut the budget request, as expected, with the result that the committee recommended a reduction to $150,000. It was reported later that Senator Strom Thurmond (R., S.C.) had argued in executive session for a total of $25,000, an amount which would have undermined the committee's purpose. In recalling the Rules Committee deliberations, Jordan stated upon the Senate floor:

> As chairman, and having only one vote, I recommended the $150,000 figure subsequently adopted after several members had proposed smaller amounts. I felt that a higher amount would not be accepted by the Rules Committee in the absence of firm evidence that plans were far enough along to

insure need for the full requested figure during the budget period. If the study progresses to the point that the necessity for more money can be shown, I will support such a supplementary request.[6]

In concurring, Majority Leader Mansfield added:

As far as the distinguished senator from North Carolina [Mr. Jordan] is concerned, I know what he did to raise the amount in committee, and I wish to say that he is just as humanitarian as they come.

In McGovern's opinion, $150,000 was a respectable amount, but nonetheless inadequate to permit full exploration of the hunger issue. He huddled with his counsel and others, debated the merits of a public stand for full $250,000 funding, and decided the tide was with them. Rising public concern could make opposition politically difficult. McGovern, in order to test his colleagues' resolve, asked Mansfield to schedule a floor debate. Such a step was unusual, as Rules has an almost sacred status with regard to control over committee budgets.

Having little to lose in going to the floor, McGovern nevertheless was concerned that he have the right kind of support to assure his success. An important ingredient would be the favorable alignment of the new Nixon administration. Nixon had chosen Clifford Hardin, President of the University of Nebraska, to be his first Secretary of Agriculture. He, like the new Secretary of Health, Education and Welfare, Robert Finch, had not yet developed a policy position on hunger. To force such a response, McGovern invited them to testify before his committee on February 17, the day before he was to carry his budget fight to the floor.

Additionally, it was important to McGovern that he gain southern Democratic support. Since June, 1968, he had been hearing of a courageous physician named Donald Gatch, who worked alone with the "untouchable" black poor of rural Beaufort, South Carolina. Gatch had been lionized in *Esquire* magazine that month, and had been something of a celebrity ever since.

Gatch had also been on the mind of Ernest Hollings, the former South Carolina governor and now freshman senator. After his election, Hollings had taken it upon himself to visit Gatch and see the conditions in Beaufort first-hand. His revulsion led him to agree to testify before McGovern's committee the morning of the debate, where he said:

South Carolina, like every southern state, is proud. I know we should be ashamed of hunger. I know as a public official I am late to this problem. But in South Carolina we are also practical. . . . As governor I had to put first things first. There were many able-bodied men standing around looking for jobs. So industrial development plus state pride resulted in the public policy of covering up hunger. . . . Let me categorically state that there is hunger in South Carolina. . . . I have seen it with my own eyes. . . . The hunger and the burden of the poor can no longer be ignored.[7]

The cynics quickly noted how easy it was for Hollings to be so courageous at the beginning of a six-year term, the public memory being seldom six months long. But McGovern knew he had a major southern ally for the first time, one willing to say in public, "Hunger is nonpartisan, nonracial. South Carolina's hunger is both white and black." Such testimony could carry the issue to unimagined heights, and food program reform with it.

The actual floor debate over the $100,000 was largely symbolic. Speaking quietly but passionately to a Senate chamber nearly two-thirds empty, McGovern was tested early by Nebraska's Senator Carl Curtis, who objected to the $90,000 budget for consultants as extravagant and irrelevant. McGovern replied to Curtis:

I have no way of knowing whether we could do it in one year either. I think that we can. Granted, one year is a short time in which to deal with a problem as far-reaching as this one. So let us not stretch out the time needlessly by crippling this committee with a $100,000 cut, one which would be penny-wise and pound foolish.

I must say to the Senator that if we cut this $100,000 we will probably not find a reliable answer to the problems of

163

hunger. We will be asking the hungry to wait a little longer.

It is a matter of conscience; it is a question of whether the Senate is going to come to grips with this problem now and face up to the needs of the hungry or whether we are going to falter along without the kind of compelling information the Senator asserts he needs in order to make an intelligent judgment.

Sensing that he was losing his audience after some 15 minutes' debate, Curtis asserted, "As far as the Senator from Nebraska is concerned, any starvation is unacceptable, I want to put an end to it." He then noted that he had asked local officials in Nebraska whether any children were starving and had always received a negative answer. McGovern waxed sarcastic:

I respectfully suggest to the Senator that he may have asked the wrong question. The question that might have been more relevant would have been, how many people in Nebraska and elsewhere are suffering from malnutrition of a serious nature? How many infants, before they are born, have suffered irreparable brain damage, bordering on mental retardation?[8]

Once Curtis capitulated, the snowball began to roll. George Murphy of California, one of the three on the original April, 1967 tour of Mississippi, spoke forcefully for restoration of the amount cut. He was followed by Senator Javits, ranking Republican on the Select Committee, then by Abraham Ribicoff, a former Secretary of HEW. Following quickly were Edward Brooke of Massachusetts, Gaylord Nelson of Wisconsin, Illinois' Charles Percy (who sparred briefly with Senator Curtis by saying that he was tempted to request even more) and others. The juggernaut seemed unopposed until Senator Ellender, resolute to the end, proposed the restoration of $15,000 in unrestricted funds and the deletion of $85,000 for consultants.

The only answer needed came from Senator Edward Kennedy, also a member of the Select Committee, in a long and eloquent defense of the proposed budget and the job to be done with it. Kennedy concluded on a note that was becoming more and more the popular view:

> We must demonstrate that we are concerned about the problems of malnutrition and starvation, and that we are dedicating ourselves to doing something about them. We must demonstrate also that where local government, state government and Federal government are failing to respond, these facts will be rooted out as well.

Once Ellender's amendment was rejected, it become obvious that McGovern's forces would prevail. Senator Mansfield thereupon offered McGovern a quick tactical opportunity for the victory that was surely his. "Would it be possible," he asked, "to ask unanimous consent to withdraw the yeas and nays on the committee amendment so that we may have a final vote on this matter immediately?"

McGovern's instinct must have been to press for a roll call that would place every name in one column or the other for all to see. While it was likely that his forces would have defeated the Rules Committee amendment on a roll call, he readily accepted the majority leader's suggestion. Thus there were two voice votes. First, the Senate rejected the amendment. Thereafter it passed Resolution 68 to enable the Select Committee on Nutrition and Human Needs to begin its activities with a $250,000 budget.

CONCLUSION

The committee system of Congress is dominated by standing committees having rigid structures and jurisdictions as well as durable personal and political relationships. A variety of circumstances, however, can stimulate political forces to establish select committees for special needs. The needs may be distinct from the traditional concerns of the standing committees, whose leaders may have failed to grasp the full significance of social changes triggering new political demands. In other cases, senior members of standing committees deliberately may ignore certain political interests, believing them inconsistent with their own political philosophies. Under such circumstances, an ambitious and politically sensitive legislator may be able to marshal sufficient support from colleagues sharing his concern to win authorization of a select committee.

To do so, he must overcome inherent strengths of existing legislative institutions. An individual embarking on this course is likely to encounter significant opposition from committee chairmen and other senior colleagues protecting their hegemony. Certainly efforts to establish a select committee could not succeed without at least tacit support from the majority party leaders.

The role of a select committee within congressional processes will depend upon two fundamental factors: what its leaders choose to make of it, and what financial support the House or Senate provides it. The first of these is solely a matter of personal creativity and ambition, which, given the attentiveness of today's mass media, may be readily apparent to the American public. The second, however, is far more complex, bringing into play at yearly intervals all of the forces of conflict which may have characterized the committee's establishment. It is the weight of the funding process that this chapter seeks particularly to illuminate. While less obvious to most people, a winning strategy in the institutional politics of securing funding is indispensable for select committee effectiveness.

1. Important 92nd Congress select committees included those in the House on Crime, Small Business, and Lobbying; those in the Senate were Nutrition and Human Needs, Equal Educational Opportunity, Standards of Conduct, Small Business, and Aging.

2. Michael Harrington, *The Other America: Poverty in the United States* (Baltimore: Penguin Books, 1963), p. 20.

3. Robert Choate, "The Hungry Have Farm Problem," *Washington Post*, October 13, 1968.

4. Harrington, *op. cit.*, p. 14.

5. *Congressional Record*, 90th Congress, 2nd Session, July 30, 1968, p. 24161.

6. This and subsequent quotations from the floor debate are from the *Congressional Record*, 91st Congress, 1st Session, February 18, 1969, pp. 1765-1771.

166

7. U.S. Congress, Senate, Select Committee on Nutrition and Human Needs, Hearing, 91st Congress, 1st Session, Washington, D.C., February 18, 1969, pp. 1165-1166.

8. During the earliest hunger hearings it became apparent that definitions were going to be important for political reasons. Eminent physicians in time supplied many acceptable definitions. McGovern himself liked to make this distinction: "Hunger is a sensation. Malnutrition is a condition."

167

IX | Congress Gets New Ideas from Outside Experts

ERNEST A. CHAPLES, JR.

It has become commonplace to expect that important legislation in the American political system will originate with the executive branch, in part because its staffing is far superior to that of the Congress. Yet many congressmen wish to be creative legislators. This chapter focuses on one congressman's effective use of outside expertise to initiate major legislation.

The author is Assistant Professor of Political Science at the University of Maryland, and wishes to thank the University's General Research Board for financially assisting a project on manpower policy from which this chapter is derived. He is co-author of The Quality of Life in America (1970) and editor of Resolving Political Conflict (1971). During the academic year 1966-1967, he was a Congressional Fellow of the American Political Science Association, serving in the offices of Congressman James H. Scheuer (D., N.Y.) and Senator Joseph D. Tydings (D., Md.).

IT IS A PERVASIVE and substantial criticism of Congress that much of its function of originating legislation has been assumed by the executive. In his annual State of the Union and budget messages and in a series of special messages, the modern President sends to Capitol Hill a set of programs which Congress considers its major agenda for the year. In consequence, the typical congressman spends much of his time deliberating upon legislative programs developed outside of Congress. Given the many demands upon his time and the paucity of his staff and informational resources in comparison to those of the executive, it is difficult for the congressman to devote either the concentration or the resources needed for meaningful, creative legislative work. As a result, Congress responds rather than initiates.

This increasing trend has caused frustration among the many legislators who originally conceived of their very candidacies in terms of changing society. Proposals for the restoration of congressional initiative commonly have focused upon improving congressional staffing and research facilities. A cooperative strategy is to pool resources by creating informal groups such as the Democratic Study Group (DSG) to develop policy research. A strategy which any individual congressman may pursue is to mobilize outside expertise. The experiences of Representative James H. Scheuer exemplify how the use of outside expertise can result in restoring congressional initiative.

REFOCUSING FEDERAL MANPOWER PROGRAMS TOWARD "NEW CAREERS"

Scheuer came to Congress in 1965 believing that America could do much better for its poor citizens. His interest in problems of poverty and education reflected the nature of his district, the South Bronx area of New York City. By almost any economic or social indicator, Scheuer represented one of the poorest congressional districts in the urban North. Virtually every major social problem of the 1960's—including poor education, high crime, deteriorating race relations, and increased pollution—was abundant.

Scheuer decided to seek membership on the House Committee on Education and Labor, and his efforts were successful. While strongly supporting the objectives of the Johnson administration "Great Society" programs, he believed that more sophisticated and practical means of implementation were essential.

At the time Scheuer joined the generally young and progressive Democratic congressmen on the Education and Labor Committee, President Johnson decided to emphasize manpower training programs as a principal vehicle for combating poverty in America. Manpower was a new program area for the national government; before the fledgling Manpower Development and Training Act was passed in 1962, the Federal effort in manpower was practically non-existent. But by 1967, more than 30 different Federal manpower programs including the Job Corps, Neighborhood Youth Corps, and Operation Green Thumb were costing the Federal government more than $3 billion per year. Most of these programs came under the jurisdiction of the House Education and Labor Committee.

In its early years the Federal manpower effort emphasized skills training by attempting to provide trainees with job skills to fill job "slots." The Manpower Development and Training Act (MDTA) sought to assist what manpower experts regard as the structurally unemployed. The program took the unemployed from industries where jobs had been discontinued and gave them new skills in industries having manpower shortages. The MDTA program assumed that a trainee had a history of work and a belief in the joys of working for one's living.

By the mid-1960's, manpower programs began to respond to a very different category of unemployed persons, the so-called "hardcore unemployed." But despite the inappropriateness of the MDTA approach, it became incorporated in most of the manpower programs of the War on Poverty.

171

While Labor Department experts and traditional manpower economists stressed skills programs and expanded employment opportunity, a renegade movement was developing among other manpower professionals. It was to be the basis for Scheuer's impact. The renegades stressed the need for a much more comprehensive look at manpower training, having concluded that established programs were not making any real impact on most of America's poor. Working from such diverse professions as psychology, education, social work, economics, and penal work, the innovators began to organize demonstration projects and to present their ideas in professional journals. An important breakthrough was the publication of *New Careers for the Poor*,[1] the first major critique of administration poverty programs and full-scale discussion of alternative approaches. Its authors were two of the group's most influential spokesman.

Pearl and Reissman argued that an effective manpower program would de-emphasize job placement and start preparing the unemployed for careers. If poor people were going to develop a more positive attitude toward work, they had to be able to perceive some future opportunities in their employment. Pearl and Reissman believed that the Federal government was shoving the poor into dead-end jobs at the bottom of the economic ladder. They sought to substitute programs which would treat the total needs of the person rather than concentrate merely on job skills for the normal working day.

The New Careers concept emphasized an individual's family needs, his health problems, his basic educational deficiencies, and the establishment of credentials for upward mobility. The program would require that personal counseling, basic educational programs, and supportive services be available for the trainees. Pearl and Reissman believed that the manpower needs of American society in education, health, law enforcement, and other public services were so great that the current and projected numbers of professionals being trained to work in these fields could not meet the demand. They foresaw an

172

opportunity to meet this demand by developing and employing underprivileged persons as paraprofessional "new careerists."

Congressman Scheuer came into contact with both the New Careers philosophy and some of its principal spokesmen during his first year in Congress. He became convinced of the logic underlying the arguments of the manpower renegades, and he read as much material on their ideas and demonstration projects as he could. Scheuer became chairman of a working group of liberal freshmen belonging to the DSG. His group was to review manpower programs and formulate a proposal to meet the needs of America's poor more effectively.

Realizing that his own staff resources were too small to develop a major new proposal, Scheuer decided to tap the willing minds and vast energies of the New Careers advocates. Without some outside assistance, Scheuer would not have been able to construct a legislative program because his project staff consisted solely of a part-time DSG employee, his own already overburdened administrative assistant and, later in the process, a legislative assistant.

Scheuer's initial goal was to assemble the New Careers advocates and to form a working body. While many of the leading advocates of manpower reform were acquainted with one another, these individuals had never been organized. Scheuer gathered a small number of the most active for a series of meetings in his home, his office, and at luncheons in the House of Representatives Dining Room. He encouraged them to organize a committee, to accept group responsibilities, and to expand their numbers by bringing new members—but only working members—into the Scheuer Advisory Council. Scheuer himself acted as legislative critic, provided the physical setting for meetings, conveyed the necessary sense of importance to the group's work, and encouraged the individuals to volunteer for more work.

Within a few months the Scheuer Advisory Council on Manpower had produced a full-scale legislative program complete with a bill, voluminous supporting evidence for the program, and material for a number of speeches by Scheuer. Their first payoff came when Congress adopted a "New Careers" amendment in its revision of the Economic Opportunity Act in 1966 [Title II, Section 205(e)], known as the Scheuer Amendment.

The odds against a first-term congressman producing a major new program bearing his name are very great indeed. The success stemmed only partially from Scheuer's diligence and astute mobilization of talent. It probably would not have been possible had not the Education and Labor Committee been extraordinarily receptive to the policy initiatives of freshmen generally. Attention to seniority and apprenticeship are usually low in this committee.[2]

Nonetheless, it was crucial that he enlist expertise to help develop his ideas, write his speeches and reports, and formulate program strategies. The New Careers manpower experts—Arthur Pearl, Frank Reissman, Russell Nixon, Douglas Grant, Arnold Trebach, Jay Fishman, and others—had the professional experience to provide the guidance needed to win support for the program.

What the New Careers advocates lacked, however, was access to the governmental decision-making process. The congressman, who recognized the promise of the New Careers concept, transformed it into legislative reality. Once the breakthrough was made, the program quickly became one of the most important components of the Federal manpower effort and one of the government's primary weapons in the war against poverty.

CRIME IN THE STREETS: A LIBERAL'S DILEMMA

Scheuer utilized outside expertise not only to revitalize manpower training but also to develop a new approach toward controlling crime. For many liberal members of Congress, increasing street crime has proven to be a vexing issue. Strengthening the police and cracking down on criminals have become popular political stances of the right wing in American

174

politics. Liberals, in contrast, have generally believed that crime reduction requires emphasis upon such causes as poor education, poverty, and hatred between the races.

Many liberals have found, however, that crime—especially street crime—is a very salient concern of their constituents. Congressman Scheuer found this to be especially true in his poverty-ridden, densely populated, multi-racial constituency. His regular contacts with constituents produced substantial evidence of the inner-city dweller's fears. Churches and schools were finding it necessary to cancel their evening programs because people would not go out after dark. The New York newspapers daily reported chilling stories of murder, rape, assault, and other vicious crimes in Scheuer's district.

The real saliency of the crime issue for Scheuer's constituents was documented beyond any doubt during his first year in office. Like most congressmen, Scheuer regularly sought the opinions of his constituents in an annual mailed questionnaire. Although the questionnaire by no means reached all the voters and the response rate was generally low and the replies undoubtedly biased, the poll did provide a crude indicator of the attentive public's perspectives on some of the major issues of the moment. The 1965 poll asked what respondents considered to be the nation's most important problem. The possible answers provided in the questionnaire included the Vietnam War, pollution, education, and poverty. Crime was *not* one of the choices provided. Nevertheless, more of the respondents wrote "crime" in the "other" slot than checked all the printed alternative choices combined. A similar constituency poll in 1966, which included a reference to crime in the streets as one of its printed choices, demonstrated an even more overwhelming concern for this issue.

The results of the 1965 poll and other experiences in his district made it clear to Scheuer that he had to deal with crime as a public policy question. Because he had won his party's primary as a reform-oriented challenger to an incumbent congressman by only a few hundred votes in 1964 and seemed likely to face another challenge by the regular Democratic organization in 1966, the political importance of a response to the crime issue seemed obvious. Nevertheless, Scheuer, like most liberals, felt extremely uneasy with the apparent options. Some public officials called for reducing civil liberties by repealing the *Escobedo v. Illinois* and *Miranda v. Arizona* Supreme Court decisions which guaranteed the rights of the accused. Others championed "support your local police" slogans and increased penalties for street crime. But none of these things appealed to Scheuer as being either practical or politically promising solutions to the problem of street crime.

The basic theme in Scheuer's eventual formulation was originally suggested by Richard Brown, the congressman's administrative assistant and most important political advisor. Brown believed that a Federal effort should stress innovation in police methods and new approaches to improving the criminal justice system. Law enforcement and criminal justice have always been primarily a local responsibility in the United States. Brown's idea was to initiate a Federal program in research and to create an institution for the dissemination of new ideas and approaches to law enforcement agencies. An agency similar in form to the National Institutes of Health would administer the new program. This idea produced the nucleus for what eventually evolved into the National Institute for Criminal Justice.

Scheuer and Brown tried out the idea on a number of interested professionals. Seeking information and suggestions, they consulted leading law enforcement officials, lawyers, judges, and academics in every discipline conceivably related to law enforcement and criminal justice. This circle of advisors grew as Scheuer's initial contacts suggested other people with related interests who might be willing to help. Scheuer lunched two or three times weekly with people who could provide him with further information and new ideas directed toward solving crime problems. Within a few months the staff compiled a mailing list of over five hundred interested people involved with

176

criminal justice. Soon thereafter Scheuer and his staff shaped their proposal into a bill which the congressmen introduced as a "trial balloon."

Response to the proposed institute was extensive, including suggested modifications in its objectives and structure. By early 1967, crime had become one of Scheuer's principal legislative concerns. The author joined the staff to work with Brown and Scheuer's outside advisors in coordinating the congressman's efforts. The staff formulated a new bill reflecting suggestions by many Scheuer acquaintances. It also coordinated the outside experts, molding them into a task force. The participants became key workers in Scheuer's campaign to attract public interest in the institute and to mobilize support for his proposal. They drafted his speeches, assisted in preparing testimony, and helped organize publicity efforts. Scheuer's staff established liaison with the President's Commission on Law Enforcement and Administration of Justice. After tedious and difficult negotiations, the project team made arrangements to have the bill co-sponsored in the Senate by Senator Edward M. Kennedy of Massachusetts, a member of the Judiciary Committee.

Due to personal initiative and the hard work of his small staff, Scheuer, a second-term congressman who was not even on the Judiciary Committee, began to be recognized as a leader in crime legislation. He was invited to give a major address at the National Crime Institute at the Illinois Institute of Technology. Invitations for similar appearances flowed into his office. National television networks asked him to discuss the problem of increased crime, and Washington's columnists and commentators turned to Scheuer for ideas on crime prevention.

It became apparent that the Johnson administration, primarily because of FBI Director Hoover's opposition, was not going to support the institute proposal. The administration's alternative, embodied in the proposed Safe Streets Act, was to provide more funds for grant-in-aid programs for state and local governments to support new research and innovation in law enforcement. As neither Scheuer nor Kennedy was considered to be friendly to the administration, their sponsorship of the institute undoubtedly lessened its attractiveness to the administration.

To counter the opposition of the administration and the House establishment, Scheuer decided to promote his ideas by a unique and dramatic exhibit in the Rayburn House Office Building. The exhibit demonstrated the principal strength of the proposal: in Scheuer's words, that "we can adapt the technology of the space age to the law enforcement process." It provided ample indication that most police methods were badly outdated and that the equipment of law enforcement officials seldom met their real needs.

To stage such a public demonstration of the potential of new approaches to police work, Scheuer needed the cooperation of the most innovative people in law enforcement software and hardware. New ideas and potential future developments included guns that would stun but not kill, infra-red detection devices, new alarm and lock systems, new olifactronic equipment, and many other exotic devices previously restricted to comic strips and science fiction novels. Far more exhibitors offered to display their wares than could be accommodated in the two lounges made available to Scheuer by the Speaker. For two days the scene resembled more a carnival than the stately milieu one would associate with a legislature.

Scheuer regarded the crime exhibit as a great success. Congressmen flocked to see the show, and the exhibit received widespread and generally favorable national television and newspaper coverage, thus enhancing Scheuer's reputation as a bright, young innovator trying to overcome a tough problem. As anticipated, however, the House leadership, the chairman of the House Judiciary Committee, and the Department of Justice were not enthusiastic about the exhibit. In general, they seemed to feel that Scheuer was playing to the press, and the carnival atmosphere did not appeal to their sense of propriety. When the time came for action, the Judiciary Committee approved the administration alternative.

In the meantime, however, Scheuer had gained co-sponsors from both parties for the institute proposal. One of his most important allies was Congressman Robert McClory of Illinois, a Republican member of the Judiciary Committee. After another series of negotiations which required modifying functions of the institute and decentralizing some of its operations, McClory made Scheuer's institute a part of the minority committee report. The coalition of McClory's Republican allies and Scheuer's liberal Democrats was successful during subsequent House debate. When McClory with Scheuer's support offered the institute as a substitute for Title III of the administration's bill, the institute amendment carried by five votes. Surprisingly, the House leadership did not pose the challenge of a roll call vote. With Edward Kennedy on its Judiciary Committee, the Senate passed the institute bill easily. The measure became law when President Johnson signed the Safe Streets Act in 1968.[3]

THE FOLLOW-THROUGH: KEEPING THE OUTSIDE EXPERTISE INVOLVED

Analysis of post-enactment developments in these two fields suggests the continuing importance of outside experts. Passage of the New Careers amendment led to Scheuer's further utilization of outside expertise in the field of manpower policy. His growing reputation as the legislative spokesman for New Careers encouraged his task force to develop a strategy for extending this approach to new areas of public service employment.

The task force convened frequently during the 89th Congress, and Scheuer met with individual members from the group nearly once a week. Professor Russell Nixon of New York University's Center for the Study of Unemployed Youth became its chairman. The two maintained regular contact in both New York City and Washington.

This continuation of efforts led to further legislative successes for the New Careers advocates. Largely through the congressman's initiative and the work of his task force, paraprofessional training was expanded in 1967 through amendments to the Higher Education Act, the Elementary and Secondary Education Act, and the Vocational Education Act. Still other New Careers provisions were incorporated into the Safe Streets and Crime Control Act, the Allied Health Professions Personnel Act, and the Model Cities Act.

Scheuer's liaison with his task force members and other interested professionals provided him with accurate and up-to-date assessments of what was happening in the New Careers projects being established. As a non-administration program, New Careers encountered numerous difficulties in its early implementation. First, the Office of Economic Opportunity decided to divest itself of responsibility for the program and to delegate New Careers to the Labor Department. Next, the Labor Department staff found it equally difficult to implement the new approach and even more difficult to provide direction to the more than forty projects funded under the original act.

What Scheuer's task force gave him was an independent line of communications to the many field projects.[4] These channels enabled Scheuer to become aware of the program's initial difficulties, since little useful information was forthcoming through regular Labor Department channels. Thus it was his own sources that allowed him to put pressure on the Labor Department to overcome these difficulties. Assisted by Scheuer's personal legislative oversight, New Careers continued to grow and prosper.

Several factors stemming from the congressman's interest and position contributed to the vitality of the New Careers program. After New Careers was enacted, he supplied key personnel who were instrumental in getting the program underway. Subsequently the Labor Department, presumably desirous of maintaining Scheuer's support within the Education and Labor Committee, supported full funding of the program and worked to get it into operation. The optimism associated with New Careers made it natural for Scheuer to maintain close working relationships with his outside advisers in this field.

By way of contrast, parallel facilitative factors were missing from Scheuer's campaign to make the National Institute for Criminal Justice fully effective. The Justice Department never became very interested in the program, and J. Edgar Hoover's opposition to the institute, which he seemed to view as a potential competitor to the FBI, made it extremely difficult to gain appropriations for it. That Scheuer was not a member of either the Judiciary Committee or the Appropriations Committee meant that he had virtually no legislative leverage with the Justice Department. His unsuccessful New York City mayoral campaign in 1969, followed by redistricting and his hard-fought primary victory over fellow Congressman Jacob Gilbert in 1970, diverted his attention from the institute's initial organization. As a result of all these factors, Scheuer did not utilize his task force on crime for any significant follow-through activities which might otherwise have resulted from his leadership in bringing about the institute legislation.

OUTSIDE EXPERTISE AND LEGISLATIVE INITIATIVE

Many members of Congress and students of the legislative process believe that Congress, in order to realize its constitutionally intended independence from the executive, must develop means to contribute more substantially to its own agenda. For this to occur, critics assert that it must come to grips with the huge information gap between itself and the executive bureaucracy.

Reducing this information gap requires a multifaceted approach. Almost certainly, the Congress would have to improve its staff capabilities and modernize its own information services. Beyond these steps, however, Congress can more adequately utilize currently available information channels outside the bureaucracy. This chapter has indicated how one new member overcame the information gap and found it possible to provide congressionally-initiated alternatives to major administration programs.

Undoubtedly, the Scheuer approach is not applicable to all situations in which legislators require better information to meet their lawmaking responsibilities. The Scheuer experience suggests that the use of outside expertise is most feasible when an existing group of professionals fails to gain a working relationship with executive agency policy-makers. We may also conclude that cooperation with outside experts is most effective when they perceive that their free labor may result in a new program bringing them personal credit. Finally, this pattern has the best chance of success when the congressman involved perceives of his legislative role as somewhat independent of the administration, his party, and the chairman of his committee.

Contacts between most members of Congress and the academic and professional communities are usually minimal at present. Practitioners of the two kinds of occupations tend to be suspicious of each other, resulting in a lack of communication between the politician and the expert. But this congressman's experience suggests that the gap is surmountable and that the payoff can be substantial for both groups. Harnessing available outside expertise can provide a member of Congress with advisers who have professional competence and are unhindered by bureaucratic restraints. Scheuer's approach is not unique, and it is likely to be pursued by more legislators who seek an independent voice for the Congress in solving America's major policy problems. It is a method whereby members individually can shape substantive answers to the challenging question posed repeatedly during the last decade: "Doesn't Congress have ideas of its own?"

1. Arthur Pearl and Frank Reissman, *New Careers for the Poor* (New York: Free Press, 1965).

2. For a detailed discussion of how the committee works see Richard F. Fenno, Jr., "The House of Representatives and Federal Aid to Education," in Robert Peabody and Nelson Polsby, ed., *New Perspectives on The House of*

Representatives (Chicago: Rand McNally, 1969). pp. 283-323, and the author's "The Utility of a Congressional Committee in Program Initiation and Legislative Oversight," *Zeitschrift für Parlamentsfragen*, 3 (December, 1972).

3. The problem of Justice Department opposition and congressional establishment resistance to the institute has never been overcome. Neither the Johnson administration nor the Nixon administration has ever put any real effort into getting the institute into operation. Moreover, Congressman John Rooney, a close friend of the late J. Edgar Hoover and Chairman of the Appropriations Subcommittee which provides funds for the Justice Department, has steadfastly refused to provide even the token funding requested by the administration for the institute.

4. Scheuer's former legislative assistant, Edward Cohen, became a program administrator for New Careers in the Labor Department. Russell Nixon's Center for Unemployed Youth and the University Research Corporation, headed by Jay Fishman and Arnold Trebach, key task force members, provided technical assistance. Economic Systems Corporation, with the author of this chapter serving as chief consultant, conducted the major first-year program evaluation. A few task force members, including Pearl, Reissman and H. Douglas Grant, directed New Careers field projects across the country.

X | Leadership: The Role and Style of Senator Everett Dirksen

JEAN E. TORCOM

Legislative leadership involves overcoming cleavages within one's own party and building winning coalitions across the two parties. Senate Minority Leader Everett Dirksen, Republican leader during both Democratic and Republican Presidencies from 1959 until 1969, sought to maximize his and his party's impact in the legislative process. This chapter focuses on his leadership strategy and offers several conclusions regarding leadership and the requirements for its effective performance.

Jean Torcom Cronin is Assistant Professor of Government at California State University, Sacramento. She is completing a dissertation on Senator Dirksen for The Johns Hopkins University. In preparation, Mrs. Cronin interviewed 27 Republican members of the Senate plus leading Democrats including former President Lyndon B. Johnson. She worked part-time in Senator Dirksen's office, 1962-1965, and on the staff of Congressman F. Bradford Morse (R., Mass.), 1968-1970. She was a Congressional Fellow of the American Political Science Association in 1967-1968, serving in the offices of Senator Thruston Morton (R., Ky.) and Representative Morse. This chapter is adapted from a paper presented at the 1971 Annual Meeting of the American Political Science Association. Special thanks for assistance are due to Senator Dirksen's staff and particularly to Glee D. Gomien, his Executive Secretary; to former President Johnson; especially to Congressman Morse, whose counsel was of incalculable value and under whose flag the author was able to arrange many interviews; and to Professor Robert Peabody for his continuing support and encouragement. Interviews were granted with the understanding that the responses would be treated anonymously.

185

AS ONE OF THE MOST colorful men in the Senate, and the focus of much attention during his long leadership, Everett Dirksen of Illinois contributed to the popular awareness of the minority leader's role. It is a flexible and creative role which a leader may shape in accordance with his own ingenuity. Voting majorities and minorities rarely conform rigidly to party lines, but are normally fluid, varying with the issue. The fluidity is attributable to the decentralization of nomination and election processes and to norms of behavior within the Senate stressing individuality and independent judgment.

Senators often envision their responsibility in terms of their state or the nation first, and not necessarily in terms of their party. While political parties are still the most important organizing and coordinating force in the Congress and have the most potent effect on voting, other pressures, such as committee loyalties, interest group activities, and personal positions on issues are also very significant.

Minority leadership activity can have great impact because majorities result not from party attachment but from legislative processes, including bargaining and compromise with members of each party. Thus the minority party in Congress frequently has the opportunity to become part of the process of building majority coalitions.

The impact of the minority party depends on a number of factors, among them the leadership and organization of each party and the margin of the majority over the minority. It may also be affected by procedures and especially by rules such as the requirement of a two-thirds affirmative vote on constitutional amendments. One factor which can greatly affect the minority leader's role is how his fellow minority party members view their party's function. Interviews during the Nixon Presidency with more than 20 Republican senators indicated that the party role is expected to vary depending upon who is in the White House. For example, one senior senator put it this way:

There are two roles, depending on the White House. If a Republican is in the White House, then it is the job of the minority party to support the administration—to offer constructive criticism of programs maybe, but to support the President.

When a Democrat is in the White House then the minority is the loyal opposition. You try to improve programs, offer alternatives, build a record for the party. Because when the Democrats are in the White House, it's the Senate party (and in the House too, if the Republicans are in the minority there too) that represents the party's viewpoint.

Several senators suggested what might be called the "watch-dog role":

I think the minority party has a job to perform that's very much like the responsibility of an attorney assigned to defend someone. I think it is their job to make the majority prove their case every step of the way. I believe that they shouldn't take anything for granted, that they should challenge everything that's been done. I think that results in much better legislation.

The function of the minority party in the Senate, especially in the Senate, is to be the party of constructive criticism—this is the basis of the two-party system. The party that's in the minority is a sort of watchdog over the activities of the majority—try to keep them in line and offer constructive alternatives.

A difference of view began to emerge between conservative and more liberal Republicans, with the latter taking a less partisan view of their role:

The Republican party in the Senate should project a positive image—I think my differences with the administration lay on this point. Where they've been positive, I support the administration. But where I think what they put forward isn't positive, I can't go along. The important thing is to be constructive. The role of the Republicans is to provide constructive ideas in a way that may agree or disagree, but the important thing is to be constructive.

187

In sum, minority members collectively have no clear definition of minority party role. As one senator said, "The Senate is made up of a hundred individuals and they all seem to go off in their own directions without paying very much attention to any kind of party discipline or to party loyalty."

The lack of overall agreement on minority party role contributes to the flexibility of the party itself and provides considerable latitude for the leadership to work out strategies for legislative participation. If, in contrast, it was widely held that the role was to oppose, and nothing else, that would severely restrict the options available to the leadership. As it is, however, the norms encompass approval of cooperation across party lines.

The minority leader has a great deal to do with how actively and effectively the minority may participate in the business of the Senate, as well as with the character of that participation. The man himself, his own view of his job, and the expectations his party members have of him, among other considerations, are crucial determinants of how he fashions his role.

THE JOB OF THE MINORITY LEADER

By far the most important situational variable defining the job of the minority leader is whether or not his party controls the White House. If it does, as has been the case since 1969, and was for the last six years of the Eisenhower administration, most minority party members expect the party to support the President's program in the Senate. If the opposition controls the White House, the expectation appears to be that the minority party may be flexible, offering support to those programs it agrees with and opposition to those which it cannot accept. Within this framework there is a significant degree of freedom for individual senators.

This functional distinction between support and opposition was recognized by the Republican senators. Mindful of the fact that a Republican occupied the White House, fully half of them, when asked, "What would you say is the job of the minority floor leader?" answered that it was his function to move the President's program in the Senate. As one senator stated:

> Well, the job of the minority floor leader is of course to try to carry the program of the President. He has that obligation and I'd feel he should be the one in the Senate that is most responsible in that regard.

Clearly, the members expect that the leader has a responsibility, when a Republican is in the White House, to try to pilot his program through the Senate. And this, of course, is a formidable task. As one senator put it, "He's in the position of a military commander who is out-gunned and out-numbered."

Still, theoretically, the minority leader accrues advantages when a member of his party is in the White House, generally unavailable when the Democrats are in control. Favors, appointments, an inside track on information of importance to senators, and other such perquisites are sometimes available to senators from the White House through the minority leader. As he is the Senate's representative to the White House, so he also is the President's spokesman to the Senate party, and from this function he gains a measure of influence over his fellow senators. This, however, does not make up for the fact that his is a very difficult role; he has the responsibility for the President's program without even a nominal majority to back him up.

The question of to whom the leader owes his first responsibility has been discussed often. William S. White, writing in the mid-1950's, argued that while there was no general agreement on what a leader should be, there was some agreement on what he should not be. Senators expect, White said, "that he who is a member of the party holding the White House will not so much represent that party as the Senate itself."[1]

Opinions expressed by Republican senators approximately 15 years later suggest that a reassessment may be in order. Particularly among conservative Republican senators, who generally support the Nixon administration and its programs, the expectation prevailed that the leader's first responsibility was to the President and his legislative proposals. Only one senator, a noted liberal freshman, expressed an attitude reminiscent of White's. His response suggested his misgivings about existing relations between Senate Republicans and the Nixon administration:

Well, the minority leader of the Senate holds his commission from his colleagues, not from the President. I think that this is an important and a basic fact sometimes forgotten both by the general public and by the White House staff.

Of course no minority leader's responsibility is defined solely in terms of his relations with the White House. He has an equal if not more important function within his Senate party. His essential role as a broker, both within his Senate party and between the Senate and the White House, is emphasized by some senators:

The job of the minority leader, as I see it, is to try to put together as many votes as possible for those causes the party's going to try to support, whether or not they happen to be on the side of the President or on the side of the minority in Congress.

Well, he's essentially a broker between at times conflicting points of view within the White House and the Senate. He's the focal point of these different points of view. His job is further complicated by the fact that the Republicans are split, for example, on the war issue. So, he's the focal point of this wide divergence of view.

Not all leaders are equally adept at performing this fundamental function. But their effectiveness as Senate leaders depends to a great extent on how well they can act as brokers between competing interests.

Finally, any discussion of the floor leader's job must acknowledge the importance of the attitudes and philosophy of the man who holds the position. Even a cursory examination of various Republican Senate leaders established the fact that it is the man and his view of the job which, more than any other single factor, determines the style and tone of his leadership.

Senator Robert Taft, "Mr. Republican" in the Senate of the late 1940's and early 1950's, shunned the floor leader's post until General Eisenhower's election as President in 1952. Taft assumed the majority leadership in 1953, perhaps as much because he wanted to exert a measure of control over the newly elected President, with whom he had vigorously competed for the nomination, as because he wanted the central leadership position. In fact, Taft had been at the center of his party in the Senate, primarily because of the force of his personality and the views he held, rather than as a result of his formal position as Chairman of the Republican Policy Committee.

In comparing Taft with Lyndon Johnson, who became Democratic leader at the same time Taft was elected Republican leader, White suggested that while Johnson worked incessantly for intraparty accommodation through endless compromise, Taft's style was just the opposite. "Taft . . . had been a great Senate leader," White argued, "precisely because his whole spirit was alien and hostile to party accommodation. Taft, in a small chamber where men are close, had been a great leader because he was, in a way, always pointedly alone."[2]

William Knowland of California, who had been whip under Taft, succeeded him as Republican leader. Except for the "laying on of hands" by Taft, it would seem unlikely, from the comments of most senators who served with him, that Knowland would have been elected leader. His conception of the role was limited, both by outlook and by inclination. Even with a fellow partisan in the White House for the entirety of his tenure, Knowland did not seem to feel any urgent responsibility to the President's programs. He saw himself first and foremost as a senator, responsible to himself and his constituency. This view obviously colored his relations with his fellow senators, and his inclination was clearly not to try to reach an accommodation within the party so that they could stand together. As one senator described his leadership:

Bill Knowland was very aloof, at least from my experience with him. He made up his own mind, he made his own plans, we had no general party meetings in those days and none of us knew when we went to the floor of the Senate what the program was. That was Bill's trouble: he ran a one-man show and every once in a while he used to amaze us by ceremoniously leaving his seat and going to another part of the chamber and then tearing the administration to pieces.

Apparently, neither Knowland nor Taft were unusual Republican leaders in that they shunned the art of compromise. Kenneth Wherry, the Nebraska Republican who served as leader in the 81st Congress, was described by the sympathetic White as "a fair to good leader—but his outstanding characteristic in the post was a flatly uncompromising attitude and a brand of Midwestern smalltown, Lions Club Republicanism so intolerant as sometimes to repel even the redoubtable Taft."[3]

Interestingly, none of these earlier Republican leaders cast himself in the brokerage role. And notably, with the exception of Taft, who served for only a matter of months before his death, none is characterized as a particularly effective leader by his colleagues. While Senate Democrats throughout most of the 1950's were being led by one of the most skillful practitioners of the delicate art of compromise, Lyndon Johnson, the Republicans in the Senate were led by men who seemed to have little appreciation of the potentialities of their leadership position.

THE DIRKSEN LEADERSHIP

Everett McKinley Dirksen was elected Republican Leader in January, 1959 and served until his death in September 1969. Dirksen served under four Presidents: Republican Dwight D. Eisenhower for two years, Democrats John F. Kennedy and Lyndon B. Johnson for eight years, and Republican Richard M. Nixon for almost one year. He was early recognized as "probably the most effective leader the Republicans had had in the Senate for years."[4] What were the ingredients of his success? What role did he try to shape, for himself and for Republicans in the Senate, especially when his party was a true minority, out of power in the White House? What was the basis of his power or influence, and what style characterized his

leadership? And finally, what factors contributed to the decline
of his effectiveness as Republican leader?

Basic Attitudes and Approach

Dirksen was an altogether different personality from any of his
immediate predecessors and his view of the minority leadership
was different as well. In contrast to them, Dirksen was uniquely
qualified for just those aspects of Senate leadership that were so
totally neglected by both Taft and Knowland. In a story written
before his selection as minority leader, the *Wall Street Journal*
said this of Everett Dirksen:

> Senate Republicans, badly outmaneuvered by a slim Demo-
> cratic majority during the past four years, will exchange the
> bludgeon for the rapier in the next Congress. The wielder of
> the new weapon: Everett McKinley Dirksen, the velvet-voiced
> senator from Illinois.

> G.O.P. senators long have looked with grudging admiration
> on the ability of Democratic Leader Lyndon B. Johnson to
> effect compromises, quickly shift position, cajole rebellious
> senators of his party and weld some semblance of unity
> between Northern and Southern Democrats. Now, in Mr.
> Dirksen, they will have a leader bound to borrow more than
> one page from the Johnson book.[5]

Emphasizing Dirksen's talents, the *Journal* story pointed up
some of Knowland's deficiencies as well as the requirements for
more effective Senate leadership. "Unlike Mr. Knowland, he
[Dirksen] ranks among the Senate's masters of extemporaneous
debate, refuses to take a position that permits no strategic
retreat and in the manner of Mr. Johnson, can turn on a dime
without losing his balance."[6]

The hallmark of Dirksen's approach was legislative pragma-
tism. With Lyndon Johnson, he was a believer in the art of the
possible. As he said once, "I am not a moralist, I am a
legislator," and a legislator's major responsibility is to pass bills.
As one Republican senator said in Dirksen's first year as leader,
"Bill Knowland saw the leadership primarily as a matter of
stating a principle and standing on it. Dirksen doesn't stand on

principle so much; he gets on the phone and lines up the votes for our side."[7] Unlike Knowland, if a proposal came down from the White House with which the leader could not agree, he would not relinquish his responsibility as leader. In the words of one conservative western senator close to him, "Dirksen would say, 'Well, I don't like it, but let's see what we can do.' "

Dirksen himself expressed an attitude toward his role which seemed to stress his responsibility, not only to his party or to the Senate, but to the Presidency as well, without too much regard for who held the White House, Republican or Democrat. "It should be remembered," Dirksen argued in 1962, "that the minority has the same stake in the well-being and interests of the whole country as the majority, and in consequence you have to refine the role of the minority so that it will include these things—to support those proposals that the administration might offer if, in our judgment, they are in the interests of the country and if they're sound."[8] Where the initiatives of the administration were not, in the minority's view, sound, then of course it was their role to oppose, Dirksen argued, but always with the interests of the country as a whole paramount.

Dirksen's view of his role, both with regard to the White House and within the Senate itself, was not unlike Lyndon Johnson's, and these attitudes did much to shape both men's leadership styles. Both saw the Presidency as the one office capable of providing national leadership. Both believed that to demean the President, whoever he may be, was destructive of the institution itself and therefore of the country's well-being. Finally, both placed greater importance on reaching an accommodation among differing points of view within their respective parties, in order to effect some positive action, than on the statement of a principle not to be compromised, which might or might not contribute to the accomplishment of the Senate's and the country's business. One Republican senator, with close ties to Dirksen, described the Illinois senator's view of his job in this way:

> Well, he saw it as leader of the Republican party, I judge, and as leader of the Senate who owed a responsibility to the President, to the party at the same time—which created a sort of ambivalence on occasion—but he saw it as a matter of serving his colleagues and leading the party in a position and discharging a responsibility to the Presidency—those three things mixed together.

Intraparty Strategy: Accommodation

Dirksen's strategy with respect to bringing his party together had four main components: (1) find out what senators want and what they will settle for (often two different things), and try to find out what can be done to effect a compromise; (2) work with and through the established party organs such as the Policy Committee and the Conference and forge a cooperative relationship with the White House; (3) communicate extensively with all members of the party in order to keep them informed and be informed himself; and (4) avoid forcing party positions on divisive issues. Perhaps the best way to illustrate Dirksen's approach to the leadership is through an explication of the circumstances surrounding his election and the way in which he met the initial problems he faced.

The results of the 1958 congressional elections, which immediately preceded Dirksen's election as leader, were nothing short of disastrous for the Republicans. The party lost 47 seats in the House of Representatives and declined from 47 senators to a low of 34, a net loss of 13 Senate seats. Not only were these results a jolt for the Republican party; the newcomers in the Senate foreshadowed a major shift in the liberal-conservative balance in the chamber. As might be expected, most of the Republican losses were among the more conservative members of the Senate party. The potential effects of those elections were not lost on the more liberal members of the Republican Senate party or on their soon-to-be new leader, Dirksen, who had moved into the line of succession for the post

195

with his selection as whip in 1957, primarily as the protégé of the powerful Styles Bridges who served as Chairman of the party's Policy Committee.

Dirksen, however, was not without opposition in his own Senate party. From the time he had first been elected to the Senate in 1950 until perhaps shortly before he ran for re-election in 1956, Dirksen had been closely associated with the more conservative wing of Senate Republicans. His now famous denunciation of former presidential candidate Thomas Dewey, in a last-minute effort to win the nomination for Taft, was only one indication of his closeness to the Taft wing in the Senate. His defense of Senator Joseph McCarthy was another, and one which particularly embittered the more moderate to liberal Eisenhower supporters in the Senate toward him. It was not until McCarthy's censure and eventual demise that Dirksen began to move away from him and, with the press of his own re-election campaign of 1956, toward a closer rapport with President Eisenhower.

When the 86th Congress convened in January of 1959, the liberals within the party were demanding change in the party's way of doing business. Their objections were basically two-fold; first, they were dissatisfied with the rigidity of the committee assignment process which was completely dictated by seniority and which therefore precluded many more junior senators from receiving any choice positions. Second, they were displeased at the prospect of seeing another leader whom they thought would carry on the distasteful Knowland tradition, and they wanted a greater voice in party affairs.

Dirksen was mindful of these attitudes and aware of the problems he would have to face as leader. No less than many of his colleagues, Dirksen had been dissatisfied and dismayed at the Knowland leadership. At the same time, he was acutely aware of the success with which Johnson led his Democratic Party and of the tactics of compromise and accommodation by which he had accomplished the feat of bringing together a dissident Democratic minority in 1953. Dirksen "had played the partisan in the party's internecine warring over the years, and he had done so on different occasions as a member of *both* major factions of the party. He saw now the need to move in a different direction, to assume a stance to which both party factions could repair. He wanted to be the leader of the Republicans in the Senate, not merely of the dominant faction of the party there."[9]

Dirksen's new desire to accommodate, however, could not head off a challenge from the more liberal wing of the party. But, as the statement of Dirksen's challenger indicates, the liberals were more concerned with replacing an inept and isolated leadership and with gaining a greater voice in party councils, than they were with actually defeating Dirksen:

> I became a candidate at the time because we'd just gone through a period under the leadership of Senator Knowland of California. There were a group of us who were against Senator Knowland for two reasons: one was that he did not keep us informed, and two, on issues . . . where he had no particular expertise (he still wanted to take the leadership to himself).
>
> Then, and this may be a party view that I thought more about then than I would now, . . . we felt that he would, . . . that he just wanted to *run* everything without ever conferring with anybody.
>
> There were, oh, 14 or so of us . . . and we decided we ought to get somebody to run to impress on the other members of the Republican side that we expected to be heard, we expected to be informed and this was a way of doing it.[10]

While Dirksen won his party's leadership by a vote of 20 to 14, calling in some of the I.O.U.'s he had collected as Chairman of the Senate Republican Campaign Committee in 1952 and 1954, he knew that he faced a divided and demoralized party. Senate Republicans had been split throughout the 1950's, liberal against conservative, internationalist against isolationalist, pro-Eisenhower and anti-Eisenhower. The 1958 elections exacerbated these divisions. Dirksen faced a formidable task in developing a strategy for bringing his party together behind his leadership.

Elements of the Strategy

The first requirement was to find out what senators want and what they will settle for and then to work out a compromise that, as nearly as possible, satisfies all of them. Thus, in response to the major criticism of the Knowland leadership, Dirksen immediately took steps to broaden the base of participation in Senate Republican Party affairs, and especially to include a major share of power for the so-called "liberal" faction. While conservatives had sufficient votes to elect as whip, Karl Mundt of South Dakota, Dirksen did not want to exclude so completely and thus further alienate the liberals. He and Bridges persuaded enough senators to change their votes to elect as whip, Thomas Kuchel of California, also by a margin of 20 to 14.

The second point of contention among liberals and all junior senators was the party's practice of making committee assignments and transfers strictly on the basis of seniority. The liberals suggested a new system for assignments along the lines used by the Democrats. One of the first moves Lyndon Johnson undertook as leader was to assure that no Democrat was given two major committee assignments until every Democrat had one. Dirksen approved of such a step, perhaps not only because he understood how grateful senators had subsequently responded to Johnson after receiving a choice committee assignment, but also because this was clearly a way to accommodate dissident senators and help to consolidate his own position as leader.

For the Republican leader, however, this required more than a unilateral decision to move. In Johnson's case, as floor leader he also served as Chairman of the Democratic Steering Committee, counterpart to the Republicans' Committee on Committees. In this position, Johnson had a major share of the responsibility for the Democrats' committee assignments. The Republicans, formally at least, did it differently. While the Leader had the responsibility for naming members of the

Committee on Committees, and while he himself sat as a member, his power was greatly circumscribed by the fact that positions were delegated on the basis of seniority.

Nevertheless, Dirksen moved to loosen the rigidity of the assignment process through the only tool a leader has, the power of persuasion. One senator described the situation this way:

> You are talking about 1959, when the seniority system got too oppressive for some of the senators and there was a good deal of agitation among the Republicans, and a number of senior Republicans, one by one, gave up one of their major committees to make room for the junior Republicans, I recall how the pressure finally got down to one . . . and he finally yielded and gave up one of his committees.

Biographer Neil MacNeil gives several examples of Dirksen's intervention on behalf of individual senators, many of whom had voted against him for the leadership. "Using all his skills of private persuasion, Dirksen negotiated assignment of Case of New Jersey to the Labor Committee, Kuchel to the Appropriations Committee, and Carlson of Kansas to the Foreign Relations Committee. Javits of New York, two years a senator, had been serving on inconsequential committees. Dirksen moved him up to the Banking and Labor Committees."[11]

In addition, Dirksen, perhaps borrowing another page from the Johnson book, was solicitous of freshman senators, understanding how important a choice committee assignment can be to them in establishing themselves at the outset. One freshman senator from a western state faced the problems of living down a campaign charge that he wanted to go to the Senate to help his friends on Wall Street. Subsequently, he learned that he had been assigned to the Banking and Currency Committee:

> I went to Dirksen and just told him, "I won't take it, I just won't take it and if you insist, then I'll resign." He looked at me with a great, broad grin and said, "Would it make any difference to you to know that for the first time in history

you have also been appointed to the Interior Committee where your [Republican] colleague is already sitting as a member?" That took the wind completely out of my sails and I had nothing more to say and accepted what was given to me.[12]

Dirksen had another tactic to help accommodate the committee desires of senators when they ran up against the wall of seniority. He used it first in his initial period as leader. Gordon Allott, in his first term as senator from Colorado, faced a re-election campaign in 1960. Allott thought it would be especially helpful to be on the Appropriations Committee, on which there were no vacancies. The minority leader, a member of the Appropriations Committee since 1951, in an extraordinary move promised Allott that he would give up his own seat on the committee in Allott's favor, if he could get agreement from the several senators ahead of Allott in seniority to waive their right to the position. Then Dirksen proceeded to talk to each of the senators and secured their agreement.

While Dirksen cherished and retained his seat on the Judiciary Committee, he otherwise shifted from committee to committee, giving up a position to a colleague who wanted it, where he could. He gave up his seat on the Labor Committee for freshmen John Tower of Texas in 1961. In all, Dirksen served on six different Senate committees, not including special or joint committees.

The second and third components of Dirksen's intraparty strategy were two sides of the same coin. He tried to work with and through the party organs in the Senate, the Policy Committee especially, to forge a working relationship with the White House, and he took care to communicate extensively with all members of the party.

One criticism of Knowland's leadership had been that he seldom accepted much responsibility for helping pilot President Eisenhower's programs through the Senate. Indeed, he was noted for those occasions on which he would leave his seat at the front of the chamber and go to another part of the Senate, there to lambast the administration for its policies. While

200

Dirksen had criticized certain policies of the Eisenhower administration, as whip he had begun to take an active part in shepherding the President's legislative proposals through the Senate. While this often called for a reverse of a former position or a sublimation of his own views, Dirksen felt it was his responsibility as Republican leader to marshal support for a Republican President.

Dirksen was fond of saying about the job he did for Eisenhower, "I carry the flag, I carry the flag." And he did. Dirksen was not bothered by charges that he altered his position. "No one will ever embarrass the minority leader," he said, "by charging him with having changed his mind or reversed his position on other occasions. One cannot have been in this man's town for twenty-eight years in the House and Senate without recognizing the verities of political life."[13]

Time and again, as whip and later as leader, Dirksen had defended Eisenhower's foreign policies, reversing his former isolationist position. He supported Eisenhower's 1957 Middle East Resolution, and much to the chagrin of his conservative backers in Illinois and the arch-conservative *Chicago Tribune*, the foreign aid program. He sponsored the President's civil rights legislation in 1957, and helped achieve a compromise to enact further measures in 1960. As leader, he "carried the flag" for Eisenhower on controversial labor legislation, helping to work out a difficult situation in the conference committee. "When other legislative leaders beg off from a difficult campaign for legislative battle he would say to his leader, 'Chief, give me that hot poker.' "[14]

But Dirksen was not only the President's spokesman to Senate Republicans. As he said so often, this was a "two-way street." Again, responding to the disgruntlement with Knowland's "uncommunicative" leadership, Dirksen went out of his way to confer with all Republican senators, both individually and collectively. He revitalized the meetings of the Republican Policy Committee, virtually dormant during the Knowland years. At their weekly lunches which followed the leadership's meetings at the White House, Dirksen took great care to report faithfully on what the President said, what was coming before the Senate, and how the President felt about legislative matters. At the same time, however, the meetings became a forum where every senator could express his own views on legislation or party policy, and these Dirksen would faithfully report to the President, giving equal representation to liberal as well as conservative senators. Thus, Dirksen successfully walked that slim line between being the President's man in the Senate and the Senate's man in the White House.

The final component of Dirksen's intraparty strategy, aimed as it was at keeping the party at least minimally together, was to avoid forcing party positions on divisive issues. Dirksen drew considerable criticism from party members outside the Senate, especially during the Kennedy and Johnson Presidencies, for what they characterized as a lack of effective opposition to the Democratic President. What they criticized was, in fact, an essential part of the Dirksen strategy as leader *not* to exacerbate the already considerable internal divisions in his Senate party. In a general sense, it was Dirksen's strategy to keep the minority reasonably well together in the Senate by compromise and by blunting issues rather than exploiting them. Facing a Republican contingent encompassing both a Javits and a Goldwater, Dirksen was astute enough to realize that any attempts to reach a "party position" on which these two men could agree would be fruitless. Thus, he avoided trying to force a false unity where none could exist and thereby retained the respect of his colleagues or at least did not invite their enmity. Dirksen, therefore, preferred to let slide those issues which produced strong tensions within the party, refraining from attempting to offer alternatives to Democratic programs. In this way, he was able to maintain good relations with both major factions of his party.

By the end of his first Congress as minority leader, Dirksen had, by all accounts, effected a tremendous change in the pattern of Republican leadership. Through an approach which emphasized tact, patience, and an extraordinary ability to get along with all the members of his party, as well as his refusal to take the side of one faction against the other, and his practice of giving all a full chance to be heard in party councils, Dirksen solidified his party behind his leadership even if not on all votes.

In an unusual address to the Senate late in the session in 1959, former Senator Margaret Chase Smith of Maine, admitting that she had opposed Dirksen for the leadership, paid him an extraordinary tribute, describing the tactics and approach which made him so effective.

At the beginning of this session, when the Republican Members of the Senate met to choose their officers, I did not support the candidacy of Everett Dirksen for the position of Senate Minority Leader. I had my reservations.

But as I have watched him perform the duties of Minority Leader I have increasingly come to conclude that his election to that position was a very wise action by the Senate Republicans. If another election were to be held today, I would unhesitatingly vote for Everett Dirksen for the position of Minority Leader.

... it has been in the execution of his duties as Minority Leader that other qualities have come to the forefront. He has shown a capacity for understanding. By that I mean not just the kind of understanding by which one agrees with another. Instead, I mean more the kind of understanding by which one can disagree agreeably—by which one can differ with another without rancor, without impugning the motives of the other, but with respect, and with willingness to listen to the other side.

He has shown a capacity for tolerance and patience. Within the ranks of the Republican senators there are varying shades of opinions on many legislative issues. Everett Dirksen has extended tolerance and patience to all opinions and views. But he has not extended tolerance and patience in a patronizing manner or with a condescending attitude. He has done this without compromising his own principles and beliefs.[15]

Legislative Strategy: Participation

While it is unlikely that Dirksen would have used these words, his legislative strategy can perhaps best be interpreted as an attempt to maximize participation in the legislative process, both for himself and for the minority party. There were, again, four main components to this basic strategy: (1) foster a cooperative relationship with the majority leader in all aspects of Senate business; (2) cooperate closely with the White House, regardless of the incumbent; (3) pay close attention to the details of legislation, both substantive and technical, as well as the parliamentary situation; and (4) take advantage of peculiar situations in the legislative process which sometimes permit and occasionally require the minority to play a decisive role.

Dirksen's strategy must be understood against the background of two kinds of factors which inevitably will shape the behavior of any Senate leader. Broadly, they are: (1) situational variables, including who controls the White House, the strength and make-up of the Senate party, the personality and tactics of the majority leader, and perhaps most important, what issue is before the Senate and how it divides senators generally; and (2) the personality, philosophy, and talents of the man himself.

Dirksen, though commanding a force far smaller than Knowland's, brought a new level of cooperation to the minority's relations with the majority. Whereas Johnson found both Taft and Knowland difficult to work with, he found Dirksen "more like me than anybody." The initiative in Senate affairs rests, of course, with the majority leader. But a highly cooperative relationship between the two leaders *can*, if developed properly, give the minority a voice in such mundane matters as scheduling and the general disposal of Senate business. Significantly, they shared the view that their job was to move the business of the Senate. Both were legislative pragmatists who believed that "half a loaf is better than no loaf," and compromise and mutual accommodation were the way to achieve legislative results. Johnson described their day-to-day working relationship:

> Well, after I evaluate the bills on the calendar I ask him [Dirksen] to make his recommendations. When I walk into the chamber every morning, he puts on my desk a memorandum stating what he thinks about each bill and what his policy group thinks and what his colleagues think—"This will be trouble," "This will be long debate," "This will have relatively little opposition," and so forth. And he marks the bills on the calendar in blue pencil. I evaluate mine and mark my calendar in red pencil. Then we exchange calendars.
>
> We have every bill that has been introduced and been considered by a committee evaluated in red and blue, and he knows my opinion and I know his opinion. I would say we spend a third or a fourth of every hour during the legislative day talking to each other and either trying to reach agreement or to ascertain the points on which agreement is not possible.[16]

Senator Dirksen, emphasizing the leaders' mutual responsibility to the nation, explained the Johnson-Dirksen relationship this way:

> We used to make medicine, as I say, over in his office. Of course we had to make book and make schedule on what came up. The Senate is a two-way street, that is one thing we are always agreed on. A minority leader with some backing could just truss up the Senate any old time with a filibuster or anything else and stop it in its tracks and the majority leader could do likewise. And so we agreed that we had to work together because the overriding interest was the well-being and the welfare of the republic. . . .[17]

Both men understood what Ralph Huitt calls "the basic skill of the politician, the ability to divide any number by two and add one."[18] And the center aisle of the chamber was not a forbidden line either. "If I couldn't get all the votes I needed," Johnson said, "it didn't matter because I'd get some Republicans. And he'd come over and try to woo some of my girls." One incident which occurred during this period is illustrative of Dirksen's desire to foster good relations with the majority leader, in order to protect his own and the minority's position. A former Senate staff member recalls an afternoon when John Marshall Butler of Maryland, described as a petulant fellow, decided to offer a motion to adjourn, an action that is always the perogative of the majority leader:

> This was the only time I ever saw Dirksen excited, and he was—upset. He came over and said, "John, don't make that motion. Lyndon doesn't want it. If you offer that motion, you know what will happen? You will erect a wall down this center aisle, between the parties, that will be unbridgeable." And Butler refrained and a half hour or so later, Johnson adjourned the Senate.

Dirksen continued this close liaison with Johnson's successor as majority leader, Mike Mansfield of Montana. Mansfield's entirely different style and more limited interpretation of his role gave Dirksen an opportunity to exercise a more active role in the Senate's business. Mansfield, in contrast to Johnson, chose to be a far more quiescent and far less demanding leader. With regard to the potential perquisites of a leader, such as manipulating committee assignments, Mansfield simply does not use them, insisting instead that he wields no instruments of authority. Of Dirksen, Mansfield said, "I need him," and the two were very close, notwithstanding differences in personality. When Mansfield was attacked by some Democrats for lack of leadership, Dirksen came to his defense. As one Republican senator close to the minority leader said, "I'm certain that they never spoke with less than complete candor to each other—and I'm sure that there were many, many accommodations reached between those two men that the Senate never fully understood and that contributed to their respective roles in leadership." Indicative of their cooperation is the frequency with which measures came to final Senate action as "the Mansfield-Dirksen substitute." Mansfield's less partisan approach to his job and his reluctance to seek and exercise power, along with his own belief in cooperation and accommodation with the minority, contributed to the enlargement of Dirksen's role.

A second component of Dirksen's strategy for maximizing minority participation was close cooperation with the White House, as well as with the congressional majority. He had followed this pattern when Eisenhower was President, of course, but he continued it with Democratic Presidents Kennedy and Johnson, sometimes to the dismay of fellow Republicans. The personalities of both Kennedy and Johnson, different though they were, and the close relationships each had with Dirksen, based on previous congressional service, promoted their receptivity to Dirksen's cooperation and counsel.

Kennedy and Dirksen, through their association in both House and Senate, developed a genuine liking and respect for one another. Knowing that in some situations cleavages in the Democratic Party would necessitate cooperation of Republicans, Kennedy took care to consult closely with Dirksen, whom he knew could be the key with some fellow Republicans. For his part, Dirksen was solicitous of the President, at times almost protective. "I never try to embarrass the President of the United States," he said in 1963. "I shall always bend over backward to make certain that he is not projected into any awkward situation."[19]

During the years of Lyndon Johnson's Presidency, the minority leader had an even closer intimacy with the White House. Whereas Kennedy consulted Dirksen mainly because he understood political necessities, Johnson relied on Dirksen because they shared ideas and outlooks and to some extent styles. In the words of a close Dirksen aide, "Both were earthy, salty men, who played the same kind of game." Their long years of association, especially as party leaders, have forged a deep friendship and mutual understanding. While they occasionally took swipes at each other, and while Dirksen vigorously opposed many of Johnson's Great Society programs, their completely honest and open relationship permitted them to disagree without rancor—in Dirksen's phrase, "never to let the sun set" on their anger. Johnson trusted Dirksen and his judgment implicitly. As President, he consulted the minority leader on most matters and talked with him almost every day. "He'd call me up," Johnson said, "and say, 'I want a drink of your whiskey,' or on the way home he'd stop by."

Dirksen, however, did not offer unconditional support to Democratic Presidents. His pattern of cooperation-opposition was set in response to a number of situational variables, the most important of which was the particular issue at hand. Thus, the support for a Democratic White House for which Dirksen became famous was primarily restricted to foreign policy. This support was a direct result of his strong feeling that the President should be the paramount figure in foreign affairs. As Dirksen said:

> ...We cannot, as a minority, show a disunited spirit to the world. We must make it manifest to the whole wide world that this country is united by the President, once a policy has been set. Therefore, we have always insisted that when a certain policy is to be pursued we should have the opportunity to criticize. We should have a chance to comment. We should have a chance to make suggestions and modifications. But once that discussion has been had and once the issue has been resolved then, of course, it is our duty to support it.[20]

In the realm of foreign policy, Dirksen came to both Kennedy's and Johnson's rescue more than once. In 1962, he helped enact a law granting the President unprecedented authority to negotiate tariff reductions. In 1963, he helped avoid Senate rejection of a treaty aimed at bolstering Latin America's economy by support of coffee export prices. Dirksen's efforts in two other controversies of the Kennedy administration were of crucial impact.

In 1962, Kennedy proposed a $100 million bond issue to rescue the United Nations from a serious financial crisis, a measure which met strong opposition in the Senate, especially from Dirksen's more conservative Republican colleagues. Notwithstanding the pressure from other members, as well as from his conservative Illinois backers, Dirksen adopted a stance and a strategy which he was to use many times. Rather than oppose the measure outright, or even give it unqualified support, Dirksen moved into the breach and sought to reach an agreement with Majority Leader Mansfield which would satisfy some of the criticisms of the opposition. Such a compromise could not, of course, satisfy all senators, and several Republicans objected strongly. But Dirksen argued, in contradiction of sentiments expressed on other occasions, "This is not a financial question. This is a moral question." He emphasized his allegiance to the Presidency: "I haven't forfeited my faith in John Fitzgerald Kennedy. I'm willing, as always to trust my President, because he is my President."[21]

Dirksen's activity was also essential to the success of Kennedy's efforts to secure ratification of the Nuclear Test Ban Treaty. This situation had several particular ingredients which compelled Dirksen to play a leading role. Because treaty ratification requires a two-thirds majority, some minority cooperation was required. Also, the lack of active leadership by the majority leader made it possible for Dirksen to fill the resulting vacuum.

While he had initially opposed such a treaty—even as Kennedy announced only that the United States would resume negotiations with the Russians to this end—he gradually sensed that there was widespread support for it within his own party. When two prominent Democrats, Senator Richard Russell of Georgia, Chairman of the Armed Services Committee, and Senator John Stennis of Mississippi, also influential in military affairs, announced their intention to vote against the treaty, Dirksen's support became critical. At this point, under these unique circumstances, Dirksen went to Mansfield with the proposal that together they approach Kennedy and persuade him to take some step that would assure wary senators that the treaty would in no way endanger national security, and that he, Kennedy, would not let down the nation's guard. Kennedy accepted a draft letter which Dirksen had prepared. The President sent this letter to Mansfield and Dirksen, and the minority leader read it to the Senate in the course of an enthusiastic speech endorsing the treaty. It was subsequently ratified by a vote of 89 to 19. This incident illustrates as well another ingredient of the Dirksen approach. A good leader must at times be a good follower. Thus, when he sensed that many Republicans supported the Nuclear Test Ban Treaty, Dirksen maneuvered himself into a position where he could lead Republicans in a cooperative effort with the White House, taking advantage of the peculiar variables of this legislative situation.

The basis of Dirksen's support for Johnson was, as in the case with President Kennedy, a firm commitment to the supremacy of the President in foreign affairs. Time and time again, Dirksen reiterated his unqualified support of Johnson's policies in Vietnam. As the Vietnam War became an ever more divisive issue in both parties, Dirksen stood out as the President's most enthusiastic backer in the Congress. Majority Leader Mansfield, unable to support the President's view in Vietnam, was to an unusual degree replaced by Dirksen as the President's spokesman to the Senate. Thus developed the unique situation in which the opposition's leader in the Senate had a more direct and intimate pipeline to the President than did his own party leader.

This situation held both advantages and disadvantages for Dirksen. His closeness to Johnson and his direct access to the White House enabled him to do things for himself and his colleagues that an opposition leader is normally unable to do. One Republican senator relates how Dirksen helped him secure Johnson's acquiescence on an appointment:

> I had a candidate for a job and Johnson didn't want him—made no bones about it—but Dirksen stayed with me and we got one or two other Democrats to help, and Johnson always said to me afterwards, "You, I didn't want that man, you forced me to take him." Well, he [Dirksen] could do that . . . he had the kind of relationship that I'm not sure they didn't call each other by their first names when they got in the White House and nobody else was around.

Theoretically, a President's own leader in the Senate has an edge over his colleagues because he serves as the source of communication and information from the White House. This is an advantage normally denied the opposition's leader. Dirksen, however, consulted frequently with Johnson on all manner of issues, giving the President advice and counsel on this position or that, or on what the chances were for this proposal or that proposal. Dirksen learned a great deal, of course, in these informal sessions and often knew the President's desires and plans before the Democratic leadership did. "You can be sure," one observer stated, "that Dirksen is aware of how to use all the information he picks up from LBJ."[22] This advantage helped him to maintain a pivotal position, not only in his own party, but within the Senate as a whole.

Part of Dirksen's legislative strategy involved, as has been indicated, an ability to take advantage of the peculiar legislative situation, and to cast himself in a central role whenever possible. He shared with Johnson many techniques of leadership: the gentle persuasion, the cajolery, and, on occasion, the hard sell. Like Johnson, he was a master tactician and parliamentarian. But unlike Johnson, Dirksen was also a legislative *technician*, for he liked to putter with both the substance and the technicalities of bills. He had developed a formidable skill at the tedious job of tinkering with the commas and the "whereases" of complex legislation, to the point where he usually knew a piece of major legislation better than even the committee members who had considered it. This attention to detail he carefully cultivated as it enabled him to move in where other senators were either not interested or too lazy, and to offer amendments which changed the substance of a bill, a little here or a little there, to work his way.

These two talents, the ability to take advantage of a legislative situation and his technical skill, are illustrated by his part in the 1964 Civil Rights Act. The primary situational factor which placed Dirksen in a central role was, of course, the fact that any Senate action on a civil rights bill would require more than a mere majority, given the inevitability of a southern filibuster.

Dirksen's strategy can be summarized briefly. He maintained a low profile while the opposing forces positioned themselves. While he had early announced his opposition to a public accommodations section and his problems with the fair employment practices portion of the bill, he did not publicize his own specific solutions. Whether this initial opposition was part of a deliberate strategy to mollify the conservatives in his own party by letting them know he was with them, while privately planning to bring them along later in a compromise, or whether it reflected his own true feeling at the time, is a matter of question that will probably never be answered satisfactorily. In any case, that is basically what happened.

Dirksen spent the first several weeks of the debate giving the entire bill a careful going-over. He was, at the same time, consulting closely with Mansfield and with Kuchel, whom he had designated as Republican floor manager for the bill. His own task was clear, but nonetheless difficult. In order to bring sufficient numbers of his recalcitrant colleagues into voting for cloture to obtain the necessary two-thirds majority, he had to negotiate sufficient changes in the bill to assure that they could support it, at least minimally. On the other hand, Dirksen's modifications could not be so severe as to gut the bill, lest liberals refuse to pay the price.

Thus, Dirksen negotiated, first within his own party at a series of Policy Committee meetings and then with the bill's managers and Attorney General Robert Kennedy. The result was that Dirksen was able to persuade the bill's proponents to accept a whole series of technical amendments and minor changes, most of which did not alter the legislation significantly. But the changes did allow Dirksen to persuade most of his colleagues that he was "getting all he could get." On the other hand, he compromised his own position on the delicate public accommodations and fair employment practices sections. The outcome was the Dirksen-Mansfield substitute, which was by no

212

means welcome by all Republicans. Dirksen had to persuade his colleagues to accept this compromise. His tactics were an indication, and his success a measure, of his effectiveness at marshaling what political scientist David Truman so aptly called the "fragments of power" available to any Senate leader. Primarily, he relied on his well-developed powers of persuasion, probably the last resort of any effective Senate leader, to convince those Republican senators who still opposed him. He once described his basic approach, emphasizing the need for patience in such situations:

> ... The gift of patience, of course, I think is a highly desired attribute because you are dealing with people; they have fixations, they have convictions about any number of controversial matters. You have to hear them out. You have to be careful not to be too precipitous or capricious in pointing out what you think the weakness in the other fellow's case may be, especially if he is on your side of the aisle politically speaking. So that requires, I think, gentle discussion and a very gentle oil-can art as I call it so that the bearings never get hot.
>
> What was it that Lincoln said—we shall sooner have the chicken by hatching the egg than by breaking it.[23]

Despite the recalcitrance of some, Dirksen was able to secure enough commitments and on June 10, 1964, the Senate successfully invoked cloture by a vote of 71 to 29. A total of 27 Republicans, including the conservative core, voted with Dirksen.

DIRKSEN: EFFECTIVE LEADERSHIP AND ITS DECLINE

Without exception, all 27 Republican senators interviewed for this study agreed that Dirksen was an effective leader. Many, representing all shades of opinion within the party, thought he was the most effective leader Senate Republicans had had, at least in their memory. At the same time, however, most recognized that his effectiveness was waning in the last years of his life. Why this change? What ingredients of his early success were lacking in the last few years?

213

Dirksen's effectiveness sprang from several sources. As was pointed out earlier, Dirksen was carefully solicitous of the needs, desires, and views of his colleagues. As one senator put it, "He knew that the art of politics is the care and feeding of egos." He consulted frequently with members of his party, and regularly with ranking Republicans on Senate committees. Almost every evening, Dirksen would have a gathering in the back room of his Capitol office where colleagues could sit around and informally discuss issues over a friendly drink. Dirksen's style was, even from the beginning, a highly personal one; he did not rely too much on others to do his spadework. But he did take the initiative in communication.

Dirksen adopted early a mediator and broker role within his party and, as we have seen, within the Senate where circumstances, the issue, and the situation permitted. He was even-handed and fair in his intraparty dealings, carefully avoiding the mistake of taking one side against the other in his own divided party. His leadership pattern followed the requirement for effectiveness that David Truman suggested:

> Given the depth and persistence of the cleavages in both parties . . . one would expect that a leader who accepted any degree of responsibility for the substantive actions of the party would almost certainly be a middleman, not only in the sense of a negotiator but also in a literal structural sense. One would not expect that he could attract the support neces-sary . . . unless his voting record placed him somewhere near the center in an evenly divided party, and one would not expect him to be effective in his role unless he continued to avoid identification with one of the extreme groups within his nominal following.[24]

At the outset, Dirksen did move visibly toward the middle of his own party. A *Harper's* magazine article written in 1959 put it this way: "Give a Minority Leader the chore of building a coalition out of the current crop of Senate Republicans and he takes on the complexion of the coalition."[25]

Dirksen's effectiveness was also in part a result of his highly heralded skill as a legislative technician and parliamentarian.

And he worked very hard at it. Senators looked to him for advice and counsel because he knew what was in a bill, what the language meant, and what the effect might be.

He was effective, too, because of his closer than usual relations with both majority leaders Johnson and Mansfield. One senior Republican referred to this relationship in explaining Dirksen's skill:

> Dirksen established a close relationship whereby he could influence the pattern of the legislative program, despite the fact that the majority leader has the power to set the program. There are times when I think he had more influence on the schedule than the majority. He might also persuade the majority leader that a particular bill needed work, or possibly change this, or that might happen to it. He could get into the Democratic Policy Committee—not physically of course, but through Mansfield.

For a Republican minority leader the fragments of power are far more scarce than for the Democratic leader, who also is chairman of his party's Policy Committee, which sets the schedule, and the Steering Committee, which makes committee assignments, and the Conference. But, while most observers have suggested that "the Democrats incline toward a highly personalized rule by the floor leader; (and) the Republicans, toward leadership by a handful of party officials,"[26] this assessment does not hold true for the Dirksen period. Neither Bridges nor Hickenlooper nor Allott—each of whom served as Chairman of the Policy Committee during Dirksen's tenure— ever presented any challenge to the supremacy of the floor leadership. While these men may have chaired meetings of the Policy Committee, it was Dirksen who led them and used them as a platform both to disseminate and gather information and views.

Opinion is divided as to whether the Republican organization, which does spread the leadership positions more widely, is a hindrance to the floor leader or not. One senator, asked this question, argued that:

It didn't hurt Everett Dirksen any—I think a lot depends on the individual leader . . . the floor leader is still the leader on the floor. The Conference chairman is a presiding officer, really, over the party conference. The Policy Committee chairman presides over the support operations of the party in the Senate. The whip of course serves as the leading assistant to the leader, so I think that there is very little dissemination of real leadership responsibility as far as the floor . . . [is concerned].

If the fragments were scarce, Dirksen was able to maximize their impact and, as one senator said, to "consolidate his power position as he went along." The minority leader has the power to make appointments to special committees and commissions, to name members of the minority party who will represent the Senate at various functions and so forth. As we have seen, Dirksen maneuvered also to have a greater impact on standing committee assignments than the formal structure would suggest he could have. And he used these things, too, to help build a "line of credit":

He knew the interests of each individual person in the Senate. He knew how to appeal to their interests. If one senator had a bill that was being boxed in or hungup somewhere in the committee, and he wanted that senator's support for another bill, he knew how to get that bill out of the box and get that senator's support on his measure.

When he went looking for support, he relied mainly on persuasion. "I need your vote on this, can you help me out?" He once described his own style in the following way: "You argue politely, amiably, and with the utmost good nature. It requires a lot of patience. You can't violently disagree, and maybe you won't succeed. Well the next day is another day, and there's the next day and the next day. You stay at it everlastingly."[27] He did keep at it, and always with a stance which allowed him to seek modifications or compromise in order to bring another senator into the fold. In this process, however, he "held no malice toward people who didn't go

216

along. He bore no resentments," one senator explained, and "he didn't carry any grudges." This attitude enabled him to look for support in all wings of his party and the Senate as well, taking care never to alienate a senator who might be his ally on the next issue.

While the "oil can" was his own self-professed favorite weapon, he could also be forceful. Over the years he did many favors for his colleagues and "he simply collected I.O.U.'s," as one senator said:

> ... and on occasion he cashed 'em out. And he could cash 'em, with great, brutal bloodiness when he did it. On occasion—one occasion I'm thinking about—he simply told a member, "You *owe* me this vote," and he collected. I saw that only once, but I saw it happen—so he had quite an arsenal of devices.

Dirksen's effectiveness, then, was the result of several factors: his legislative skill and knowledge of bills, his persuasiveness, his evenhanded and communicative relationships with his colleagues, his leverage with the majority and the White House, his ability to do countless favors for his colleagues and his care to do them, as well as his willingness to use all the perquisites and powers at his disposal. These factors compounded one another and added to his overall influence. Perhaps an additional factor should be mentioned. In the Senate especially, where members prize their independence, and where it is generally agreed even the most skillful leader cannot force his party to take a course they do not wish to take, Dirksen's effectiveness lay partly in his ability to follow. When he was effective, it was because he didn't let himself get too far away from the center of thinking within his party, and he did not try to force issues on them. While this stance frequently required him to change positions, he did not mind. He chided his critics by insisting, "I am a man of principle, and one of my basic principles is flexibility."

Effectiveness Declining

Several of the variables that created the situation in which Dirksen operated so well during the late 1950's and early-to-mid-1960's changed. Dirksen himself changed, and perhaps began, as early as 1965 or 1966, to take his press notices too seriously. The decline in his effectiveness, which was so evident by the time of his death in 1969, is attributable to several factors.

First, the character of his party in the Senate was changing. After the 1964 election, Republicans in the Senate were down to 32. By 1969, when the 91st Congress convened, their numbers were up to 43. The increment included mostly young, "new breed" Republicans who looked with dismay on the style Dirksen represented, a style which they felt gave the party a bad image nationally. Between 1966 and 1969, the center of gravity within the party shifted to the left with the addition of such new senators as Percy of Illinois, Cook of Kentucky, Mathias of Maryland, Brooke of Massachusetts, Goodell of New York, Saxbe of Ohio, Hatfield and Packwood of Oregon, and Schweiker of Pennsylvania. These more liberal senators were dissatisfied, not only with Dirksen's style, but also with what they viewed as the negative and far too conservative position he represented. Increasingly, they resented his efforts to continue to speak for the party when what he spoke was anathema to them. His continued support for Johnson's Vietnam policies, for example, especially annoyed those "dovish" Republicans who wanted their party to differentiate itself from the Democratic President in the eyes of the electorate. One liberal Republican talked about Dirksen's role in the Policy Committee:

> Well, there were many times I would say ... [when] a position was announced by Senator Dirksen at a Tuesday luncheon of the Policy Committee that, ah, he'd been over at the White House that morning visiting with the President, and he'd said *this* to the President, or he'd said *that* to the President, which sounded to the average listener, as a

commitment. And there was a feeling of "Well now wait a minute; you may have said that for your own role or your own position, but you didn't . . . why do you imply that you said it for me?"

This statement reflects change in Dirksen's own role and job performance. A staff member who was very close to him suggested that perhaps as early as 1966 he began to change. Whereas early in the 1960's, his sessions with the press were as spokesman for his party, increasingly they became one-man performances, an opportunity for Dirksen to put on "a show." Certainly it was clear at the end that he no longer consulted as much with his colleagues as he had. As his national notoriety increased, his attention to the details of his leadership job and especially the aspect of consultation and communication with members decreased. The example of Johnson's nomination of Abe Fortas to be Chief Justice of the United States in 1968 illustrates this point, as well as the fact that Dirksen's closeness to the Democratic President could be a disadvantage at times. Dirksen had consulted with Johnson on this appointment and had promised his wholehearted supported for Fortas, even while he knew that Senator Robert Griffin of Michigan and several other Republican senators, including Dirksen's son-in-law, Howard Baker of Tennessee, had resolved to fight any Johnson nomination in order to preserve this option for the incoming President, whom they, of course, thought would be a Republican. What Dirksen did not know was the extent of Griffin's support within the party; not having done his homework in this instance, he dismissed the younger senator's efforts.

By the time the Senate reconvened after the political party conventions that summer, it was clear that Griffin could successfully filibuster Johnson's nomination. By mid-September, Griffin had enough firm commitments to forestall cloture. The matter had passed completely out of Dirksen's hands because of his failure to maintain close consultation with his colleagues. Griffin had most Republicans behind him. In the end, Dirksen had to go back on his word to the President, for which Johnson chided him. But to both men it was clear that the nomination was lost, and Johnson withdrew Fortas' name. The incident, however, was a keen embarrassment for the minority leader, illustrating that his once paramount position within the party and the Senate could be successfully challenged.

Dirksen's effectiveness also declined because he became increasingly absorbed in his own pet projects including his recordings and his constitutional amendments regarding school prayer and the "one man, one vote" decision of the Supreme Court. Gradually, his leadership evolved into what one senator described as "a one-man, vest pocket kind of leadership role." Interestingly, the objections senators had to Dirksen's leadership were of much the same nature as the objections he and his colleagues had had to Knowland's operation some ten years before.

CONCLUSIONS

A minority leader's role and style depend on a combination of factors, including his personality and political attitudes as well as the legislative situation in which he operates on a given issue. In performing his role, Dirksen tried to maximize participation for the minority and for himself in the legislative process.

The Dirksen experience supports several conclusions about Senate leadership. First, the notion that effective leadership requires an ideological "middleman" is confirmed. Dirksen was most effective when his views placed him in the middle of the Senate Republican party, able to deal equally well with both liberal and conservative factions. While his decline in effectiveness is not easily related to voting scores, his "middleman" position in the party is indicated by two *Congressional Quarterly* tabulations. *CQ* tabulates the percentages of support for, or opposition to, the so-called "conservative coalition," as well as each senator's support and opposition regarding bills on which the President has taken a position. From 1959 through 1968, Dirksen, with only the exception of 1960, was in neither the highest support group nor the highest opposition group on conservative coalition scores. In the same vein, with only the exception of 1965, when he was among the highest Republican supporters of President Johnson, Dirksen was in neither the highest support group nor the highest opposition group on Presidential support scores. While these findings are not offered as conclusive proof, they are an indication that Dirksen, more often than not, was in neither of the extreme groups of his party.

Second, an effective leader must also be a mediator or broker among competing interests or views. In the case of the minority leader, his impact may depend on his ability to forge a consensus among a sufficient number of his colleagues so that he may hold a balance of power in a given situation and, from this position, exact modifications or compromises on pending legislation.

Third, Republicans seem to desire their leader to be highly communicative, to engage in frequent consultation with all members, and to be willing to listen to all sides of a question. Members do not necessarily require that the leadership be "shared" literally, although this is the term which Dirksen's successor, Hugh Scott, uses to positively distinguish his leadership from that of Dirksen. Clearly, even at the height of his effectiveness, Dirksen did not, in fact, "share" his duties or his central role with anyone. He took care to consult members on their views, and to not take off on his own without advising and informing his membership. Thus, the effective leader, as revealed by both the Johnson and Mansfield experiences as well, must at least give the appearance that he seeks to know what everyone thinks and that he lets this counsel inform, if not shape, his decisions.

Fourth, the floor leader may choose to centralize the leadership function or share it with other formal party leaders. Dirksen's successor, Hugh Scott, purposefully tries to give some of the leader's functions to the whip, Robert Griffin, whom he designated assistant Republican leader. The Dirksen experience, in contrast, illustrates that Republicans can tolerate and even applaud a highly personalized and centralized leadership, with the condition that extensive communication exists.

Fifth, a minority leader, especially when his party is small and the opposition also controls the White House, must in order to be effective and have any impact on Senate affairs, have a close working relationship with the majority leader and the White House. If he has such a close relationship, in a body which stresses a cooperative attitude, he can magnify his role appreciably over what it might be if he isolates himself. Clearly, much of Dirksen's effectiveness and much of his impact was a result of just this factor.

Finally, one may tentatively conclude that the character of the Senate has changed appreciably since the decade of the 1950's. That was a decade of such Senate "giants," if you will, as Taft, Bridges, Eugene Millikan, Richard Russell, Walter George, and others. This is not to say simply that a shift has occurred along conservative to liberal lines. Rather, it suggests that the kind of politician who comes to the Senate today is different, and that the kind of forceful, personalized leadership characteristic of Johnson's and Dirksen's tenures is no longer as fitting as it was in the 1950's and perhaps the early 1960's. One or two comments of younger senators are instructive. Referring to both Johnson and Dirksen, one said:

> They were the last of what might be called the old structured highly stylized leaders who could say, "This is the policy and it's been given from on high and everyone fall into line," and if everyone didn't want to fall into line they were able to exert certain pressures and influences.

It may be that in the future we will witness more of the low-key, less demanding, and less flamboyant leadership of men such as Mansfield and Scott, and that the days of the Dirksens and Johnsons are gone. To be effective in the future, Senate leadership will have to come to terms with the increasing independence and prominence of the younger members.

1. William S. White, *Citadel: The Story of the U.S. Senate* (New York: Harper & Row, 1956), p. 96.

2. *Ibid.*, p. 105.

3. *Ibid.*, p. 106.

4. The *New York Times*, April 4, 1960.

5. *The Wall Street Journal*, November 5, 1958.

6. *Ibid.*

7. Quoted in William Barry Furlong, "The Senate's Wizard of Ooze: Dirksen of Illinois", *Harper's Magazine*, Vol. 219 (December, 1959), p. 45.

8. "A Personal Interview," *The Christian Science Monitor*, January 7, 1962.

9. Neil MacNeil, *Dirksen: Portrait of a Public Man* (New York: World, 1970), p. 155.

10. Brookings Institution Round Table Discussion on the Senate, 1965.

11. MacNeil, *op. cit.*, p. 165.

12. Brookings Round Table Discussions, *op. cit.*

13. Mary McGrory, *The Washington Star*, August 10, 1960.

14. *Ibid.*

15. *Congressional Record*, Vol. 105, Part 14, p. 18488.

16. "An Interview with Senator Majority Leader Johnson", *U.S. News and World Report*, Vol. 48 (June 27, 1960), p. 89.

17. Interview with Joseph McCaffrey, ABC-TV, February 7, 1965.

18. Ralph K. Huitt, "Democratic Party Leadership in the Senate," in Huitt and Robert L. Peabody, *Congress: Two Decades of Analysis* (New York: Harper & Row, 1969), p. 145.

19. Jerry Landauer, *The Wall Street Journal*, August 15, 1963.

20. *The Christian Science Monitor, op. cit.*

21. MacNeil, *op. cit.*, pp. 195-196.

22. "Dirksen and LBJ—Strange Allies", *U.S. News and World Report*, Vol. 63 (December 11, 1967), p. 75.

23. Interview with Joseph McCaffrey, *op. cit.*

24. David B. Truman, *The Congressional Party: A Case Study* (New York: John Wiley, 1959), p. 106.

25. Furlong, *op. cit.*, p. 45.

26. Donald R. Matthews, *U.S. Senators and Their World* (Chapel Hill: University of North Carolina Press, 1960), p. 145.

27. *The Washington Star*, Sunday Edition, June 27, 1965.

XI | Can the Incumbent Be Defeated?

FARIBORZ S. FATEMI

Incumbents campaign constantly, and they normally win new terms of office. This chapter, based on Democratic senators' re-election campaigns, explores the motivations of repeated candidacy, the assets of incumbency, and the causes of victory and defeat. It concludes that with effective fund-raising, skillful media presentation, and dependable organization, a legislator will have long tenure.

The author is a political and urban affairs consultant with broad experience in incumbent Democratic senatorial campaigns. He also served as a campaign aide in the Presidential campaigns of 1960, 1968, and 1972, as well as in Senator Robert F. Kennedy's 1968 Presidential primary campaign. In 1964 he was an advisor to Young Citizens for Johnson-Humphrey and assisted Michigan's John Conyers, Jr. in his winning campaign for the House. He was a Congressional Fellow of the American Political Science Association in 1962-1963. As a Fellow of the American Society for Public Administration in 1968-70, he worked in the Office of the Assistant Secretary for Equal Opportunity, Department of Housing and Urban Development. In 1963-1967 he was an Assistant Professor of Political Science at Wayne State University. The author thanks Diane V. Brown for wise counsel and assistance.

SENATOR ROBERT F. KENNEDY held that "an honorable profession calls forth the chance for responsibility and the opportunity for achievement; against these measures politics is a truly exciting adventure."[1] Involvement in many campaigns has led me to the conclusion that politics must be approached primarily as an art, rather than as a science. It has been said that "An art is not learned like a science by insight into laws but by experience." This chapter is based upon observations gained by experience. My objective in this discussion is to present some general observations by which the reader may gain insight into the multiple factors which determine the outcome of an incumbent's campaign. These factors are not clearly separable, and their relative impact cannot be measured precisely.[2] Recent Democratic senatorial campaigns will be illustrative.

Statistical analysis indicates that it is overwhelmingly likely that the incumbent will be re-elected, returning to Congress one step ahead in the pecking order of seniority which brings power and prestige. In only five election years since 1954 have more than four incumbent senators been defeated in primary or general elections. In the House of Representatives, approximately 400 of the 435 incumbents will seek re-election, and, on the average, 370 of them will win. Such statistics suggest that the power of congressional incumbency may bring victory even when presidential or other candidates sharing the ticket are being rejected.

MOTIVATIONS OF CANDIDACY

Service in Congress is a demanding occupation, and campaigning commonly is an exhausting experience. Yet the number of senators and representatives who establish and maintain congressional careers is impressive and suggests that the motivations for candidacy are strong. Some even claim that the desire to stay in office is the greatest motivational force driving a senator or a congressman.

The prospect of a likely victory itself becomes an inducement to seek re-election and to win handsomely. A wide margin of victory provides more than personal satisfaction. It discourages future opponents and increases one's attractiveness as a candidate for higher office. A Washington political observer once said, "Each member of Congress is wont to consider himself a sort of autonomous principality sent forth to Washington by an adulatory constituency."

"Potomac fever" must be acknowledged as another potent motivation for continuing congressional candidacy. The power of the Washington scene is contagious, and many lawmakers are chronically affected by it. To be a senator or congressman is to live an exciting though highly pressured life from which withdrawal is normally a reluctant step.

Along with the enjoyment which members derive from their office and their association with others in government who have power, the retirement system and the congressional salary are further incentives to seek re-election. The retirement system, established in the Legislative Reorganization Act of 1946 and liberalized several times subsequently, permits senators and representatives to contribute to a pension fund which yields considerable benefit if retirement follows a minimum of six years in office. Annual benefits increase with length of service to a maximum of three-fourths of a member's final salary. The current salary is $42,500 for senators and representatives.

Finally, possession of a seat in Congress offers the incumbent an opportunity for public service and national leadership not matched in most other occupations. Unless he chooses to accept appointment to a high administrative or judicial post, to run for an office which he regards as an advancement, or to retire, the member of Congress is likely to take to the hustings in defense of his job.

With the motivation for continued candidacy so obvious, it is not surprising that generally all but the most senior members will continue to seek office. Some, however, arrive at the realization that they have just so many useful years in public service, and having given it all they have, they get out. Statistics on House members indicate that in the last three decades

227

incumbents most frequently have left office to retire or to seek a higher office. The next most important reason for leaving Congress is death, followed by defeat in primary or general elections.

THE RISKS OF POLITICAL LIFE

Although it is very difficult to defeat an incumbent, it can be done and has been done increasingly in recent years. Just within the last decade, defeats in primary and general elections accounted for more House incumbents leaving office than retirement, death, or candidacies for higher office. In 1970, 20 House incumbents with an average of 14 years' service were defeated in primary or general elections. More significantly, 9 incumbents each having more than 20 years' service were defeated in party primaries. In 1972, including those running against one another in districts realigned after the 1970 census, 26 House incumbents were defeated in primary or general elections. Among them were 4 committee chairmen. There were as many defeats in primaries as in the general elections. The trend toward increasing defeats of incumbents can also be observed in the Senate. Three of the five elections years since 1954 in which more than 4 incumbents were defeated were 1968, 1970, and 1972. In my work I have observed a number of factors contributing to the defeat of incumbents. The following half dozen, however, are not meant to be inclusive or in any order of priority.

My first observation concerns a question which all incumbents confront, namely: Do they seem to serve the attitudes and interests of their constituents in a manner most satisfactory to that constituency? Two cases illustrate this point. Senator Albert Gore (D., Tenn.), running for his fourth term in 1970, and Senator Ralph Yarborough (D., Tex.), running for his third term in 1970, faced opponents' charges that they did not represent the attitudes of their respective states. Their opponents focused their attacks upon the Senators' votes against President Nixon's southern Supreme Court nominees, against his policies on Vietnam, against legislation to prohibit bussing, in favor of gun control, and against school prayer amendments. These two senators, with national reputations and solid records, who had sought to discern and to serve the national interest on these issues, were forced to fight for re-election on the narrower basis of whether they or their opponents best represented the social attitudes of their constituents.

Senator Gore's media director, Gene Graham, a Pulitzer Prize-winning Tennessee reporter, expressed it best when he said:

> Bill Brock [Senator Gore's opponent] might represent the attitudes of the working man and his family perfectly on the social issues [race, bussing, crime, gun control, prayer in schools, etc.] but they know Gore is the man who will vote to protect their economic interests. What we are trying to do is to force that working man and his family to recognize the conflict between their attitudes and their interests.

Senator Gore referred to himself during the campaign as a "progressive." He had led the fight against the Nixon administration on taxes, economic policies, the administration's policy priorities, the Vietnam War, Pentagon spending, and development of anti-ballistic missiles. Yet, during the campaign he consistently had to answer charges made on behalf of his opponent that he was anti-Tennessee, anti-American, anti-white, anti-God, and anti-prayer. As David Halberstam reported: "His [Brock's] newspaper ads and television ads are hitting away daily at the most emotional issues they can touch."[3] In the end a majority of Tennesseans voted on the basis of their social attitudes rather than their economic interests, and Albert Gore lost. "Can you imagine it," the Senator said after the results were in, "coming down here to find out not what the people wanted, what they needed, but what their fears were?"

Senator Ralph Yarborough's fate was parallel, although his loss came in a primary fight with a relatively unknown Houston millionaire, Lloyd M. Bentsen, Jr., who much earlier had served six years in the House. Every night during the campaign, 30-

and 60-second spots were shown on prime-time television suggesting that Senator Yarborough was "un-Texan" and "pro-violence." After a scene from the Chicago Democratic National Convention of 1968 in which demonstrators battled police, Bentsen would say, "Those were the supporters of Eugene McCarthy rioting . . . Senator Ralph Yarborough endorsed McCarthy for President. Did he represent your view?" Another claimed that Senator Yarborough was against prayers in school and asked, "What's wrong with prayers?" Every night Bentsen would be on television telling the people of his opposition to school bussing, of his desire for peace in Vietnam without "bugging out," and of his intention to be tough on the "law and order" issue. All of this was designed to show Senator Yarborough as "ultraliberal" and out-of-step with the people of Texas—"a Senator from Texas, not for Texas"—and it took its toll.

In the beginning Bentsen was not taken seriously by many people. A month before the primary, a San Antonio columnist wrote that it could "end in a slaughter for Bentsen." However, Senator Yarborough could not match Bentsen's spending in the primary. Moreover, he was saving his scarce resources for the general election. Bentsen said he spent about $800,000 in his campaign against Yarborough. Senator Yarborough reported spending $275,096. By the time he started to counteract Bentsen's slick imagery campaign, it was too late.

While other factors to be discussed later also contributed to the defeats of Senators Gore and Yarborough, the job was made easier because the incumbents were made to seem out-of-step with their states' thinking and attitudes. There are those who say that the wise incumbent will not stray far from what is seen to be the political center. Yet others just as vehemently will claim that it is better to stand for one's principles than to give in to rampant emotionalism.

A second threat to incumbency is the issue of a candidate's age and health. Senior incumbents seeking re-election have found one of the major issues to be their age. This issue became

230

a liability for Senator Paul Douglas (D., Ill.) when he ran unsuccessfully for re-election in 1966 against Charles Percy. It was also a factor in the defeat of Senator Wayne Morse (D., Ore.) when he ran for a fifth term in 1968, as well as one of the factors in the defeat of Senator Yarborough.

A younger opponent will try to make the voter perceive that he is more energetic, has more fresh ideas and, therefore, can serve the constituency better than the incumbent. After the 1970 senatorial campaign in California, the Field Poll indicated that 43 percent of those who supported Democratic Representative John V. Tunney for senator said they did so because he was "a younger man with younger ideas" than Republican Senator George Murphy. A recent and low-cost way to demonstrate youthful energy while gaining widespread publicity is walking across one's state to communicate with the people, as Lawton Chiles (D., Fla.) and Dick Clark (D., Iowa) did in their winning campaigns of 1970 and 1972.

The seasoned incumbent may try to turn the issue of his age to his own advantage. The longer one stays in Congress, he will say, the more seniority one gains, and with it more prestigious and powerful committee assignments and the ability to influence the Federal bureaucracy to be more responsive to the needs of one's constituency.

A third observation is that a paramount national issue may damage an incumbent's campaign. The re-election campaign of Senator Wayne Morse in 1968 provides an excellent illustration. Senator Morse had served since 1944 and was running for a fifth term. His record as a senator had won him a reputation for honesty, integrity, and great independence. Above all, Wayne Morse was fearless, and Presidents as well as his legislative colleagues and opponents found him a formidable adversary. As early as 1953, Senator Morse started to speak out against the general role of the United States in Southeast Asia, and as our involvement intensified in the late 1950's and into the 1960's, he spoke more frequently against our commitment in South Vietnam.

When he ran for re-election in 1968, the Democratic Party in Oregon, as across the nation, was split over Vietnam policy. The Senator survived a tough primary fight. But the bitter primary left many animosities unresolved and exhausted many campaign resources, money in particular. These factors were crucial in causing his defeat, which was by a margin of only 3,000 votes out of 800,000 cast. While the opposition campaign of Republican Robert Packwood did not seem particularly powerful, Packwood continuously tried to make an issue of their difference in age. He also was helped immensely by the Democratic Party's division over Vietnam. In such a close election, persisting factional differences can upset an incumbent.

A fourth observation concerns the role of personal organization in incumbent campaigns. By personal organization I mean an organization that is responsive only to the candidate and his needs and is distinctive from party organizations or the political arm of labor or other interest groups. Most of the campaigns about which I have first-hand knowledge have lacked strong personal organization. An exception has been the Kennedy family of Massachusetts, whose concept of "Kennedy secretaries" will be discussed later.

In 1970, Albert Gore did not have an organization throughout the state of Tennessee, nor had he sought to build one. Customarily people would help him and then disappear until the next campaign. While no one can say with certainty what the outcome would have been had Senator Gore had a strong personal organization on which he could depend, it is likely that, in an election in which only 50,000 votes out of more than 1,000,000 cast separated the victor from the vanquished, a strong organization on the model of the Kennedys' would have reversed the results.

Senator Ralph Yarborough also lacked a personal organization. When he faced opposition in his primary in 1970, he looked to his traditional base of liberals, unions, and Mexican-Americans to pull him through. In the beginning the Senator perceived his opponent as a minor threat and campaigned only on weekends, with little money invested in radio and television spots. By the time it became clear that his opponent was a real threat, and the Senator started to campaign full-time with extensive use of radio and television, the damage had been done. No doubt, had there existed a strong, Kennedy-style organization to go door-to-door, to propagate the Senator's record, and to counteract his opponent's attacks during the early months, his campaign could have been successful.

A fifth observation, perhaps the hardest to measure, is that the prevailing national political mood affects an incumbent campaign. What constitutes that mood? It is, for example, emotional exhaustion caused by years of change and crisis. It can be a sense of aimlessness brought about by lack of national leadership. Then too, new issues such as bussing and environmental protection may disrupt old voting patterns. Some see these changes as producing an anti-incumbent trend, an attitude of "when in doubt throw the rascals out." However, others might say, "Things have been bad so long that we might as well stick with the idiot we have rather than switch to an idiot who might be worse."

In the final analysis, the political mood could bring to the forefront some newly organized segment of society demanding a reorientation of politics toward new programs, new leaders, and a different style of representation. This would not augur well for incumbent campaigns. Prominent examples in 1972 were the defeats of Republican Senators Gordon Allott by Floyd K. Haskell in Colorado and J. Caleb Boggs by Joseph R. Biden, Jr., in Delaware, both caused in part by environmental issues.

A final observation, also very hard to quantify, concerns fate and luck. It could be said of some politicians that rain never falls on their rallies. Senator Robert F. Kennedy once said: "In order to win any political office fate must be kind to you and above all you have to be lucky. The higher the office the greater must be your luck." Political history is filled with examples of candidates who seemed to have a natural tendency to be lucky, while others have seen fate intervene time after time to prevent them from achieving their goals.

As the foregoing shows, incumbents are not invincible, and one or two factors—either local or national—or a combination of factors could play havoc with their re-election campaigns.

ASSETS OF INCUMBENCY

The occasional incumbent defeat does not diminish the fact that the incumbent possesses numerous and varied advantages. He begins with a psychological advantage. He has the experience of having won approval in the last election, successfully handling the difficult issues and choices. An incumbent is likely to demonstrate knowledgeable self-confidence, and he knows his job. Not the least of his advantages is that everything he does in his job can be related to campaigning, that is, seeking voter approval. Incumbents, in effect, run for office throughout their terms. Herbert Alexander writes, "It is virtually impossible to separate any politician's activities into those which are part of his present position and those which may be pointed toward a future position or campaign."[4]

Furthermore, incumbent status creates confidence and respect among the people and brings allies, funds, services, and the opportunity to expound upon achievements in office. The incumbent will have won or deepened the support of many individuals by personal attention lavished on them and their problems, by his casework, and by his legislative record. He may even have found it possible to arrange a committee hearing in his constituency, thereby demonstrating his skill or impact.

It is often said that the most difficult task in campaigning is to become known to the voters. The incumbent will have overcome this hurdle before the campaign begins, since his exposure to the public is frequent and promoted by media attention. On countless occasions in the course of his term, an incumbent provides interviews and comments. He utilizes the facilities and expertise of the House and Senate recording studios to produce radio and television tapes. An incumbent may even write a regular newspaper column. Finally, he will make countless presentations before virtually every type of organization in his state or district.

Also, the perquisites of the office provide great advantage over the typical challenger. The senator or congressman continues to draw his $3,540 monthly salary while campaigning. The government pays his Washington and field staff and maintains and equips as many as three district offices. His regular staff, aided by the Congressional Research Service of the Library of Congress, provides professional issues research. The franking privilege enables him to mail materials free of charge, as long as they are official business and not directly campaign oriented, to persons on his mailing list or, in the case of congressmen, to all residents in his district. Under this privilege, *Congressional Record* reprints and newsletters are sent, perhaps daily or weekly, to newspapers and thousands of constituents. He may also utilize the franking privilege in conducting constituency polls. He may distribute a quota of such publications as the informative *Department of Agriculture Yearbook* and HEW's *Infant Care* to selected constituents. To match the benefits of franking privileges and the perquisites of office, it is estimated that a senatorial challenger in a large state would have to spend about $150,000.

In addition, senators and congressmen are eager to assist one another in return for future favors; they frequently visit one another's states and districts and provide testimony of their colleagues' effectiveness. Having half a dozen of your colleagues present at a fund-raising dinner not only enhances both the attendance and one's prestige, but also fills the incumbent's campaign coffers. The magnitude of these events is indicated by the Citizens Research Foundation's report that, in 1968, candidates and committees at all levels collected at least $43.1 million from fund-raising dinners—$21.5 million raised by Republicans, $19.9 million raised by Democrats, and $3.6 million raised by the American Independent Party.[5] While presumably half of these funds were delivered to the presidential campaign, huge sums from fund-raising dinners went to incumbent Senate and House campaigns.

Incumbents have still further advantages in raising money. The congressional campaign committees of both parties allocate most of their funds and services to incumbents, usually in proportion to the severity of their challengers' threats. Such support may be worth as much as $10,000 to $15,000 for a Senate race, and $5,000 for an important House race. In 1970 the Democratic Senatorial Campaign Committee spent $628,671, and its Republican counterpart spent $968,534.[6]

Moreover, interest groups tend to concentrate upon those incumbents whose voting records and legislative activities have been favorable to them. Growing campaign costs have increased reliance upon large contributions from such sources. A report by the Citizens Research Foundation indicated that in the non-presidential 1970 elections, organized labor reported spending $5.2 million; business and professional groups, $5.1 million; peace groups, $624,113; and miscellaneous political committees, $5.8 million. This heavy spending has tended to nourish the image of office-holders being indebted to their financial backers rather than free to follow their consciences or the wishes of their constituents.

Furthermore, such groups can provide more than financial support. Those national organizations having strong local branches can mobilize support at the grass-roots level and provide public relations experts, lawyers, clerical staff personnel, and office equipment. Their conventions and publications provide opportunities for favorable communication with great numbers of potential supporters.

Finally, incumbents generally have an advantage in raising money because success attracts money. While some people donate for ideological or partisan reasons, others do so to gain access to legislators, and the latter are especially sensitive to the vote-drawing assets of incumbency. Nonetheless, even incumbents can have difficulty raising money. In the elections of

236

1970, Albert Gore had financial problems because too many people thought he was likely to lose. Yet Senator William Proxmire (D., Wis.) found that the overwhelming likelihood of his re-election inhibited potential contributors. On balance, however, the incumbent normally is in a superior position to attract funds.

IMPLICATIONS OF CAMPAIGN COSTS

There is no way of knowing how much money is required to win an election. But in less expensive days, Will Rogers reportedly said, "It takes a lot of money to even get beat with." One thing is certain: Today's campaigns for Congress and the Presidency are increasingly expensive. The Citizens Research Foundation reported that in 1952 the total cost of campaigns for all elective offices in the United States was about $140 million. That cost rose to $155 million in 1956, $175 million in 1960, $200 million in 1964, and $300 million in 1968.[7] The 1972 estimate is $400 million.

Costs have mounted as techniques have become more sophisticated. Reliance upon the broadcast media, which are ideally suited for mobilizing the mass society and large constituencies, and upon professional political operatives employing pollsters, computer experts, direct-mail specialists, and television consultants in particular have pushed up expenses.

Big-city machines no longer are in complete command of working class votes. One-third of the electorate regard themselves as independents. The Gallup Poll in 1968 reported that 84 percent of the people said they would vote for a candidate and not a straight party ticket. In these circumstances, a candidate running for office no longer talks to his party chairman first, but to a good pollster or media man who can handle his campaign for him.

David Broder and Haynes Johnson, perceptive political correspondents for the *Washington Post*, describe the situation this
way:

> In a day of instant, vivid, and personal communications, new
> political operatives who specialize in media campaigns have
> replaced the old-line party organizations. The media firms
> raise money independently of the parties, choose issues
> independently of the parties, advise and counsel candidates
> independently of the parties, determine strategy inde-
> pendently of the parties. They can even organize and deliver
> get-out-the-vote campaigns independently of the parties.[8]

Roger Ailes, one of Richard Nixon's top television producers,
was reported to have commented in 1968, "This is the
beginning of a whole new concept. This is it. This is the way
they'll be elected forevermore. The next guys will have to be
performers."[9] Yet in 1970 the majority of candidates handled
by top media consultants lost, and heavy spending for political
broadcasts did not guarantee election success for either Republican or Democratic candidates for Congress. Senatorial candidates spent $13,631,960 and, as described throughout this
chapter, produced some of the most controversial and costly
media campaigns in history. In a number of states they
saturated prime-time television and radio with spots aimed at
building favorable images of themselves and discrediting their
opponents. Elections for the House of Representatives also
resulted in heavy broadcast spending which totalled
$5,185,388.

After the 1970 elections there was indication that the "image
campaign" featuring great television and radio expenditures was
undergoing a re-evaluation. Perhaps Senator Gaylord Nelson
(D., Wis.) summed up the problem best in a Senate debate:

> A two-dimensional, eighteen-inch-high candidate, presented
> with all the candor of a laundry product or a dancing dog act
> does little to assure a concerned public of the relevance and
> responsiveness of the political process in this country.[10]

Because of their experience, incumbents are best able to time their fund-raising with overall campaign strategy in mind, knowing that without money there can hardly be a campaign. An incumbent who starts his basic fund-raising well before the election by direct mail and individual solicitations, testimonials and fund-raising dinners will find himself in the enviable position of being able to develop a realistic campaign budget. In this way he will have cash on hand at the time of maximum need and will not be competing with other candidates for the same sources when the crunch is most severe. Early fund-raising will also help prevent the situation in which the incumbent pays for billboards in April, which he must do, and then finds he has no money for radio or television, or in which he pays the printing bills and finds that there is no money for election day get-out-the-vote activities. Money at the right time, astutely spent, can have an immense impact on an election, yet it is only one of the many determinants of the outcome. If money were always the controlling factor, the access of incumbents to financial resources would make it a wonder that they ever lost.

TWO SUCCESSFUL CAMPAIGNS

The senatorial campaigns of Philip A. Hart (D., Mich.) and Vance Hartke (D., Ind.), each running for a third term in 1970, demonstrate that winning is based in large part on matching techniques to circumstances.

About 18 months before the election, quietly but very diligently, both Senators had some of their full-time campaign staff raising money as part of their duties. Fund-raisers were held, individual and direct-mail solicitations were conducted, and as the money came in, budgets were formulated. In addition, each Senator started to make frequent personal appearances in his home state.

While neither Senator had any primary opposition, Hartke faced a rough fight in the general election against Republican Congressman Richard Roudebush. Although the Senator's record on the issues was thought to have broad voter support, he was hurt at the beginning of the campaign by an opposition allegation that he had accepted an illegal campaign contribution in 1964. The decision was made to concentrate his resources on polling, on media, and on developing a campaign organization. The media campaign lacked punch and was not very memorable; the campaign organization never lived up to expectations because it could be only as effective as its personnel. Despite these shortcomings and a heavy media blitz by his Republican opponent that reportedly cost $364,825, Senator Hartke won a narrow victory. The result could be attributed to the Senator's people-to-people campaign style and his opponent's less energetic campaign and media over-kill.

Traveling day and night, criss-crossing Indiana repeatedly, Hartke counteracted his opposition by a vigorous personal campaign. By his skillful stump speaking, he more than made up for deficiencies in his campaign organization. His opponent's hard-hitting advertising rebounded to Hartke's favor by creating a sympathy vote. Night after night a television spot shown in prime time depicted a black-pajama-clad Viet Cong soldier pointing a gun at the viewing audience. The narration detailed Hartke's votes against the Vietnam War, implying that by these votes he "was giving support to the Viet Cong, who are killing our boys." This type of image manipulation back-fired and helped re-elect the Senator.

In Michigan, Senator Hart, already strong, became an overwhelming favorite. He ran a low-key campaign with a good organization, emphasis on his record, and a moderate amount of media exposure. He had considerable party and union help and enjoyed statewide popularity. He was further helped by the fact that GOP nominee Lenore Romney, wife of the then Secretary of HUD and former Governor, had been badly weakened by a primary in which conservative Robert J. Huber had received 48 percent of the vote. Thereafter Mrs. Romney had further difficulty developing issues which would be effective against Senator Hart, and her campaign never became a threat.

To direct his media campaign the Senator hired Charles Guggenheim, one of the most prominent specialists in political television commercials. He is especially noted for cinéma verité, which involves following a candidate to film actual campaign appearances. In one of the spots, the Senator was shown handling the issue of law and order in a stress situation. This issue was a major one across the country. One scene was Detroit's Thirteenth Precinct Police Station, Hart appearing with coat off and tie undone. The police officers gathered around the Senator, firing questions right and left and engaging him in debate. Hart calmly but firmly answered the sensitive questions, the spot ending with the officers agreeing with him. Such spots were perfectly suited to the kind of soft-sell campaign being waged. Senator Hart won in what seemed to be an effortless manner.

THE IMPORTANCE OF ORGANIZATION

Winning often depends on organizational impact. Particularly noteworthy is the system of "Kennedy secretaries" developed by Senator John F. Kennedy and now used by his brother, Senator Edward M. Kennedy.

In every major town in Massachusetts having substantial numbers of Democratic and independent voters, a Kennedy secretary has the responsibility to organize and report political activities. These reports, collected frequently from all over the state, bring political trouble-spots to the attention of the Senator. During an election year, the organization is expanded so that every precinct with heavy Democratic and independent registration has designated Kennedy secretaries. Each one not only has the job of explaining the Senator's position on the issues to his friends and neighbors, but also has a quota of votes to produce on election day. This sort of organization seeks to leave nothing to chance. In the event of a feud with a local party organization, the Senator's personal organization could either ignore or supplant that party organization. If harmony prevails, each organization complements the other. This kind of painstaking organizing not only wins elections time after time but also allows the Senator to know exactly what is going on throughout his state in non-election years. Furthermore, such an organization assists in overcoming the kinds of threats to incumbency previously described.

Despite the obvious value of the Kennedy-style grass-roots organization, it is virtually unique. In most instances, incumbents as well as nonincumbents lack a standing corps of campaign workers, and a campaign organization will have to be built. It need not be difficult for an incumbent to secure and designate volunteer coordinators in the most important counties or election districts of his state. People are most likely to respond favorably if they are asked to participate in the political process on a continuous basis, rather than once every six years or once every two years. Building such an organization takes time, hard work, and ingenuity, but an incumbent has all the resources to accomplish this. He is in office for a certain time and has staff help available, plus the many perquisites of his office.

In the ideal campaign, once enough money has been raised, there should be an early poll to find out how the voters feel about the candidates and the issues. At the same time a media campaign should be created, based on the campaign issues, and an organization should be developed and deployed. Generally the incumbent should have the advantage of having assembled a winning team of workers who can be re-activated.

In reality, however, some campaigns emphasize fund-raising and media at the expense of developing issues and building a dependable organization. Others will concentrate too heavily on issues or otherwise lose impact by getting these fundamental elements out of proportion. It is useful to bear in mind a seasoned campaign consultant's remark that "There are two ways to get out the vote: one is persuasion, the other is organization. Either one is enough if it works completely, but only the most naive ignore one or the other." Most will agree that the key to any successful campaign is determining one's resource allocation to the best advantage in terms of money, organization, media, and timing.

ADVANCING

Advancing is an aspect of organizational work which is characteristic of presidential campaigns, coming into vogue in senatorial campaigns conducted in the very largest states, and likely to be increasingly applied. Published accounts of advance work are few and fail to convey its significance. They do, however, provide colorful impressions:

> The campaign advance man is a staple of modern political folklore. He is the scout for the candidate's wagon train, as well as a political strategist, tour director and carnival barker. It is his exigent assignment to schedule a rally to his candidate's best advantage, drum up enthusiasm, charm local party leaders and, when the occasion demands, get tough with local officials.[11]

> ... The nearest thing the Western World has to a Chinese coolie. The advance man arranges for halls, podiums, luncheons or dinners, keys to the city, press conferences, hotel accommodations, rendezvous between the visiting poo-bah and his local political underlings, or a pitcher of water for the dignitary's bedside table. He referees disputes over who will sit where at ceremonial functions, and tries to discourage bores or potential troublemakers who might embarrass the official presence.[12]

From most of the writings one could readily gain the impression that advance work should not be taken very seriously, as it only furthers the carnival atmosphere of campaigning for political office.

Advance work is a relatively new concept in political campaigns. Few legislators other than the Kennedys have really understood its role, and few treat advance work as a professional aspect of campaigning. In talking about the 1958 re-election campaign of Senator John F. Kennedy, his political confidante, Kenneth O'Donnell, said that the team tested various techniques of advance work in that campaign and sought to perfect them so that the techniques could be used in his bid for the Presidency in 1960. It was in that campaign and in Robert F. Kennedy's winning New York Senate campaign in 1964 that advance work developed as a professional aspect of campaigning.[13]

Advance work generally consists of a number of very important elements. The advance person usually arrives at the proposed campaign stop from one to four days before the candidate. He carefully checks the schedule for the candidate's visit to see that it is feasible within the time framework allowed and that the events scheduled are worthwhile. If there is to be a rally at the airport, extensive preparations must be made. A motorcade to take the candidate, his party, the press, and local VIP's to the event must be organized. Several cars and sometimes busses plus police escort can be involved. Hotel arrangements must be made if the candidate and his party plan to remain overnight in the area. All "crowd events" at which the candidate appears—rallies, motorcades, parades, dinners, get-togethers with local officials and VIP's—must be checked to be sure that no details have been overlooked. There must be similarly careful preparation for appearances before editorial boards of newspapers and television and radio programs.

There is more to advance work, however, than overseeing details. Good advance work has broad impact on campaigns and can provide significant advantages. Every time a candidate makes an appearance, the advance person, working with the local organization, must try to make it a success. Sometimes an advance person will find himself in a locale where the organization is quite weak or there is no organization. A capable advance person will mobilize all local resources to maximize the effectiveness of the candidate's appearance. It is more than likely that when the advance person leaves, either there will be an organization where none existed before, or an existing organization will have been greatly strengthened. Furthermore, the local organization will have been helped to see what its deficiencies are and can keep working in order to improve itself.

244

Advance work which ensures the success of the candidate's appearance and generates enthusiastic crowds will give local supporters a tremendous psychological lift. Uncommitted voters seeing or reading about the candidate's great reception will find it hard to resist the urge to join the candidate's bandwagon. Jerry Bruno expressed the reaction well when he wrote, "Those stories create a sense of momentum or of failure. Those stories may persuade money-givers to go with a winner or hold back from a loser."[14]

Many times one hears the comment that if a candidate cannot run his campaign effectively, he cannot be expected to run the office he is seeking. Advance work can convey a professional image. An efficient and well-organized campaign appearance will leave the voter with a good impression. He will sense that the candidate is decisive and capable of handling any office.

Effective advance men use both persuasion and diplomacy in dealing with elected officials, party officials, the press, and the general public. This aspect of advancing is probably the most difficult, most sensitive, and least understood of all. Yet it can play a key role in the success or failure of a candidate's visit. It is not easy to train people in the arts of persuasion and diplomacy, yet when choosing a person to do advance work, the candidate ought to seek these foremost qualities. While some advance men tend to be tough with local people, my experience suggests that diplomatic tact avoids costly alienation.

Occasionally an advance person will find that the candidate's local supporters are fighting among themselves, disagreeing on everything except the candidate. By subtle persuasion, he must get them together to make the candidate's visit a success. He must avoid favoring or ignoring any individual or group. The media are usually quick to observe which local dignitaries greet a candidate. The absence of prominent people could embarrass the candidate. Also it would damage the campaign psychologically by suggesting that the candidate lacked the leadership or prestige to unite all groups behind his candidacy.

An advance person must decide sensitive questions such as who is to ride in the car with the candidate, who will sit next to him on the platform, who will get close to the candidate at various functions, and who should be avoided at all costs. In the final analysis, the advance person is the point of the lance for the candidate. He is the candidate's eyes and ears. He is the candidate's representative on the scene, the person who will have greatest contact with local people. His performance will be a determining factor in how they view the candidate. In such politically sensitive situations, the value of good advance work is immense.

Each advance person learns by bitter experience to proceed by certain rules. The following rules are a useful guide:

- Assume that anything can go wrong and probably will. Accordingly, always provide for back-up systems, including back-up sound systems in case the first one fails, an alternate band, extra cars.
- Check every detail personally.
- Involve the local people as much as possible in planning the campaign stop, so that they feel that they are part of a team.
- Never exclude anyone because he did not support your candidate from the beginning or during the primary or because he supported someone else. Always ask for people's assistance, and include everyone who wants to help.

Good advance work can make possible what appears to be impossible, stave off potential catastrophe and create the impression of great support. In a close election it can be the difference between victory and defeat.

WITH HUMPHREY IN CALIFORNIA

The pressures and impact of advance work can be well illustrated by Vice President Hubert H. Humphrey's final trip to California in the presidential campaign of 1968. In the last

246

week of September, I went to work for the Vice President as one of his advance men. I had worked for Senator Robert F. Kennedy in the primaries, had decided to leave politics for a while after his assassination, but felt strongly motivated to work against the candidacy of Richard Nixon.

The campaign had not gone well in the month of September. The polls showed Humphrey far behind. Campaign trips were generally disorganized and the crowds were sparse. The violence associated with the Democratic National Convention in Chicago tended to stigmatize the Vice President and seemed to haunt his campaign efforts across the country.

By the middle of October, there was visible improvement. The campaign trips were better organized and seemed to be much smoother. The crowds were growing larger and friendlier, and relations among the party's factions were improving considerably.

I arrived in California the night of October 29, about five days before Humphrey was scheduled to visit the state. The tentative schedule for his visit began with arrival at Los Angeles International Airport on the Sunday before the election. After an airport rally, he was to go to the Beverly Hilton Hotel for an overnight stay. A press reception which Humphrey might attend was scheduled for that evening. He also was to speak by telephone hook-up to a fund-raising event in San Francisco. The next day there was to be a ticker-tape motorcade through downtown Los Angeles at noon, and a live telethon that evening. After the telethon the Vice President was to fly to Minneapolis to cast his ballot the next morning.

The proposed ticker-tape parade appeared to be the only problem spot on the schedule. Los Angeles is probably the most difficult city in the country in which to conduct such a motorcade. There is no natural downtown such as New York City's Wall Street or Chicago's Loop and hence no place where a parade-minded crowd was assured. A flop the day before the election would be disastrous. The polls at this

247

point showed Humphrey narrowing the gap or even pulling ahead. A triumphal motorcade in crucial California could increase his momentum.

Mike O'Donnell, who was heading our advance team, was favorably inclined toward scheduling the motorcade, but wanted assurance that it could be done successfully. We reflected on the Vice President's previous trips to California, which had not gone particularly well. In one instance bad scheduling had caused Humphrey to waste a great deal of time driving on the freeways from one event to another. On another occasion, the airport arrival was disorganized. Furthermore, liaison with local political leaders had been inadequate. Mike asked me to take care of this political work, to check whether it was feasible to hold the motorcade, and to take responsibility for the airport arrival.

I had some knowledge of California politics, and fortunately was introduced to a congressman's aide who was most knowledgeable concerning the rivalries, pettiness, egos, and virtues of California politics. Her assistance was invaluable to me in handling the basic political work. We made lists of all prominent Democrats, officeholders, and independents throughout the state, including well-known supporters of Senators Robert F. Kennedy and Eugene McCarthy. I called all of them, giving them the Vice President's schedule and inviting them to the airport and to be in the receiving line to greet Humphrey. I also asked them their opinions of the schedule and made sure they knew how to reach me if any questions should arise. In a number of instances, this was the first time that a national staff person from Humphrey's campaign had contacted these individuals. It was decided, moreover, that Martin Stone, who was a former co-chairman of the McCarthy campaign in California, and Paul Schrade, a United Auto Workers regional coordinator who had supported Robert Kennedy, would ride with the Vice President from the airport to the hotel. The next day Mrs. Helen Chavez, the wife of farm labor organizer Caesar Chavez, and Sig Arywitz, secretary-treasurer of the Los Angeles County Federation of Labor, would ride with the Vice President from the television studio to the airport. When Humphrey arrived, all the factions of the California political scene were waiting to greet him. All were there for the single purpose of helping elect the next President.

In order to investigate the possibility of having the motorcade, it was necessary to hold a series of meetings with the local people who would be involved. Included were Don O'Brien, one of the most skilled political operatives, who headed southern California for Humphrey; Stephen Reinhardt, national committeeman; Carmen Warschaw, an unusually astute national committeewoman; and Leon Cooper, southern chairman of the Democratic State Central Committee. While opinion was divided as to whether to have the motorcade, there was consensus that if it were successful, it might provide just the momentum Humphrey needed to carry him to victory. Of course, if we were not successful, it could become the biggest disaster of the campaign. There was, however, the precedent of the highly successful motorcade for Senator Kennedy in May. Moreover, should this motorcade be a success, the crowds cheering the Vice President would be seen election eve on all the television network news programs, and the viewing audience might have that image in their minds as they went to the polls the next day. It was decided to go ahead.

The motorcade route was quickly decided, handbills printed, and radio spots purchased. We decided that Senate candidate Alan Cranston, Assembly Speaker Jess Unruh, and Congressman Edward Roybal, as well as the vice presidential nominee, Senator Edmund Muskie, would ride in the parade car with Humphrey. I was fortunate to pick up 12 bands at nominal cost. The bands consisted of a fire engine from the Red Garter Saloon with a calliope on it which led the motorcade, the Mamas and the Papas, rock bands, mariachi bands and a bazouki band. For the bands needing them, we arranged for portable generators and flat-bed trucks. Slowly but surely, the preparations for the motorcade were completed.

The decision was made early that the only people greeting Vice President and Mrs. Humphrey at the airplane ramp would be Alan Cranston, Jess Unruh, and their wives. Protocol, of course, called for a number of others to be in the greeting party at the airport, so a receiving line was planned within this VIP area. In order to prevent overexuberance and possible charging of the plane ramp, which can occur when people are caught up in the excitement of the moment, barriers were erected between the ramp area and the larger VIP area. The plan was that after Cranston and Unruh greeted the Vice President, we would open up the barriers, and he would proceed down the receiving line to a portable podium where he would make some informal remarks.

I arrived at the airport only to discover that the lectern had not been delivered. As this was Sunday afternoon, it would be nearly impossible to find another one. I also learned that Larry O'Brien, National Chairman of the Democratic Party and chairman of the campaign, would be coming to the airport and wanted to go aboard the plane to talk to Humphrey. The weather was fine, the crowds were gathering, the VIP's were arriving, and 20 minutes before the planes were due to land, someone found a lectern.

Firm arrangements had been made that only Cranston, Unruh, and their wives be allowed in the ramp area. The security people were not to let anyone through unless they checked with me. About 10 minutes before Humphrey's plane was to land along with three other planes filled with newsmen, Chairman O'Brien arrived at the VIP area, heading for the plane. Walking with his arm around the national committeewoman, a close friend, he strolled right into the ramp area. Immediately chaos started to break loose. A long-time rival of the national committeewoman charged me and said, "If she is in the ramp area, then I have to be there, too. If I can't go in

250

the ramp area, then I am leaving." One after another, local political personalities joined in insisting upon their own inclusion, similarly threatening to leave.

Moments before touchdown, a beautifully orchestrated greeting was on the verge of disintegration. Unable to get word to the chairman that the plans were being disrupted, we quickly worked out a solution by which some local politicians would be allowed in the ramp area, staying in the background. The crisis passed.

While all this was taking place, there was a sudden downpour which seemed as if the sky had opened up. While the hard rain lasted only about three minutes, it seemed an eternity as everyone was thoroughly soaked. Now we had to get umbrellas in case it was raining when the Vice President arrived—one more thing to add to the confusion!

The plane landed, and the rain stopped. The chairman went up to speak to Humphrey; then the Vice President came down the ramp and was greeted by Cranston, Unruh, and their wives. I led him over to the receiving line, where he shook hands with everybody. The Vice President was received warmly; it was an enthusiastic crowd. He made a nice speech; it was very short.

Nothing further developed until the next day, just prior to the parade. The weather was fine, and as early as 10:00 a.m., reports were coming in that large crowds were gathering along the route of the motorcade. Earlier we had decided that Senator Muskie would ride with the Vice President, along with Cranston, Unruh, and Roybal. The Secret Service agent on the scene, however, told me that because of security precautions only the Vice President and his running-mate would be allowed in the convertible. Indicating to him that this was contrary to the arrangements we had made with the agent in charge, I asked him to communicate with his superior to verify the original plan. Because of malfunctioning radio equipment, the agent on the scene was unable to contact the agent in charge. Without further orders, this meant that

Cranston, Unruh, and Roybal would not have a car in which to ride and could not be in the parade. Awaiting the arrival of the motorcade, I began trying to find another convertible. I was on the verge of commandeering the first one that came along or even of getting one of the flat-bed trucks, kicking off the band, and using it.in the parade.

While all of this was going on, Cranston arrived and wanted to sit in the Vice President's car, but the agent told him it was impossible. Soon after, Unruh arrived, and Cranston explained to him that the agent would not allow them in the car. Unruh said to me that he thought they were to ride with the candidate. I told him that there was a mix-up in the agent's orders and that we were trying to resolve it.

Sirens indicated that the Vice President was approaching. Ted Van Dyke, the Vice President's aide in charge of the traveling party, was first to arrive. I grabbed him and very quickly explained the situation. Since there was no time for further communications, the consensus was simply to hurry Cranston, Unruh, and Roybal into the waiting convertible. We did exactly that.

It was a fantastic parade. The official crowd estimates were 225,000, while some newsmen reported 100,000. On election morning, R. W. Apple wrote in the *New York Times* feature article:

> Vice President Humphrey ended his exhausting and often disheartening quest for the Presidency today with a triumphal lunch-hour motorcade through downtown Los Angeles. . . .
>
> Standing on the trunk of a convertible with his running-mate, Senator Edmund S. Muskie of Maine, beside him, he was acclaimed by a crowd of nearly 100,000 as confetti, ticker tape and flower petals cascaded down from the buildings. . . .
>
> With confetti in his hair and on the shoulders of his blue suit, the Vice President leaned over and said to a friend, "I feel great, just great, because this is the best it can be."[15]

Both the airport and motorcade incidents illustrate that there is often, at the last minute, a deviation from plans, and that what is required of an advance man is a tough, serious, and professional job requiring persuasion and diplomacy. It can be crucial in such situations to have an advance man on the scene who understands the local problems yet speaks for the campaign team.

Having so many people turn out for the downtown parade involved the hard work of many people and a great deal of luck. Everything had come together perfectly at this one parade. But suppose this had taken place a month earlier in Chicago or Philadelphia or on a previous California trip. The psychological impact would have been immense. It would have shown that the Vice President had the momentum to win. It would have encouraged contributions from otherwise reluctant sources. A massive turnout is infectious, and could have been repeated, for it tends to create a band-wagon effect. One wonders what the outcome of the election might have been if the campaign's advance work had been as effective a month earlier.

CONCLUSION

With an early and effective fund-raising effort, with a dependable organization, and with a media effort presenting the issues in a manner which binds it all together, a campaign can overcome most challenges, no matter how much the opponent spends. If all these factors were put together by an incumbent who services his constituency with energy, ability, and imagination, mending his political fences as problems occur, it would be nearly impossible to defeat him.

If one wants a career in Congress, one has to love to campaign. The higher the office to which a legislator aspires, the more grueling, costly, and extensive his campaign will be.

The campaign is the crucible of American legislative politics. It tests the candidate's effectiveness in relating to individuals and groups in face-to-face encounters and through mass media. It tests his response to society's wants and fears. Its results shape not only the politician's future but also the course of the country.

1. Pierre Salinger, Edwin Guthman, Frank Mankiewicz, and John Siegenthaler, *"An Honorable Profession": A Tribute to Robert F. Kennedy* (Garden City, N.Y.: Doubleday, 1968), p. viii.

2. As a consultant, I have had access to privileged information while dealing with my clients or working in campaigns. Under no circumstances do I want to reveal such information, nor is it my intention to malign or make light of the candidates or the campaigns about which I have personal knowledge.

3. David Halberstam, "The End of a Populist," *Harper's*, CCXLII, No. 1448 (January, 1971), p. 39.

4. Herbert E. Alexander, *Financing the 1968 Election* (Lexington, Mass.: D.C. Heath and Co., 1971), p. 54.

5. *Ibid.*, pp. 188-189.

6. These and subsequent 1970 campaign finance data are from Robert A. Diamond (ed.), *Dollar Politics* (Washington, D.C.: Congressional Quarterly Inc., 1971), pp. 21, 23, 59, and 61.

7. Alexander, *op. cit.*, p. 1.

8. *Washington Post* (December 19, 1971), p. A22.

9. Joe McGinniss, *The Selling of the President 1968* (New York: Trident Press, 1969), p. 155.

10. *Congressional Record*, 91st Congress, 2nd Session, 1970, p. 38532.

11. *Time* (January 24, 1972), p. 16.

12. Larry L. King, "My Hero LBJ," *Harper's*, CCXXXIII, No. 1397 (October, 1966), p. 54.

13. Jerry Bruno, widely considered "the father of advance work," detailed his experiences with the presidential campaigns of John F. Kennedy, Lyndon B. Johnson, Robert F. Kennedy, and Hubert H. Humphrey in Jerry Bruno and Jeff Greenfield, *The Advance Man* (New York: William Morrow & Co., 1971).

14. *Ibid.*, p. 136.

15. *New York Times* (November 5, 1968), p. 1.

254

Index
Names of members of Congress are italicized.

Abourezk, James G., 117, 120n
ACORNS, 74, 75
Adams, Brock, 141-142
Ailes, Roger, 238
Albert, Carl, 102, 113, 115, 137, 138, 145
Alexander, Herbert, 234
Allott, Gordon L., 200, 215, 233
AMERICAN POLITICAL SCIENCE ASSOCIATION, vii-x, 26;
  Congressional Fellowship Program, vii-xvii
AMERICANS FOR DEMOCRATIC ACTION, 144
Anderson, John B., 146
Apple, R.W., 252
Arends, Leslie C., 146
Arywitz, Sig, 248
Ashbrook, John M , 4, 97n
Aspin, Les, 116

Badillo, Herman, 109
Bailey, Douglas L., 81, 85, 91, 98n
Baker, Howard H., Jr., 147-148, 219
Begich, Nicholas J., 117, 120n
Bentsen, Lloyd M., 229-230
Biden, Joseph R., Jr., 233
Bingham, Jonathan B., 138
BLACK CAUCUS, 96n
Blackburn, Benjamin B., 133-134
Blatchford, Joseph H., 5
Boggs, J. Caleb, 157, 159, 233
Boggs, T. Hale, 115, 116, 120n
Bolling, Richard W., 29, 102, 129-130
Bridges, H. Styles, 196, 215, 222
Brock, William E., III, 229
Broder, David, 238
Brooke, Edward W., 164, 218
Brown, Richard, 176, 177
Bruno, Jerry, 245, 254n
Buckley, James L., 147
Burch, Dean, 80
Bush, George H.W., 14, 17
Butler, John Marshall, 206

Cahill, William T., 98n
CAMPAIGNING, 1-21, 226-254;
  advance man's role, 16, 243-253;
  assets of incumbency, 234-237;
  campaign management firms, 16, 98n, 238, 241;
  candidate's role, 14-16, 239-241;
  challenging incumbents, 5-6, 12, 226;
  costs, 7, 12-13, 16, 230, 235, 236, 237-239, 240;
  finance, 10, 12-13, 235-237, 239;
  headquarters, 11;
  incumbent defeats, 228-234;

  media, 12, 16-17, 229-230, 238, 240, 241;
  organization, 8-11, 17-20, 241-243;
  polling, 7, 235;
  strategy, 6-20, 239-241
CANDIDACY;
  candidate backgrounds, 3-5;
  motivation for, 5-6, 170, 226-228
Carlson, Frank, 199
Case, Clifford P., 199
CASEWORK, 27, 53-72, 234;
  high-level, 68-70;
  routine, 54-65:
    categories, 55-58;
    congressman's role, 63-65;
    organizing for, 59-61;
    receiving requests for, 58-59;
  urban and rural, 65-68
Celler, Emanuel, 125
Chavez, Caesar, 248
Chavez, Helen, 248
Chiles, Lawton, 231
Chilsen, Walter J., 24
CHOWDER AND MARCHING CLUB, 74, 75, 90
Church, Frank F., 5
Clark, Dick, 231
Clark, Joseph S., 91, 127, 154, 156, 157, 158
Clay, Henry, 125
Cohen, Edward, 183n
Colmer, William M., 96n, 113
COMMITTEE ASSIGNMENTS, 29, 30, 83, 106-120;
  committees on committees, 107-118, 126, 134, 139, 140, 141, 146, 198-199;
  making assignments, 109-118, 120n, 199-200;
  seeking assignments, 107-109, 152, 171
COMMITTEES, 99-167;
  congressman's role in, 103-106, 118-119;
  seniority in, 121-150;
  subcommittees, 101-102, 103, 105, 127, 128, 131, 140, 154;
  types, 100-103, 114-115, 152, 165-166
COMMITTEES, HOUSE;
  Agriculture, 83, 106, 109, 111, 114, 145, 153, 155;
  Appropriations, 30, 83, 101, 111, 112, 114, 131, 181, 183n;
  Armed Services, 112, 114, 116, 146;
  Banking and Currency, 114, 117;
  District of Columbia, 115, 141-142, 143;

Education and Labor, 83, 109,
114, 115, 171, 180;
Foreign Affairs, 83, 101-102,
114;
Government Operations, 145,
146;
Interior and Insular Affairs, 111,
117;
Internal Security, 83, 152;
Interstate and Foreign Commerce,
114;
Judiciary, 114, 123, 178, 179,
181;
Merchant Marine and Fisheries,
83;
Public Works, 29, 83, 101, 114;
Rules, 79, 83, 96n, 101, 105,
106-107, 112, 113, 114, 123,
130, 146;
Select Committee to Study House
Rules X and XI, 102-103;
Standards of Official Conduct,
83;
Ways and Means, 100, 107, 111,
112, 114, 115
COMMITTEES, JOINT;
Atomic Energy, 100;
Congressional Operations, 103;
Economic, 100
COMMITTEES, SENATE;
Agriculture and Forestry, 153,
155, 157, 159, 160;
Appropriations, 199, 200;
Armed Services, 200;
Banking, Housing and Urban Af-
fairs, 199;
Foreign Relations, 93, 199;
Interior and Insular Affairs, 120n,
200;
Judiciary, 177, 179, 200;
Labor and Public Welfare, 154,
155, 156, 157, 158, 199, 200;
Rules and Administration, 158,
159-162, 165;
Select Committee on Nutrition
and Human Needs, 47, 100,
151-167:
establishing, 156-158;
funding, 158-166;
Special Committee to Investigate
Organized Crime in Interstate
Commerce, 152
COMMON CAUSE, 131, 144, 147
Conable, Barber B., Jr., 140
Conyers, John, Jr., 140
Cook, Marlow W., 159, 218
Cooper, Leon, 249
Cotter, William R., 117
Cranston, Alan, 249, 250, 251, 252
Curtis, Carl T., 163-164

Dawson, William L., 67
de Grazia, Alfred, 133
DEMOCRATIC CAUCUS, HOUSE,
107, 109, 137-146, 148-149

DEMOCRATIC CAUCUS, SENATE,
141, 148-149
DEMOCRATIC STUDY GROUP
(DSG), 74, 75, 76, 77, 78, 85, 87,
92, 95, 96n, 97n, 136, 137, 138,
144, 170, 173
Dewey, Thomas E., 196
Dirksen, Everett M., 185-223
Dole, Robert J., 159
Dominick, Peter H., 159
Douglas, Paul H., 231

Eisenhower, Dwight D., 192, 196,
197, 200, 201, 207
Ellender, Allen J., 102, 157, 160,
161, 164, 165
Ellsworth, Robert F., 79
Erlenborn, John N., 146
Evans, Frank E., 145
EXECUTIVE-LEGISLATIVE RELA-
TIONS, 53-72, 76-77, 90-92,
129-130, 148, 154-155, 162,
169-183, 186-222

Fannin, Paul J., 157
Fascell, Dante B., 138
Finch, Robert H., 93, 162
Fishman, Jay, 174, 183n
Ford, Gerald R., 75, 80, 85, 119n,
143
Fortas, Abe, 219-220
Fraser, Donald M., 114-115
Freeman, Orville L., 155
Frelinghuysen, Peter H.B., 80
FRESHMAN EXPERIENCE, 23-36,
123, 124, 174;
building one's record, 31-34;
orientation to the House, 25-26;
travel, 27-28
Fulton, James G., 142

Gardner, John W., 147
Gatch, Donald, 162-163
George, Walter F., 222
Gilbert, Jacob H., 181
Goldwater, Barry M., 79, 202
Goodell, Charles E., 218
Gore, Albert A., 228-230, 232, 237
Graham, Gene, 229
Grant, H. Douglas, 174, 183n
Green, William J., 116
Griffin, Robert P., 219, 221
Guggenheim, Charles, 241

Halberstam, David, 229
Halleck, Charles A., 80
Hansen, Julia Butler, 139
Hardin, Clifford M., 162
Harrington, Michael, 152-153, 154
Harrington, Michael J., 112-113, 116
Harris, Fred R., 141
Hart, Philip A., 157, 239-241
Harthe, R. Vance, 239-240
Haskell, Floyd K., 233

Hatfield, Mark O., 147, 157, 159, 218
Hebert, F. Edward, 112, 116
Heckler, Margaret M., 2
Hickenlooper, Bourke B., 215
Holifield, Chet, 145-146
Hollings, Ernest F., 163
Hoover, J. Edgar, 177, 181, 183n
Horton, Frank, 146
Huber, Robert J., 240
Huitt, Ralph K., 205
Humphrey, Hubert H., xv-xvii, 25, 119, 141, 246-253

Ingersoll, Charles J., 125

Javits, Jacob K., 147, 157, 160-161, 164, 199, 202
Joelson, Charles S., 30
Johnson, Haynes, 238
Johnson, Lyndon B., 93, 114, 154, 171, 179, 191-194, 196, 198, 199, 204-211, 215, 218, 219-220, 221, 222
Jordan, B. Everett, 159-161

Kastenmeier, Robert W., 33
Keating, Kenneth B., 75
Kemp, Jack F., 5
Kennedy, Edward M., 159, 164, 177, 178, 179, 241
Kennedy, John F., 158, 192, 207, 208-210, 241, 243
Kennedy, Robert F., 154, 156, 158, 212, 226, 233, 244, 247, 248, 249
Knowland, William F., 191-194, 196-197, 201, 204, 220
Kuchel, Thomas H., 198, 199, 212

LaFollette, Bronson C., 24
Laird, Melvin R., 24, 75, 80
LEGISLATIVE REORGANIZA-
    TION ACTS;
    1946: 102, 127, 227;
    1970: 127, 138-139
LeTendre, Andre, 34
Lincoln, Abraham, 125, 213
Lindsay, John V., 79, 80, 82
Lowenstein, Allard K., 4, 18
Lukens, Donald E., 4

MacNeil, Neil, 125, 199
Madden, Ray J., 113, 130
Mahon, George H., 30
Mansfield, Michael J., 147, 162, 165, 206, 209, 212, 215, 221, 222
Martin, David T., 102, 103
Martin, Joseph W., Jr., 2, 123, 149n
Mathias, Charles McC., 79, 90, 92, 98n, 141, 146, 218
Mathias, Robert B., 5
McCarthy, Eugene J., 230, 248
McCarthy, Joseph R., 196

McCarthy, Richard D., 29-30
McClory, Robert, 179
McCormack, John W., 136, 137
McGovern, George S., 47, 156-165, 167n
McMillan, John L., 141-144
McSpadden, Clem Rogers, 112
Mead, Margaret, 159, 160
MEMBERS OF CONGRESS FOR PEACE
    THROUGH LAW (MCPL), 91
Miller, Norman, 27
Millikin, Eugene D., 222
Mills, Wilbur D., 30, 114-115, 139
MINORITY   LEADERSHIP,   SEN-
    ATE, 186-223;
    evaluation, 220-222;
    intraparty strategy, 195-203;
    legislative strategy, 204-217;
    role conception, 188-195, 200-
    201
Mizell, Wilmer D., 5
Mondale, Walter F., 157
Morgan, Thomas E., 102
Morse, F. Bradford, 79, 81, 91
Morse, Wayne L., 231-232
Morton, Rogers C.B., 75
Mundt, Karl E., 198
Murphy, George L., 164, 231
Muskie, Edmund S., 249, 251, 252

Napolitan, Joseph, 16-17
Nelson, Gaylord, 24, 32, 157, 159, 164, 238
Nixon, Richard M., 17, 19, 24, 44, 57, 74, 75, 90, 93, 162, 192, 238, 247
Nixon, Russell, 174, 179, 183n

Obey, David R., 24-36
O'Brien, Don, 249
O'Brien, Lawrence, 9, 250
O'Donnell, Kenneth, 243
O'Donnell, Mike, 248
O'Konski, Alvin E., 36n
O'Neill, Thomas P., 145
OUTSIDE EXPERTS, 87, 160, 169-
    183

Packwood, Robert W., 139, 147-148, 218, 232
Patman, Wright, 125
Pearl, Arthur, 172, 174, 183n
Pearson, Lester, 93
Pell, Clairborne de B., 159
Percy, Charles H., 5, 157, 161, 164, 218, 231
Peyser, Peter A., 141
Poage, William Robert, 145
Pollock, James K., 122, 127, 132
PRESS RELATIONS, 28, 38-51;
    elements of the media, 42-45;
    learning from the press, 40-42;
    methods of gaining coverage, 45-
    48;

organizing to make news, 48-50; value to the member, 38-40
Price, Hank, 48
Prouty, Winston L., 157, 159
Proxmire, William, 237

QUESTIONNAIRES, 28, 175
Quie, Albert H., 26

Reinhardt, Stephen, 249
Reissman, Frank, 172, 174, 183n
Reuss, Henry S., 33
REPUBLICAN CONFERENCE, HOUSE, 77, 80, 85, 94, 139, 140, 141, 146, 148-149
REPUBLICAN CONFERENCE, SENATE, 141, 148-149, 195
Reuther, Walter, 155
Rhodes, George M., 116
Ribicoff, Abraham A., 164
Riegle, Donald W., Jr., 143, 150n
Rogers, Will, 237
Romney, Lenore, 240
Rooney, John J., 183n
Roosevelt, Franklin D., 159
Rosenthal, Benjamin S., 145-146
Roudebush, Richard L., 239
Roybal, Edward R., 249, 251, 252
Russell, Richard B., 41, 209, 222

Saloma, John S. III, 55
Saxbe, William B., 218
Scheuer, James H., 170-183
Schrade, Paul, 248
Schweiker, Richard S., 90, 92, 98n, 218
Scott, Hugh D., Jr., 221, 222
SENATE LEADERSHIP, 185-223
SENIORITY, 83, 108, 112, 119, 121-150, 152, 196, 198, 199, 200, 226;
    effects of, 128-135;
    reform, 135-150:
        in 91st Congress, 136-139;
        in 92nd Congress, 139-144;
        in 93rd Congress, 144-148
Sibal, Abner W., 79
Smith, H. Allen, 74
Smith, Margaret Chase, 203
Smith, William P., 158, 159, 160-161
S.O.S., 74, 75
STAFFING, 25-26, 32, 48-50, 53-72, 74, 81, 85, 90, 96, 96n, 97n, 123, 124, 128, 158, 160, 173, 176, 177, 181, 235

Stafford, Robert T., 79, 80, 81, 82, 94
Steiger, William A., xi-xiii
Stennis, John C., 209
Stevenson, Adlai E., III, 146-147
Stewart, William H., 155
Stone, Martin, 148
Stratton, Samuel P., 145

Taft, Robert A., 190-193, 196, 204, 222
Taft, Robert, Jr., 91, 97n, 147-148
Talcott, Burt L., 132
Talmadge, Herman E., 141, 157, 161
Teague, Olin E., 139
THE GROUP, 96n
Thurmond, J. Strom, 161
Tower, John G., 200
Trebach, Arnold, 174, 183n
Treleaven, Harry, 17
Truman, David B., 213, 214
Tunney, John V., 231
Tupper, Stanley R., 79

Udall, Morris K., 26, 136, 137
Unruh, Jess, 249, 250, 251, 252

Van Dyke, Ted, 252
Vander Jagt, Guy A., 143-144

Waggonner, Joe D., 114-115
Waldie, Jerome R., 137, 142-144
Wallace, George C., 44
Warschaw, Carmen, 249, 250
WEDNESDAY GROUP, HOUSE, 73-98;
    adaptation to Republican administration, 90-92;
    effectiveness, 92-96;
    operations, 86-90;
    organization, 78-86;
    reasons for, 74-78
WEDNESDAY GROUP, SENATE, 92
Weicker, Lowell P., Jr., 48-49
Wherry, Kenneth S., 192
Whitaker and Baxter, 16
White, F. Clifton, 17
White, William S., 130, 189, 191
Whitten, Jamie L., 140

Yarborough, Ralph W., 157, 228-233

258